The Contested Identities of Ulster Protestants

The Contested Identities of Ulster Protestants

Edited by

Thomas Paul Burgess
Senior Lecturer, School of Applied Social Studies,
University College Cork, Ireland

and

Gareth Mulvenna
Visiting Research Fellow, School of Politics,
International Studies and Philosophy,
Queen's University Belfast, UK

First published 2015 by
PALGRAVE MACMILLAN

Palgrave Macmillan in the UK is an imprint of Macmillan Publishers Limited,
registered in England, company number 785998, of Houndmills, Basingstoke,
Hampshire RG21 6XS.

Palgrave Macmillan in the US is a division of St Martin's Press LLC,
175 Fifth Avenue, New York, NY 10010.

Palgrave Macmillan is the global academic imprint of the above companies
and has companies and representatives throughout the world.

Palgrave® and Macmillan® are registered trademarks in the United States,
the United Kingdom, Europe and other countries.

ISBN 978–1–137–45393–8

This book is printed on paper suitable for recycling and made from fully
managed and sustained forest sources. Logging, pulping and manufacturing
processes are expected to conform to the environmental regulations of the
country of origin.

A catalogue record for this book is available from the British Library.

Library of Congress Cataloging-in-Publication Data
The contested identities of Ulster Protestants / edited by Thomas Paul Burgess and
Gareth Mulvenna.
    pages cm
Summary: "'Flags', 'Emblems' and 'The Past'; three seemingly insurmountable challenges
which continue to hinder the peace process in Northern Ireland. For many, the
responsibility for the impasse that scuppered the Haass talks and brought violent
protests to the streets of Belfast appears to rest with the perceived intransigence of the
Protestant, Unionist and Loyalist communities to embrace change. That this community
is itself riven with internal rancour and discord should come as no surprise. Issues
of social class, denominational alignment, political aspiration and national identity
have historically divided what outsiders have often mistakenly viewed as a collective
cultural, religious and socio-political entity. This study explores the statement by Henry
McDonald that this is '...the least fashionable community in Western Europe'. A diverse
group of contributors including prominent politicians, academics, journalists and artists
investigate the reasons informing public perceptions attaching to the Protestant,
Unionist and Loyalist communities in Ulster"—Provided by publisher.
    ISBN 978–1–137–45393–8 (hardback)
    1. Protestants—Political activity—Ulster (Northern Ireland and Ireland)   2. Protestants—
Ulster (Northern Ireland and Ireland)—Attitudes.   3. Unionism (Irish politics)
4. Peace-building—Northern Ireland.   5. Peace-building—Ireland.   6. National
characteristics, Irish.   7. Ulster (Northern Ireland and Ireland)—Politics and government.
I. Burgess, T. P., editor of compilation.   II. Mulvenna, Gareth, 1980– editor of compilation.
DA990.U46C674 2015
305.6'80409416—dc23   2014028155

Typeset by MPS Limited, Chennai, India.

For Mary and Ruby Burgess
TPB

To my mother and father, my brother Andrew, and Paula who is my rock
GM

Contents

List of Tables

Preface

Whilst attending a perfectly respectable dinner party in the second city of Ireland, the espresso-fuelled topic of conversation turned to, of all things, the validity of cultural expression.

After close on twenty years as a taxpaying citizen of the Republic, I am, it seems – for good or ill – forever to be designated as 'The Prod from Belfast'. (An unpleasant trait often associated with Cork is that anyone sojourning deep into the heart of the so-called 'Rebel County' will forever be considered a 'blow-in' no matter how long their duration of domicile.) As such, I could anticipate, as I so often have done before, what was coming straight down the tracks at me.

Didn't I believe that those aspects of triumphalism inherent within the core of northern Orangeism, undoubtedly stymied initiatives such as the much lambasted 'Orangefest'?[1]

It was not unreasonably posited that this legacy would inevitably scupper any attempts to move toward a more inclusive, mainstream 'carnival-like' Twelfth of July celebration aimed at promoting those positive aspects of Protestant/loyalist/unionist cultural identity.

It required just a small leap of lazy stereotyping then to press forward the inevitable premise.

At this point, a young woman with impeccable Irish Republican credentials spoke up forcefully, and advanced her sure and certain hypothesis that there did not exist – neither could there *ever* exist – any legitimate or worthwhile expression of a valid or meaningful cultural contribution emerging from the Ulster unionist or loyalist tradition.

She cited as her logic for this pronouncement that – unlike, say the great Protestant poets, playwrights and novelists who embellish the literary history of the Republic – no repressive, sectarian or reactionary state could ever produce art or cultural expression of worthwhile or lasting merit.

As if by way of empirical evidence, a quick inventory was offered. An entire pantheon of outstandingly successful musicians, writers and actors were presented, all of them first- or second-generation Catholic Irish and many of them drawing their very inspiration from the muse of Celtic mysticism, Catholicism, dispossession and suffering.

To further support this, she asked us to consider if any enduring and influential artists had emerged from apartheid Afrikaans society, the Zionist Israeli state or indeed Nazi Germany for that matter?

No. Great art in general, and edgy, subversive popular culture in particular, remained exclusively the unimpeachable birthright of the dispossessed, the revolutionary and the freedom fighter.

And woe betide anyone from the liberal intelligentsia who might dare to suggest otherwise.

I forced a smile of course – through gritted teeth – feeling that any spirited defence on the matter would render me a bellicose Paisleyite and monarchist lick-spittle ... once I had left the room, naturally.

Instead I resorted to my tried and tested response when faced with the need to defend an entire community of fellow Northern Protestant Irishmen and women in their absence. I fell back on an infinitely more interesting period in my life as a travelling minstrel of sorts.

'Did I ever tell you about the time that Elvis Costello called me an Orange bastard?'

That never fails to do the trick.

As I had learned during my own experience as a songwriter, performer and musician with my band 'Ruefrex' throughout the 1980s, the music establishment and press prefer their Paddies Catholic, nationalist and one-dimensional.

We had been performing on the Tyne Tees TV show *The Tube* as part of the 'Red Wedge' initiative. This was a collective of British popular musicians (Billy Bragg, Tom Robinson, The Communards, Madness, The Smiths, et al.) who attempted to engage young people with politics in general – and the policies of the Labour Party in particular – during the period leading up to the 1987 General Election and in the hope of ousting the Conservative government of Margaret Thatcher.

Elvis already had form here. He had been peevish toward us working-class Belfast Prods earlier that year when – as support act to those lovable cockney 'Oirishmen' The Pogues – he had turned up on our tour backstage to squire his future wife, bass player Cait.

Now it could just be that 'Orange bastards' espousing non-sectarian, socialist solidarity in their song lyrics and interviews was a little too much for Mr MacManus to come to terms with. If so ... he was not alone.

We learned later that our band were to be removed from a US tour support slot with The Pogues for ... well ... 'not being Irish enough'.

To cap it all, I endured the ignominy of having my songs described as '... *over-burdened by the weight of [my own] Loyalist imagery*' by *The New Socialist* magazine.[2]

Back at the dinner party in Cork, of course, no one was particularly interested in the finer points of sociopolitical fissures within the Ulster

Protestant monolith. 'Oooh ... Elvis ... oooh ... Shane ... what were they really like ...?' being the most common inquiry.

The incident, which was by no means an untypical one, evoked for me an oft-remarked observation that has been made by – amongst others – the late, lamented James Hawthorne (ex-controller of BBC Northern Ireland). He suggested that '... the Catholic case is sometimes more lyrical because it is about change', whilst '... the conservatism of the Protestant ethos, not well articulated, is of less interest'.

Whether or not this is the reality, it's clear that the role of those who profess to speak as the 'voice' of what *Observer* journalist Henry McDonald has called 'the least fashionable community in Western Europe'[3] would scarcely have found a sympathetic ear in a popular music culture that venerates the marginal, the subordinate and the subaltern.

Historically, southern Irish popular opinion has rarely worked up much of a sweat one way or the other over the cultural mores of Protestants North or South. Even the dynamics driving 'The Troubles', and their aftermath, have often been located in over-simplified politico-cultural terms, which cast all Catholics as nationalist, republican and Irish and all Protestants as unionist, loyalist and British.

Can community difference and its cultural legacy in modern Ireland really be still simply a matter of 'Planters' and 'Croppies' ... with the latter having all the best tunes?[4]

This easy analysis has also been largely shared by British public opinion, partially informed as it is by popular media and the arts promoting a wholly subjective rendering of the situation. Dramatic representations of the Protestant community resonate with portrayals of taciturn, emotionally retarded prison wardens or RUC men. Or tattooed, hormonally driven knuckle-draggers, pumping iron in the gym whilst their Catholic counterparts commune with their cultural bequest, through dance, language and song.

News coverage seems to feature community representatives and politicians who are either tight-sphinctered, monosyllabic '*no*'-merchants or those who seem to have arrived straight from a seventeenth-century Puritan witch-burning summit (the Iris Robinson debacle being a notable, if surreal, exception to the rule).

In fact, in almost every representation synonymous with this community – sport; politics; the arts; the historical legacy of both world wars; industrialisation and labour; broadcasting, current affairs and media; questions of language and dialect; their relationship with the US diaspora and their perceived insularity in the face of ethnic diversity and difference – the Ulster Protestant/unionist/loyalist persona as portrayed or perceived by northern nationalists, southern partitionists or UK 'mainlanders' is uniformly both limited and limiting.

Aspects of loyalism *have* emerged to dispute old shibboleths. The former leader of the Progressive Unionist Party, Dawn Purvis, challenged mainstream unionism as having a blinkered view of the causes of the conflict. She described it as one which selectively omitted sectarian misrule. Ominously, she terminated her tenure soon afterward in the face of hard-line paramilitary non-revisionism. (Ironically, in her current position as Programme Director of the Marie Stopes Clinic, she now attracts the ire of fundamentalists from both traditions.)

It remains undeniable that certain expressions of Protestant cultural identity rarely escape the constraints and representations of triumphalism. However, recognising that past Stormont supremacy had a material basis built from the sectarian abuses of a Catholic minority also requires a postscript that many journalists, cultural commentators and artists seem reluctant to allow: that same thwarted cultural development and expression within the northern Protestant community, which renders it the butt of many an easy joke, can also be explained in the collapse of heavy industry, in the breakdown of working-class neighbourhoods, in the reaction to a terror campaign waged against them (frequently by their *own* organisations) and in draconian constitutional, political and legal reforms implemented in Northern Ireland over the last 30 years.

Attempts to articulate this experience nationally or internationally have not been uncomplicated or well received. The now infamous 'flags' protest is another example perhaps of a misguided and misrepresented attempt to voice legitimate concerns regarding the erosion of political and cultural identity.

Mahatma Gandhi observed that 'No culture can live if it attempts to be exclusive'. Bearing this in mind then, journey with us now through the contested identities of Ulster Protestant culture, so that we may perhaps better understand some of the reasons as to how things became – and remain – anchored in this sorry state of caricature and negative stereotype.

T. P. Burgess

Notes

1. 'Orangefest is a "Celebration of Culture"', *Belfast Newsletter*, 29 June 2010.
2. 'Review, *Flowers for all Occasions* and *Paid in Kind*, Ruefrex', *The New Socialist*, June 1986.

3. Henry McDonald, 'Return of the Angry Young Prods', *The Observer*, 2 October 2005.
4. Sean Campbell, '"Pack Up Your Troubles": Politics and Popular Music in Pre- and Post-Ceasefire Ulster', *Popular Music Online* (2007) ISSN 1357-0951, <http://www.popular-musicology-online.com/issues/04/campbell-01.html> [accessed 1 May 2014].

Acknowledgements

The editors would first and foremost like to thank those who contributed to this volume. We are particularly grateful to those who were supportive of the book idea from its inception. These friends include Pete Shirlow, Ken Harland, Graham Walker, Richard English, Tony Novosel, Connal Parr, Colin Coulter, Robert Niblock, Peter Herrmann, Katy Hayward, Aaron Edwards, Eamonn Hughes and Wesley Henderson.

Notes on Contributors

Editors

Thomas Paul Burgess is from Belfast's Shankill Road and holds degrees from the Universities of Ulster, Cork and Oxford. His PhD was titled 'The Reconciliation Industry; Community Relations, Community Identity and Social Policy in Northern Ireland'. He is a senior lecturer at University College Cork where he serves as Director of Youth and Community Work. He has spent periods, variously, as schoolteacher, Community Relations Officer in local government in Antrim, and researcher for the Opsahl Commission of Inquiry into political progress in Northern Ireland. As a songwriter and performer with his band, Ruefrex, he released seven singles and three albums, all critically acclaimed for their political commentary on the Northern Irish conflict with particular reference to the Protestant/unionist/loyalist communities. The main emphasis of his academic research has been carried out in relation to social policy developments in the areas of education, cultural identity, community work, youth work, community relations and conflict resolution in an Irish, British and European context and he has published widely in these and other areas. He has worked as a commentator for a number of national newspaper publications and broadcasters.

Gareth Mulvenna is currently Visiting Research Fellow at Queen's University Belfast School of Politics, International Studies and Philosophy. His PhD thesis (QUB, 2009) was titled 'The Protestant Working Class in Northern Ireland – Political Allegiance and Social and Cultural Challenges Since the 1960s' and sought to raise awareness of the Protestant working-class experience in Northern Ireland from pre-Troubles to post-conflict. He has written on the history of Belfast's Protestant working class for *Irish Studies Review* and is currently writing a book about Ulster's loyalist 'Tartan' gangs of the early 1970s and the emergence of groups such as the Young Citizen Volunteers and the Red Hand Commando. The book, which will be published in 2016 to coincide with the one hundredth anniversary of the Battle of the Somme, is titled 'From Young Citizens to Volunteers'. He has also been commissioned to write for a number of publications, including *The Guardian/Observer*, on the subject of contemporary loyalism and the Protestant working class in Northern Ireland and has contributed to *Channel 4 News* items relating to the 'flag protests' in Belfast. Outside academia he has worked as a Parliamentary Researcher for the Northern Ireland Assembly Research and Information Service and as an archival researcher with the Northern Ireland Historical Institutional Abuse Inquiry – the largest inquiry of its kind in UK history.

Contributors

Fidelma Ashe is a senior lecturer in politics at the University of Ulster and member of the Institute for Research in Social Science. She has published widely in the area of gender studies. She is co-author of *Contemporary Social and Political Theory: an Introduction* (Open University Press) and author of *The New Politics of Masculinity* (Routledge). Her forthcoming book *Gendering Conflict Transformation in Northern Ireland: New Themes and Old Problems* will be published by Routledge. She is currently a co-researcher on a United-States-Institute-of-Peace-funded project that is examining gender and conflict transformation in international contexts.

Stephen Baker is a lecturer in Film and Television Studies at the University of Ulster and a member of the Centre for Media Research. He has published widely on media and television representations of class in the British context with particular emphasis on contemporary programmes such as *Shameless*. He is an authority on the depiction of Ulster loyalism in contemporary 'Troubles' cinema and is the co-author (with Greg McLaughlin) of *The Propaganda of Peace: the Role of Media and Culture in the Northern Ireland Peace Process* (2010) and *The British Media and Bloody Sunday* (Intellect Books, forthcoming 2014).

James Greer is currently a Visiting Research Fellow at Queen's University Belfast School of Politics, International Studies and Philosophy in which he is undertaking a project entitled 'The Ulster-Scots Contribution to Political Thought in Ireland, Since 1600'. The project has the twin objectives of producing work to further public engagement with this broad topic, and scholarship examining the tradition's diverse strands of political thought and agency in the development of the North of Ireland since 1885. His PhD thesis (QUB, 2011) is entitled: 'Losing the Province: a Localised Study of Ulster Unionism, 1968–74'. The thesis analysed the parallel destabilisation of Northern Ireland and the fragmentation of unionism – utilising a comparative framework to detail local variations of political violence and political change within a broader study.

Eoghan Harris is a journalist, fiction writer, director, columnist and politician. He currently writes for the *Sunday Independent*. He was a member of Seanad Éireann from 2007 to 2011, having been nominated by the Taoiseach Bertie Ahern. He has held posts at various and diverse political parties throughout his career. He was a Marxist ideologue of the Workers' Party and its predecessor, Official Sinn Féin. He was also an adviser to former Taoiseach John Bruton and an adviser to the Ulster Unionist Party. At one stage an Irish republican, he is now a bitter critic of modern day Sinn Féin. Harris is also noted for his screenwriting work; he lectures at the Irish National Film School, and teaches a screenwriting workshop.

Billy Hutchinson is the leader of the Progressive Unionist Party in Northern Ireland and a long-standing community worker in North Belfast. As a teenager in the 1970s he was a member of the Ulster Volunteer Force (UVF) and a founding member of its youth battalion, the Young Citizen Volunteers (YCV). While serving a life sentence for murder he became politicised through his relationship with the UVF commanding officer in Long Kesh, Gusty Spence. As part of a generation of UVF ex-prisoners such as David Ervine and Eddie Kinner, Hutchinson played an integral part in selling the Belfast or 'Good Friday' Agreement to the loyalist community. He was elected to Belfast City Council in 1997 and to the Northern Ireland Assembly in 1998. In 2014 he was re-elected to Belfast City Council and continues to advocate a political path for the loyalist people.

Reverend Brian Kennaway is an ordained Minister of the Presbyterian Church in Ireland and retired in January 2009. He is a serving member of the Judicial Commission of the Presbyterian Church of Ireland. He has been active in the church, serving on a number of church Committees of the General Assembly. He is the author of a number of books and articles on Orangeism. He is the President of the Irish Association for Cultural, Economic, and Social Relations, and a member of the Board of the Institute for British Irish Studies (IBIS). He is currently a member of the Parades Commission.

Caireen McCluskey obtained both her LLB and PhD at the University of Ulster. She was called to the New York State Bar in 2012. Her doctoral thesis, completed in 2013, examined domestic abuse, based on a review of research indicating continuing endemic levels of violence in

Northern Ireland, through the lens of post-structuralist feminist theory. Her research interests include gender politics and discourses of gender and violence.

Sam McCready is a senior lecturer within the School of Sociology and Applied Social Studies at the University of Ulster, where he has worked for over 30 years. He is Head of Subject for Community Youth Work and is also co-director of the Centre for Young Men's Studies. His research interests are linked to the Centre, and recent publications include *Taking Boys Seriously* (2012) which was a five-year longitudinal study funded by Department of Education NI and Department of Justice NI. The research looked at issues relating to boys' underachievement, wider concerns about boys' health and well-being and how experiences of violence in post-conflict society impact upon education and learning. He is currently chair of Playboard NI and also acts as advisor to the Youth Services Sectoral Partnership Group (YSSPG) as well as other voluntary commitments in youth work.

Henry McDonald is a writer and is the Irish editor for *The Observer*, the sister paper of *The Guardian*. He has written extensively about the Troubles, its precedents, its consequences, its demographics and such. He was born in the nationalist Markets area of Belfast and attended St Malachy's College. McDonald was formerly involved in the Sinn Féin Workers' Party, a left-wing republican party that emerged out of the Official IRA in the early 1970s. He travelled to the German Democratic Republic (East Germany) with the youth wing of SFWP around 1980. Much of his writing concerns Northern Irish paramilitaries such as the UDA and the INLA. He has written on loyalist paramilitary groups and has co-authored books on the Ulster Volunteer Force and Ulster Defence Association with Jim Cusack. He has also written a biography of Ulster Unionist leader David Trimble.

Alister J. McReynolds is the author of *Legacy, The Scots Irish in America* and also of *The Ulster Scots and New England*. Recently he has co-written a new Introduction to the 2012 publication *Robert Dinsmoor's Scotch-Irish poems*. McReynolds earned his MA at the University of Ulster, having gained his initial BA and two postgraduate diplomas from Queen's University, Belfast. He is currently an Honorary Research Fellow with the Centre for Irish and Scottish Studies at the University of Ulster. McReynolds has spent over 30 years as a teacher in his native province of Ulster, 14 of those years being engaged as Principal of a Further Education College. He was awarded Honorary Membership of the

City and Guilds of London Institute as recognition of his contribution to vocational education in Northern Ireland. Currently he continues to lecture part-time with the Open Learning Department in Queen's University Belfast. In the past five years McReynolds has lectured across the United States including at the Smithsonian Institution in Washington DC. Nearer to home he was the presenter of this year's Ulster-Scots-Agency-sponsored Whitelaw Reid Lecture in Belfast. He lives with his wife Eileen and their family at Magheragall in Co. Antrim.

Robbie McVeigh is a researcher and activist. He has taught on racism and anti-racism at Queen's University Belfast, the University of Ulster and UCD. He has researched racism and ethnicity in Irish society and is the author of many books including *The Racialisation of Irishness: Racism and Anti-Racism in Irish Society* (1996), *Theorizing Sedentarism: the Roots of Anti-Nomadism* (1997), *Travellers, Refugees and Racism in Tallaght* (1998) and is co-editor with Ronit Lentin of *Racism and Anti-Racism in Ireland* (2002).

Malachi O'Doherty is a journalist, author and broadcaster in Northern Ireland. He was, perhaps, the longest-running commentator/columnist on any Irish radio programme, having been a regular on Radio Ulster's 'Talkback' from its creation in the mid-1980s until a revamp of the programme in 2009. He provides regular political and social commentary for BBC NI's Current Affairs section. His political journalism has been published in many Irish and British newspapers and periodicals. In the mid-1990s he worked on and presented several television documentaries on Northern Irish culture and politics, for Channel 4, the BBC and UTV.

Graham Reid was born into a working-class family in Belfast, Northern Ireland. He left school at age 15, and served in the British army but returned to education and graduated from Queen's University in 1976. He became a teacher at Gransha Boys' High School in Bangor, County Down but left in 1980 to concentrate on his writing career. His first play, *The Death of Humpty Dumpty*, is a story about an innocent man who gets caught in the crossfire of the Troubles in Belfast. Characters in his work *The Hidden Curriculum* were based on pupils and teachers from the school he taught at. His trilogy, fondly referred to as 'the Billy plays', for the BBC's *Play for Today* series, were his breakthrough works. These are *Too Late to Talk to Billy* (1982), *A Matter of Choice for Billy* (1983) and *A Coming to Terms for Billy* (1984). The lead in these television plays was a young Kenneth Branagh, who had previously worked in Reid's futuristic play *Easter 2016*, which was screened as part of the BBC's *Play for Tomorrow* series. In 1992 he wrote a screenplay for the movie *You, Me & Marley* and in 2013 the much-anticipated fourth part of his 'Billy' series, *Love Billy* was commissioned and produced by the Lyric Theatre, Belfast.

Neil Symington has been a community youth worker for 15 years. He started his career in West Belfast and has since worked all over Northern Ireland. He studied youth and community work at the University of Ulster Jordanstown. He has worked with young people from all backgrounds, engaging with them often on sensitive/challenging issues. He has worked for a number of local voluntary organisations such as Newstart Education project and the Upper Springfield Development Trust, as well as regional voluntary organisations such as Barnardos, Opportunity Youth and the HIV Support Centre. For the past seven years he has worked for the NI Youth Forum as a participation development worker. The main area of work is to support, motivate and enable young people to have their voices heard on issues that are important to them. Over the last three years the focus of his work has been on the issues of sectarianism and racism, managing and developing a range of projects focused on improving relationships between young people from different backgrounds. Through his work he became increasingly interested in the role bands play in the lives of young people within Loyalist communities, which led him to develop a small research project, *Sons of Ulster*.

John Wilson is Professor of Communication at the University of Ulster, where he has held the positions of Head of School of Psychology and Communication and Dean of the Faculty of Social Sciences and Education. He studied at Ulster, Nottingham University and Queen's University Belfast where he received his PhD. He has also held visiting professorships at several major US universities, including Illinois, Washington, Seattle and Florida. His main research interests are in sociolinguistics and pragmatics, in particular political language, and he has published extensively in these areas including several books. He has just completed a book for OUP entitled *Talking with the President: the Pragmatics of Presidential Language*. For a period of time Wilson was also Director of the Institute of Ulster Scots Studies, and editor of a book series on Ulster and Scotland (Four Courts Press: Dublin). During this time he worked with an international research network on the impact of Ulster Scots on the global stage, including their role in the USA where they were often called Scotch or Scots Irish.

Introduction

Thomas Paul Burgess and Gareth Mulvenna

'Flags'
'Emblems'
'The Past'

Like Macbeth's three witches incanting 'Double, double toil and trouble; Fire burn, and cauldron bubble', these three seemingly insurmountable challenges continue to hinder the Northern Ireland peace process.

And for many, the responsibility for the impasse that scuppered the Haass talks and brought violent protest onto the streets of Belfast seems to lie directly with the apparent intransigence of the so-called and supposedly monolithic Protestant-unionist-loyalist bloc, or 'PUL community', and its apparent inability to embrace change in these matters. That this imagined ethnic bloc is itself riven with internal rancour and discord should come as no surprise. The term PUL itself is a modern concoction which has been used by commentators as shorthand to describe an entire community while reflecting the class and cultural differences inherent within it. While being far from a perfect moniker, the editors have decided that this acronym be used for the purposes of reference in this introduction.

Issues of social class, denominational alignment, political aspiration and national identity have historically divided what outsiders have often mistakenly viewed as a collective cultural, religious and sociopolitical monolith, a perception which could not be further from the truth. Allegiances between the main actors within the 'PUL' communities are tentative and rarely, if ever, enduring. Furthermore the mandatory coalition at Stormont has alienated and polarised a phalanx of opinion and allegiance across the entire unionist tradition.

1

Following the failure of the Haass talks, an exasperated Deputy First Minister Martin McGuinness claimed that the Orange Order, the Progressive Unionist Party and the Ulster Volunteer Force were '... one and the same thing'.[1] He was roundly reproached by the Orange Order for doing so. Yet behind closed doors, McGuinness claimed, 'mainstream Unionists' agreed with his analysis.[2] Whether this was an adroit political manoeuvre on his part – or the frustrated lament of a political pragmatist – what his comments did serve to reiterate was the gulf existing between those 'mainstream Unionists' with their hands on the levers of power and those 'dispossessed' whose core constituency lay within the loyalist working classes. These divisions were additionally exacerbated along socio-economic lines, as commercial and civic classes fiercely rounded on protesters who insisted, and continue to insist, that their political representatives are sleepwalking into an irredeemable diminution of their cultural identity.

It is arguable whether a single text could hope to exhaustively reflect the diversity of opinion and experience that exists within the PUL communities. Susan McKay, with her study *Northern Protestants*, attempted to do just that but ended up creating a deeply self-flagellating tome that failed to reflect the positive aspects of Northern Ireland's Protestant communities.[3] *Northern Protestants* was more a personal exorcism of Protestant self-loathing than a credible attempt to provide that community with a voice. Some participants felt let down by their representation in McKay's book and viewed the work as an 'opportunity missed'.

As co-editors of this book on Northern Ireland's broad Protestant community we saw a unique opportunity to let people speak directly; whether they themselves were from a Protestant, unionist or loyalist background, or alternatively, were outsiders with an interest in Northern Ireland's (and indeed Ireland's) social and political progress. The book's varied collection of insights and observations, drawn from an eclectic group of politicians, broadcasters, academics, artists and former paramilitaries demonstrates how we set out to 'take the pulse' of a grouping who are clearly struggling with the internal and external pressures and requirements of a transitional period in which previous certainties have been challenged, affecting all aspects of their place in the 'new order' of things.

While Irish nationalism translates more cohesively in a global context, it is true that in almost every aspect of civil society – sport; the arts; broadcasting; education; history and the relationship with our near neighbours in the Republic of Ireland and Great Britain (as well as further afield) – the 'PUL community' has presented a bewildering diversity of opinion and affiliation that serves only to perplex those who seek to understand it. Unfortunately it is often those who are the most bellicose in reinforcing an easy negative stereotype who succeed in being afforded the chance to represent this collective's true character to the wider world.

A brief journey through the contested identities

One of the most stubborn challenges to progress in Northern Ireland has been the conundrum of the Protestant working class and loyalism. Devoid of mature political leadership and with a devastating legacy of educational underachievement, drug abuse and violence it is frequently left to underfunded and often non-funded community workers to keep people in communities such as the Shankill, inner-east Belfast and Ballysally afloat. It has become apparent that many in Northern Ireland's middle class and beyond would prefer that these people reside in a social and political cul-de-sac where they would remain, unable to tamper with the brittle peace that has formed since the ceasefires of 1994. In that respect Northern Ireland has created its very own 'chav' problem, whereby people who are on the fringes of society are easily parodied and easily dismissed. There is a sense however that the period in the wake of the 'flag' controversy has borne witness to something of a 'loyalist spring'.

Previously voiceless constituencies have sought out the power of social media to convey their message. That it is unrefined at present is hardly the point – that the fledgling process of democratising social and political debate is underway is the real headline here. Of course, rather than welcoming this manifestation of popular expression from within one of its core constituencies, mainstream unionists had at first attempted to demonise and further marginalise this voice. Then, fearing electoral damage at the ballot box, they sought to placate it behind closed doors, much to the chagrin of republicans.

The most recent mobilisations by loyalist protesters at Twaddell Avenue and Belfast City Hall have been driven by groupings who understand more fully the role that media plays in the dissemination of their views. They have also taken a leaf out of the Sinn Féin playbook in embracing the agenda of the dispossessed and the marginalised, citing civil rights and liberties at every turn. The experienced journalist Malachi O'Doherty has written in this book about his involvement in media 'workshopping' with young loyalists. Many of these young people have found that their private lives have been amplified, distorted and used as fodder by the local Sunday tabloids. The protests have led to an increasing climate of non-violent politicisation among young loyalists, yet the negative aspects of the Protestant working class appear to be of more interest to the hacks in the *Sunday World* and *Sunday Life*. O'Doherty's chapter outlines the difficulties and frustrations encountered by young people in the loyalist community as they attempt to counter these negative stereotypes.

The high-profile role that women have taken in these protests is also noteworthy. In their contribution Ashe and McCluskey explore the complex processes through which PUL gendered identities are constituted and suggest that a continued analysis of gendered protests by unionist and loyalist women has the potential to draw out further insights about the impact of women's political resistances on gendered-power relationships in the PUL community, which has been traditionally dominated by masculine narratives.

Additionally, the place of the Orange Order and Orange culture in Northern Irish society has moved to centre stage, particularly in relation to Parades Commission designations and subsequent stand-offs regarding territorial claims and rights. Rev. Brian Kennaway, a controversial commentator on the Orange Order, evaluates the Twelfth of July 'flagship' events and 'Orangefest' as a means of attracting tourists on what is generally considered to be a divisive and controversial date in Northern Ireland's calendar.

And whilst the Order may at times appear outmoded, outdated and out of touch, there can be no gainsaying the important role that the marching band culture plays in the lives of young working-class loyalists in terms of community belonging and rites of passage. Sam McCready and Neil Symington present the case for the defence, highlighting the transcendence of meaning of the band culture for young people, above simple notions of perceived triumphalism. A tapestry of community emerges and the pieces illuminate the complexity of what culture means to the Protestant working class.

Nevertheless, old shibboleths have undoubtedly departed the scene. Previous convictions regarding the totemic leadership of Rev. Ian Paisley (in both a religious and secular setting) have been severely tested, not least by the revelations of Church and party infighting that emerged from a recent BBC television documentary. There is perhaps an even wider rift developing between the political classes and huge swathes of disaffected PULs. James Greer uses his chapter to demonstrate that 'while unionism is in the midst of another cycle of its particular form of pessimism it is important to note it is not alone in struggling to articulate a vision for the future, or an honest reckoning with the past. Across all communities in Northern Ireland economic peace dividends have been sporadic or insecure, and Irish nationalism and republicanism have many unanswered questions about their own Troubles narratives. The current political landscape may have secured an uneasy peace, and may be supported by an ethnic-bloc style of power-sharing, but recognition of its inadequacies is spreading', further stating that 'Further afield, the constitutional reconfiguration of the UK and political and economic crises in the EU point to broader uncertainties and challenges. How unionism responds to these evolving local, British and European circumstances will dictate its future. A re-engagement with unionist history highlights the continuity and strong structural roots of old mindsets, but it also points to the potential for Ulster Protestants to move beyond the default-settings when facing the challenges of a rapidly changing world.'

Fundamentalist beliefs vie with progressive aspiration, secular realities with religious conviction. The hunger for practical, day-to-day political administration regarding jobs, health and housing is frustrated by a slavish allegiance to an unbending sense of identity which the community still perceives as being under attack from without and within.

Questions of Britishness, Irishness and Northern Irishness are still viewed as mutually exclusive and diametrically opposed. The battle for cultural supremacy raging within council chambers and media platforms has, for the most part, usurped the violent conflict of the past.

These restrictive alignments pay scant regard to a wider historical legacy that may actually offer liberation from limited and limiting national identities. In his chapter Eoghan Harris looks at a number of what he terms 'moral milestones ... which saw the South put aside its stereotypes of northern unionists and see them for the first time as fellow human beings and acceptable agents of their own history'.

Observers may have felt that the establishment of Irish language classes in the heart of Loyalist East Belfast, spearheaded by Linda Ervine, the sister-in-law of former UVF man and Progressive Unionist Party leader David Ervine,[4] augured well for a more fluid embracing of identity and place. However, George Chittick, the Orange Order's Belfast County Grand Master, was quick to denounce the move and dissuade Protestants from taking such classes, again revealing the scope of divergence and discord within the PUL communities. Indeed some argued that this resistance to embracing a traditional cultural facet of the 'other' community demonstrated that large elements of this community continue to be actively suspicious and hostile toward difference and change. In his chapter Robbie McVeigh casts a critical eye on the origins of these controversies and outlines the choices that he feels the PUL community faces for the future.

Whereas the largely Catholic constituency of Irish-America has managed to maintain a veneer of coherence and homogeneity, the Protestants of Ireland have been largely disowned or denied by their diaspora in the United States. The apparent confusion around designations of Scotch/Scots/Irish within the US and at home does little to ameliorate the problem. These debates are contained in the illuminating and essential contribution to this volume by John Wilson and Alister McReynolds.

Within the arts community, administrators and artists alike have struggled to represent or reflect an artistic expression that sits easily within the subdivisions of these communities. This is further exacerbated by the embarrassment and rancour engendered through Newtownabbey Council's attempts to ban The Reduced Shakespeare Company's 'The Bible: the Complete Word of God (Abridged)', on the grounds that it was blasphemous.[5] Or DUP MLA William Humphrey's claim that,

> The Protestant working class unionist community see their culture as culture, and the concept of 'the arts' is not something which the Protestant working class community in this city buys into at any great level.[6]

Such knee-jerk reactions on the part of influential faith-based minorities, and sweeping statements by elected representatives serve only to reinforce the accepted stereotypes of this community as anti-intellectual, backward-looking religious fundamentalists. Humphrey's observation of course ignores the significant canon of artistic work by writers from a Protestant working-class background such as Sam Thompson, Graham Reid, Gary Mitchell, Robert Niblock and Marie Jones, among many others. Indeed the fact that, around the same time that Humphrey made this accusation, there was a Shankill 'people's history' play entitled *Crimea Square* being staged at a venue only a few hundred yards from his constituency office, was a delicious irony; it was ignored by the media, who were only too keen to carry his words of admonishment and belittlement.

Stephen Baker's contribution to this volume, 'Loyalism On Film and Out of Context', describes the fatalistic and negative stereotyping of working-class Protestants in television and film – a trend which is lambasted by figures such as Humphrey, but at the same time enabled by their entrenched outlook.

If there was once a narrow vision surrounding 'little Eire' during the de Valera years, that has perhaps been replaced by representations of a 'little(r) Britain' as 'seen' through the eyes of the loyalist working class in Northern Ireland. Baker appeals for loyalists to take the power back by representing themselves; getting involved in the arts. Again it is a question of confidence. How free from the shackles of traditional unionism is the loyalist working class?

Other contributors chose to represent their sense of PUL identity in terms of personal biography. In doing so they perhaps reveal a view of their homeland, their community and their identity that remains heavily rooted in past experience and nostalgia for simpler, more certain times. And whilst the state that they grew up in was certainly a sectarian one, it is salutary to learn how the change and upheaval they lived through influenced and affected individuals, setting them on particular life courses, informed by their notion of identity and duty.

Billy Hutchinson's chapter in particular provides a more nuanced narrative describing his decision to join the fledgling loyalist paramilitaries in the early 1970s. While much emphasis is rightly placed on the victims of violence in Northern Ireland, little is known about the motivations and experiences of those who chose to pick up the gun. Hutchinson describes a normal childhood and British working-class way of life prior to the late 1960s and outlines how he believes that it was this very existence in itself which was under threat when republicans enforced their campaign of terror on the people of Ireland and Britain.

Graham Reid, from a similarly normal working-class background in Belfast, recalls the 'big black cloud'[7] which the advent of violence heralded. Rather than pick up a gun, Reid chose the pen; and drew bittersweet but unsentimental portraits of Belfast's Protestant working class. Enveloped by the great tragedy of tit-for-tat violence in Northern Ireland, the Martin family in Reid's much-loved 'Billy' plays live out a life which is mired by domestic concerns – family, love, jealousy – rather than the contemporary scenario. For the first time the Protestant working class could see themselves portrayed on television in a manner which was similar to the great tradition of Northern 'kitchen sink' dramas played out by their counterparts in cities such as Leeds, Liverpool or Glasgow.

In conclusion, a work of this nature can but hope to reflect the central premise of the project; namely to explore somewhat the multifaceted aspects of the 'PUL' communities and by doing so, in some small way encourage readers to question the stereotype, look beyond the lazy denunciation and reject the cliché. There are many complex facets informing the shared identities of these groups, some of which are visited here. However, as the old Ulster adage would have it, 'If you're not confused, you haven't understood the situation' and this certainly holds true for the often perplexing and frustrating portrayal of those 'PUL' allegiances and aspirations, reservations and antagonisms, that continue to be presented to the wider world in a dangerously over-simplistic manner.

June 2014

Notes

1. 'McGuinness: Unionists Agree Orange Order is Linked to UVF and PUP', *BBC News* [website], 17 January 2014, <http://www.bbc.co.uk/news/uk-northern-ireland-25770465> [accessed 1 May 2014].
2. Ibid.
3. Susan McKay, *Northern Protestants: an Unsettled People* (Belfast: Blackstaff Press, 2005).
4. 'Growing Appetite Among Protestant, Unionist and Loyalist People to Learn Irish Language, Says Wife of Former PUP Leader', *Belfast Telegraph*, 9 October 2014.
5. 'Bible Spoof Play Ban Makes Northern Ireland a Laughing Stock', *Belfast Telegraph*, 24 January 2014.
6. 'Belfast Theatres Have Little to Offer Working Classes and Protestants in Particular, Claims DUP MLA William Humphrey', *Belfast Telegraph*, 9 October 2013.
7. G. Reid, 'Author's Note', *Love, Billy* (programme) (April 2013), 11.

1
Beginning to Talk to 'Billy': Revising Southern Stereotypes of Unionism

Eoghan Harris

> And we are here as on a darkling plain
> Swept with confused alarms of struggle and flight,
> Where ignorant armies clash by night.
> (Matthew Arnold, 'Dover Beach')

Introduction

Here's the question. For 77 years the Irish Republic rode roughshod over the political wishes of northern unionists by persisting with a constitutional claim on Northern Ireland.[1] Yet in 1998, by a massive majority of 94 per cent, those who voted for the Good Friday Agreement in the Irish Republic suddenly gave up that claim. How did such a convulsive change come about?

Controversially, I believe that change was largely driven by a small platoon of revisionists who waged a long war of political persuasion – but who only won that war because of a moral revulsion in the Irish Republic, marked by a number of milestones, which saw the South put aside its stereotypes of northern unionists and see them for the first time as fellow human beings and acceptable agents of their own history. Most southern nationalists saw revisionists as supporters of unionism, a charge that could hardly be denied since revisionists supported the principle of unionist consent and rejected the majority stereotype of unionists as suffering from false consciousness or racial hubris. But it made for a bitter war as well as a long war.

The big set-piece battles in that long war were won by a few famous revisionists, notably Conor Cruise O' Brien (*States of Ireland*), Ruth Dudley Edwards (*The Faithful Tribe*) and John A. Murphy's Seanad speeches of the 1970s. My own contribution was closer to that of a guerrilla, but

I believe my area of operations covered a wider range of activities than almost any other participant. In support of this I would point to this far from exhaustive list of activities: revisionist pamphlets for the Workers' Party (*The Irish Industrial Revolution*, 1977); stage plays on Protestant themes (*Showband*, 1982; *Souper Sullivan*, 1985); pro-unionist polemics in RTÉ ('Television and Terrorism', 1987); a weekly column in the *Sunday Times* largely addressed to northern unionists (1993–2000); pamphlets advising unionists on media ('Selling Unionism', 1995); contributions to David Trimble's Nobel Prize speech (1998); contributions to a feature film (*A Love Divided*, 1999), three documentary films about the maltreatment of Protestants in the Irish Republic (*Coolacrease, Cork's Bloody Secret* and *An Tost Fada/The Long Silence*, 2008–2012); and most recently a major revisionist speech entitled 'Towards 2016'.

The Arms Trial of 1970 was my wake-up call. The spectre of sectarian strife in the form of the Provisional IRA had shown its fascist face. In common with a handful of revisionists in the Republic, I resolved to do all in my power to thwart their malign plans. From then on hardly a week passed without me taking part in some political skirmish with supporters of irredentist Irish nationalism. And that intense participation in an almost 30-year struggle gives me some authority to make three core assertions. I believe that between 1970 and 1998 the Irish Republic changed its mind about unionism because it changed its mind about unionists. I believe this change was both political and moral, but that the moral change was by far the most important. I believe the change was marked by ten milestones, some of which historians depending on documents alone might see as merely marginal events. For example, I believe the Kingsmills massacre left an indelible mark on the moral psyche of the Irish Republic, whereas rhetorical nationalist posturing, like the New Ireland Forum of 1984, left not a trace behind. Arising from that evaluation, the essay that follows has three aims.

First, to chronicle ten moral and political milestones which in my view helped push anti-unionist prejudices to the margins of public life. Second, to show that what Eamon Dunphy famously dubbed 'Official Ireland' – the politicians, journalists and academics of the Irish Republic – continually lagged behind some of the smaller socialist parties as well as the general public in promoting pluralism. Third, to show that even a resolute revisionist like me did not find it easy to embrace the unionist case with complete empathy.

The darkling plain of prejudice 1921–66

My own life mirrors the Irish Republic's journey from myth to reality. I was born in Cork in March 1943. A month later, on April Fool's Day, as millions were fighting and dying in Europe, de Valera's *Irish Press* proclaimed with perfect seriousness: 'There is no kind of oppression visited on any minority in Europe which the six-county nationalists have not also endured.' And no, it was not an April Fool's joke. That kind of selfish myopia was by now normal in a southern political culture that had been in retreat from reality since 1921. It was a culture marked by two distortions which might be designated the pathology of anti-partitionism and the schizophrenia of stereotypes. Let me start with the pathology, defined in psychology as an inability to either change or to see the other clearly. From the foundation of the state Irish nationalists refused to face the reality of unionist opposition to a united Ireland.[2] Only 9 of the 338 published pages of debates on the Treaty of 1921 were on Northern Ireland.[3] The new state publicly paid lip service to Wolfe Tone's brotherhood of Protestant, Catholic and Dissenter, but adopted an ideology of anti-partitionism that stereotyped unionists as bigots rather than brothers.

Even a liberal republican like my father shared the general nationalist delusion that northern unionists suffered from two fundamental flaws. First, they were victims of what Marxists call 'false consciousness', i.e., they didn't know what they really wanted. Second, they suffered from feelings of racial superiority – a charge that would be recycled in the 1970s by some historians calling them *Herrenvolk*, a reference to racist South Africans. In passing, it should be noted that southern prejudice was not confined to unionists. Publicly, northern nationalists were lauded as our lost brethren. Privately, the Free State Cabinet found them an irritating nuisance, no more than a political and rhetorical stick to reinforce the Republic's territorial claim on Northern Ireland, later enshrined in Articles 2 and 3 of the 1937 Irish Constitution.[4] A schizophrenic stereotyping of northern unionists was the close companion of pathological anti-partitionism. Southern nationalists held two totally conflicting stereotypes of unionists in their heads. The first was that of a noble Protestant patriot, whom I shall call 'Henry' in honour of the Presbyterian United Irishman, Henry Joy McCracken; the second was that of a sectarian Orange bigot, whom I shall call 'Billy' in honour of William of Orange. Although 'Henry' had not been seen much since 1798, Irish nationalists frequently summoned him, for purely rhetorical purposes, to take his place on southern political platforms. However, when 'Henry' the Republican failed to appear, southern nationalists would swiftly dump his stereotype and replace it with that of 'Billy' the Bigot.

Southern antipathy against 'Billy' was somewhat mirrored by a soft sectarianism in its treatment of 'Billy's' southern cousin, 'William'. Official Ireland claimed the Republic had always treated southern

Protestants well – and what brave 'William' would publicly complain it did not? Accordingly, any reference to the catastrophic numerical decline of Protestants (by one third between 1911 and 1926) was totally taboo. From the early 1980s southern revisionists found that publicly admitting that some southern Protestants had suffered discrimination, however unpopular, brought two pluralist benefits. First it showed northern unionists that a few hardy souls in the Republic were ready to challenge the Catholic-nationalist narrative. Second, it subverted that most precious of southern myths: that bigotry only began at the border. Here Kevin Myers' 'Irishman's Diary' in the *Irish Times* made a major contribution by exposing the enforced exodus of rural Protestants during the period 1919–23. Although antipathy against 'Billy' was the norm among the majority of southern nationalists, a substantial minority referred to themselves as 'real republicans' to distinguish themselves from sectarian Catholic nationalists. For many years I saw myself as a 'real republican' too. Eventually, however, I could see why unionists were sceptical about the sincerity of 'real republicans' as long as they held onto myths like false consciousness and refused to accept the principle of consent.

My father was such a 'real republican'. He strongly opposed the famous Fethard-on-Sea boycott of Protestant shops in Wexford in 1957. But his pluralism seemed to stop at the border. He still saw Billy as through a glass darkly. No matter how often Billy told us he rejected Irish unity, even 'real republicans' refused to believe him. Some day he would share our dream, Tone's Republic of Catholics, Protestants and Dissenters. Even Conor Cruise O'Brien was not immune to 'real republican' rhetoric. As late as 1966, in *Embers of Easter*, he could write that 'the territorial division of the island between these people [Gaels] and the children of the Scottish-settlers in Ulster, was the slightly distorted expression of a long-standing spiritual division which men like Tone and Pearse lived and died to close'.[5] However that same year, 1966, marked a watershed. The dark forces of Provo nationalism would soon force O'Brien to fundamentally change his mind – and he in turn would eventually persuade the rest of us in the Irish Republic to change our minds too; but nobody in 1966 could have imagined the bloody milestones that would mark the journey across the darkling plain.

The war of ignorant armies 1966–98

In 1966, the Irish Republic celebrated the fiftieth anniversary of the 1916 Rising, with re-enactment dramas on RTÉ. The same year saw the start of the Northern Ireland Civil Rights Association. As a trainee producer in RTÉ, and also an active member of the Dublin Wolfe Tone Society, I was involved in both events. In August 1966, at a secret meeting in Maghera, attended by the left-wing leadership of the IRA, together with trade unionists and academics, I was selected to read a long document from the Dublin Wolfe Tone Society which set out the strategy for the newly formed Northern Ireland Civil Rights Association. The strategy stressed the peaceful principles that should govern the NICRA campaign. I still remember a phrase to the effect that the whole strategy would fail 'at the first sound of a bomb or a bullet'. The founders of NICRA shared the general nationalist consensus that Billy was being manipulated by British and unionist puppeteers. But they also pragmatically believed in not provoking him with talk of Irish unity during the struggle for civil rights. That is why NICRA opposed the provocative People's Democracy march to Burntollet. They feared it would bring out not 'Henry' but 'Billy'. They were right. In 1970, the Provisional IRA stepped onto the stage, determined to force Billy to do what he did not want to do.[6] The Irish Republic remained ambivalent for a few bloody years and then began the slow journey towards reality. What follows is a chronicle of ten moral and political milestones that marked that journey. They omit later atrocities like the Omagh bomb, because by then reality had kicked in.

Note: the adjective preceding the word 'milestone' indicates whether 'political' or 'moral' carries the most weight.

The Arms Trial of 1970 was the first political milestone. At its core was the tribal figure of Charles Haughey, who was openly contemptuous of Ulster Protestants, and seemed willing to risk civil war to promote his political career. So as early as 1970, the Republic had to take sides. By not taking Haughey's side it took the first small step towards realism. But if Haughey was nakedly tribalist, even a liberal like Garret Fitzgerald had problems with unionists too. In his 1973 book, *Towards a New Ireland*, he repeats the Republic's deep-rooted delusion that Billy suffered from false consciousness and secretly hankered after a united Ireland. 'Even today, the deep-rooted but rarely admitted belief that ultimately Irish unity must prevail, lies at the heart of many Northern Protestant attitudes.'[7] At least Fitzgerald's delusions about 'Billy' were benign. That was not true of some of the most senior figures in the British politics. In 1972, while Prime Minister Harold Wilson was being filmed for an RTÉ programme on the Liverpool dock strike, he tried to ingratiate himself with the RTÉ team by making ribald off-the-record remarks about unionists. Wilson's delinquent attitude towards Northern Ireland was confirmed by

Dermot Nally, Assistant Secretary to the Irish Government. At a lunch at Downing Street in 1976 he heard Wilson ask the Irish Taoiseach, Liam Cosgrave point-blank: 'Wouldn't it be better for everybody if we just let them kill each other in Ulster?'[8]

The second political milestone was the speech in the same year as Wilson's remark, 1972, by Tomás Mac Giolla, President of Official Sinn Féin at Carrickmore, County Tyrone. Given the different degrees of delusion about unionists held by Haughey, Fitzgerald and Wilson around the same time, Mac Giolla's courageous speech shines like a pluralist star in the darkling plain of delusional beliefs about unionists. People have talked about the Provisionals trying to bomb 1 million Protestants into a Republic; but they would not – could not – and no one can – and no one as far as we are concerned would try – to bomb them into a socialist republic. That would be the ultimate contradiction and the ultimate stupidity. Admittedly, Mac Giolla's speech is not completely free of the false consciousness myth, as seen in a reference to 'understanding the justified and unjustified fears of the Protestant working class'.[9] But for its time (1972) and place (Tyrone) it was strikingly pluralist in two respects: it opposed standing down Stormont on democratic grounds, and it categorically condemned the IRA's irredentist campaign. At the time it was seen as a landmark in left-wing and republican circles – for the first time a republican leader had implicitly accepted the principle of unionist consent.

The third political milestone was Conor Cruise O' Brien's *States of Ireland*. It was by far the most influential revisionist intervention in what would turn out be a 30-year struggle for minds and hearts in the Irish Republic. I was not an immediate convert. For another two years I resisted what I saw as O'Brien's retreat from the 'real republican' aspiration to Wolfe Tone's noble republic. It took me until 1974 to fully accept that 'Billy' was entitled to the principle of consent. 'Billy' still remained a political abstraction, was still a bigoted mask rather than a human face – but all that was about to change, and in the most tragic circumstances.

The Kingsmills massacre, 5 January 1976, was the fourth massive moral milestone. It left an indelible impression on the psyche of the Irish Republic, as any person of adult age at the time can confirm. Both as a man and a Marxist, I was revolted by RTÉ's grim pictures of the pathetic traces of the ten slain workers – bloody false teeth, lunchboxes, workmens' helmets. My revulsion was shared by most people in the Irish Republic. Paul Durcan's moving poem, *The Mini-Bus Massacre*, summed up the national mood. For the first time, many people in the Republic experienced an epiphany that became a permanent empathy.

They moved from hating 'Billy' the bigot to compassion for 'Billy' the victim. Even six years later, when my play *Show Band* was staged in Dublin and Cork, the audience spontaneously applauded after the former IRA man Frankie McCann recalled why the Kingsmills massacre had finished him with Irish nationalism forever:

> FRANKIE: Nothing seems important enough when you've seen that. You never see a tricolour flying without looking for the stains where they washed out the other stuff. You never hear the word Republic without listening for the sound of the safety catches coming off. You never feel the things you felt about Ireland any more. You just watch out she doesn't kill any more of the kids she never should have had because she is one murderous mother.

The following year, 1977, saw another small sign of the shift in the republican-socialist view of 'Billy's' political rights. This was the relatively muted response to the provocative revisionist sentiments in my pamphlet; *The Irish Industrial Revolution* (1977) published by Sinn Féin and the Workers' Party. There were only a few resignations after this reworking of what was then called 'the national question'. 'For us the national question can only be formulated as peace among the divided working class in the two states in Ireland so as to allow a united industrial revolution in all Ireland and the overthrow of Anglo-American imperialism and ultimately the construction of an Irish Workers' Republic.'[10]

The fifth moral milestone was the Republic's mixed reaction to the 1981 H-Blocks crisis. Although most people in the Republic sympathised with the hunger strikers, a substantial minority did not. For example, John A. Murphy refused to stand in silence in memory of Bobby Sands at a Munster Hurling Final – and survived. The same year, Tish Barry's RTÉ film *Victims of Violence*, which sympathetically featured RUC widows, was widely acclaimed and won a Jacob's Award. By then, as Ireland's leading pollster, Jack Jones, pointed out, IRA violence had created a major revulsion in the Irish Republic; against the IRA and against Irish unity.[11] In sum, just as northern nationalist support for Sinn Féin was rising in the wake of the H-Blocks, southern nationalist sentiment was going the other way. Like many northern nationalists John Hume seemed to feel betrayed by this shift in southern sympathy. In a 1981 interview with Seamus Deane he first flirted with a version of the *Herrenvolk* slur ('Would it have been reasonable to suppose, for example, that you can't have civil rights in Mississippi because the whites might oppose it?') but then went on to what was really bothering him: the shift in sympathy in the Irish Republic: 'Also I resent the concern evinced so frequently by Southern "liberals" for the Unionist position alone, without reference to the rest of the Northern community. They are one of the most right-wing forces in Europe – nobody else would stand for them, anywhere.'[12]

Seamus Deane, the epitome of a supportive interviewer, was also moved, as a northern nationalist himself, to patronise the soft pluralists of the Irish Republic. Nothing sums up the growing gap between northern and southern nationalists better than Deane's patronising dismissal of the Republic's new sensitivity to the sufferings of northern Protestants. Maybe the south of Ireland does not quite understand the difference in the theological ferocity of Calvinist anti-Catholicism and the much more socially directed anti-Catholicism of Anglicanism? The New Ireland Forum (1984) was a sop to Hume. But it was a backward step at a time when the Republic's benign brand of soft republicanism was replacing tribal slogans. As O' Halloran says, the Forum's rhetoric gave 'respectability to the tattered remnants of an irredentism which had become anachronistic and devalued in its tradition form'.[13]

The sixth moral milestone was the acclaimed 1985 production at the Abbey Theatre of Frank McGuinness's play, *Observe the Sons of Ulster Marching Towards the Somme*. Later that year the Abbey also staged (to somewhat less acclaim) a controversial play of mine called *Souper Sullivan* about mass conversions to Protestantism during the Famine on the Mizen Head in Co. Cork. Father John Murphy's warning to the stubborn converts who refused to return to Rome was clearly read by audiences as a metaphor for what might happen to northern Protestants if forced into an Irish Republic.

> FR MURPHY: You will have to huddle in Sullivan ... poor Protestants going the road, creeping by the hedge ... and we will creep in like the sea till you are cold, cold and then you will be gone like the labourers and no one will write your history for you will have no history and no one will tell your story for you have no story ... Listen to the wind blow ...

The Enniskillen bombing of 1987 marked a seventh moral milestone. But while the bombing revolted most people in the Irish Republic, it did not revolt some radio producers in RTÉ, who refused to condemn the bombing at a trade union meeting. As a result I resigned from that union and wrote an analysis called 'Television and Terrorism', which warned about the dangers of a 'leaky consensus' against Irish nationalism, and supported the Section 31 ban on Sinn Féin. The appendix to the document proposed 13 new programmes to promote pluralism. These included a documentary 'on the role of William of Orange in creating a Dutch Republic against the Spanish and their Inquisition, so as to place in context the historical fears of "Popery"'.[14] On the lighter side I looked for 'a frank and funny' examination of what Protestants and Catholics thought of each other growing up in the North and South, and the myths and fantasies on both sides. RTÉ took no notice.

The eighth milestone, both moral and political, was Tomás Mac Giolla's speech to the Workers' Party Annual Conference in 1988. The WP was now attracting middle-class support in Dublin, where it would win six seats, indicating that the party's pluralism was a plus factor. Mac Giolla's speech, into which I had some input, for the first time in Republican circles accepted that unionists were neither manipulated puppets, nor pitiable victims, but historical actors in their own right. 'This party wants to talk to the Protestant people of Northern Ireland. Every other party in Ireland, from Fianna Fail to Fine Gael, from the SDLP to Provisional Sinn Féin, wants to talk about them. Every faction in Britain from Thatcher Tories to Livingstone Trotskyites seems to want to talk around them or behind their back, or talk them into a corner or a cul-de-sac, as if they were some primitive tribe whose redundant religious rites and curious cultural riches should be sanitised and studied, as if they were exhibits in a museum rather than a living people – a living people whose courage and endurance has seen them take the genocidal butchery of some 200 small farmers and workers in Fermanagh without retaliation, and who gave an awesome display of tolerance and forgiveness as they knelt among their dead after Enniskillen.' Ken Maginnis, the Official Unionist MP for Fermanagh–South Tyrone, responded in kind:

> In his summary of the Protestant principles of private conscience, rebellion against Rome, and industriousness, coupled with his appeal in his final speech to the Ard Fheis, for Protestants to use these truths to confront hypocrisy in Ireland, Mr Mac Giolla has been keeping the good wine to the last.[15]

Compare Mac Giolla's generous and pluralist speech with what Official Ireland's favourite historian, Professor Joe Lee was saying a year later, 1989, in his magnum opus *Ireland 1912–85: Politics and Society*. Although Lee was not a narrow nationalist, and could legitimately call himself a 'real republican', his book still contained passages on unionism and Protestantism that seemed to come from another age:

> Ulster unionists did cherish a siege mentality. But the psychological requirements of the Herrenvolk were such that if those claims had not existed they would have had to invent them to justify the degree of institutionalised discrimination against Catholics.[16]

Arthur Aughey's *Under Siege* (1989)[17] was a welcome antidote. Here was proof that unionism could produce a fresh and sophisticated analysis of its own complex history and political culture. Reading Aughey, I finally realised that unionists looked to the state for legitimacy whereas nationalists looked to the nation. Furthermore, unionists were not simply clients of the Crown, still less a *Herrenvolk*, but heirs to a British republican tradition. In the background it was not hard to hear echoes of the Putney debates and the democratic demands of the Levellers. At this remove, I cannot say how much Aughey's analysis influenced a pamphlet I published the same year, 'The Necessity of Social Democracy'.[18] As this marked my break with socialism, it presented an updated social-democratic rather than Republican-socialist definition of the 'national question'. Significantly, while some southern commentators like Justin Keating challenged my rejection of socialism, none took public issue with my revision of the 'national question'.

The national question in today's terms can only be defined as supporting the democratic right of northern unionists to decide their own political destiny; defeating the Catholic sectarian campaign of the Provisional IRA to set up a one-party state; and uniting all progressive forces on the island in pursuit of peace and plenty in the context of a social democratic Europe from the Atlantic to the Urals. Two years later, in 1991, my old UCC friend, Gearóid Ó Crualaoich, seemed to follow up Aughey's insights with a powerful essay on 1916.[19] He argued that Irish republicans were Romantics and unionists were Puritans, but that in some fundamental sense 1916 was 1688 if regarded in the right light – both being declarations of independence in their different ways. And I experienced something close to an epiphany as I read his noble attempt to reconcile unionism and real republicanism. The aspiration to a life lived in freedom, with justice for all under the rule of law, and with the fair sharing of the produce of human labour, cannot be incompatible with the deepest desires of all who truly cherish the memory and the myth of Easter Week 1916 or of the Glorious Revolution of 1688, and we can even dare to envisage a sense in which 1916 is 1688.

The ninth political milestone was the 1990 election of Mary Robinson as President of Ireland. She had courageously rejected the Anglo-Irish Agreement, which won her the regard of many unionists. She had defeated a respected former SDLP politician, Austin Currie, whose nationalist credentials had failed to energise the southern electorate. Accordingly she was the living, breathing embodiment of the new spirit of pluralism which was now firmly – and as future events would prove – permanently embedded in the people of the Irish Republic.[20] I was proud to have played a significant part in her election, but I was still on sentry duty. In 1990 I began a weekly political column in the *Sunday Times* which reached an influential unionist readership in Northern Ireland. Many began to respond by post. It was a conversation which was carried on up to and beyond the Good Friday Agreement, and since 2000 it has been continued in the *Sunday Independent*. From the start I tried to win the trust of unionists by acting with good authority. That is, by saying things that were bound to annoy my own side. My first column, a few weeks after the first IRA ceasefire, was called 'Why the Protestants Won'. The provocative opening produced a solid northern Protestant postbag:

To put it plainly: the Protestants have won, and won against awesome odds. At first the world saw you as Afrikaners keeping down the natives. The British trendy left cast you as colonists. The South saw you as the next thing to Satan and the sight of your humble homes, and the dark mills in which you worked, seemed not to disturb the stereotypes. You had no case, and no face. Sectarians and fascists, bigots banging drums, the sleep of reason that brings forth ministers. The South shrugged. You deserved what you were going to get. But, of course, nobody deserved what you got. Not that holocaust of horror, fathers cut down in farmyards, children crying on blood-stained doorsteps, the false teeth of the slain workers among their lunchboxes. All through the 1970s the South stared in silent shock as the bloody hammer of the Provisionals rose and fell on the Protestant anvil. We waited for you to break. But you did not break. And something stirred, like grace, and we started to shed our illusions.[21]

The tenth moral milestone was Gusty Spence's expression of 'true and abject remorse' announcing the loyalist ceasefire of 1994. For the first time the South saw 'Billy' with a warm and human face. After that, David Ervine of the PUP featured regularly in my *Sunday Times* columns. He soon became a hugely popular spokesperson for progressive working-class unionism in the Irish Republic. However, apart from Gusty Spence,

Ervine and Ken Maginnis, unionists did poorly when dealing with the mass media. In 1995, I wrote a pamphlet for the Young Unionists called 'Unionism and the Mass Media', which tried to explain why Sinn Féin spokespersons seemed more successful than unionists at getting their message across on television to Irish, British and American audiences.[22] The principal reason, I believed, was that people reared on the Bible respected text rather than context. Unionists are too wedded to text over tone, to what is said rather than who says it, to the song not the singer. Second, unionists' spokespersons are perceived by audiences to lack an attractive theory of political change. Third, and of greater importance than the preceding two perceptions, is the sense that unionist spokespersons seem more concerned to make a case than tell a story.

Around this time, in the 1990s, I became active in trying to shift stereotypes of unionists in the fraught area of feature films. Brian McIlroy in *Shooting To Kill* argues that unionists were under-represented in feature films – a charge echoed by Padraic Coffey in a similar study.[23] British socialist directors like Ken Loach (with whose producer I had had a blazing row in the run-up to his first film, the aptly named *Hidden Agenda*) while waving a red flag, seemed to favour those who waved a green flag, while ironically ignoring the existence of the only industrial working class on the island – the unionist working class. Irish directors weren't much better. In 1998 I had a sharp exchange in the *Irish Times* with Neil Jordan about his movie on Michael Collins. Jordan had signalled his political take on the project the previous year, telling the *Irish Times* he was doing a film, professing that 'I don't think it will make Conor Cruise O'Brien very happy, you know?'[24]

Back in 1996, I had destroyed my own chance of making a movie on Michael Collins by breaking with the designated director Michael Cimino after he had talked to nationalists, but not unionists, in Belfast. So I was in no mood to mince my words with Jordan. My main problem was his anachronistic use of a car bomb to kill northern unionist policemen – a scene that was cheered by Provo supporters in some cinemas. Finally, in 1999, I returned to the Fethard-on-Sea saga, bringing the idea for a feature film on the boycott to my old comrade Gerry Gregg. The result was *A Love Divided*. Like *Michael Collins*, it too played to packed audiences. The national consensus was still somewhat leaky, but at least it leaked a lot less than it had 30 years before.

Postscript: the amazing grace of the Good Friday Agreement and its aftermath

The Good Friday Agreement of 1998 recognised 'the birthright of all the people of Northern Ireland to identify themselves and be accepted as Irish or British, or both'. My long stint on sentry duty for unionists was acknowledged when I was asked to address the UUP Conference, where I put my misgivings aside and called the Agreement 'an amazing grace'. David Trimble accepted some of my suggestions for his Nobel Prize speech. But one of the most quoted lines, referring to 'a cold house for Catholics' is usually only partially quoted by those critical of unionism.[25] The full paragraph does not exonerate nationalists either. Ulster unionists, fearful of being isolated on the island, built a solid house, but it was a cold house for Catholics. And northern nationalists, although they had a roof over their heads, seemed to us as if they meant to burn the house down.

The Good Friday Agreement and the Irish Republic's removal of the constitutional claim on Northern Ireland should have allowed me to step down from duty. But noxious Irish nationalism never sleeps. As late as 2008, Gerry Adams told a fundraising dinner in New York, 'Few human beings of my acquaintance are as petty and mean-spirited as those in the Afrikaner wing of unionism.'[26] Two years later, in 2010, one of the Republic's most popular historians, Tim Pat Coogan, was still stereotyping northern unionism – and unionists.

> Philosophically unionism is based on supremacy, on fear and distrust of the natives, and a quotient of false righteousness akin to the notion of manifest destiny that their ancestors used to justify their extermination of the American Indians. The fundamental unionist mind-set is a provincial one, aping British mores in Belfast bowler hats.[27]

Countering that kind of smug tribalism drove me, in the first decade of the new millennium, to draw attention to Old IRA atrocities against Protestants, three of which featured in RTÉ films: *Coolacrease, Cork's Bloody Secret* and *An Tost Fada/The Long Silence* (2008–11). The positive reactions to all three films confirmed my belief that most of my Roman Catholic countrymen are anxious to make amends for any past misdeeds. By doing so, they invite reciprocal moves from northern unionism. Acting with good authority, however, always means taking the first step. That was the burden of my speech, 'Towards 2016', at the annual Liam Lynch Commemoration in Kilcrumper cemetery in 2011. Reaching out to 'real republicans', I also gave them a reality check:

> Liam Lynch never faced the fact that the fundamental problem was not merely to break the connection with England but to create a connection with Northern Protestants – who rightly feared a repressive Roman Catholic Republic.[28]

When I finished, to muted heckling and polite applause, a fattish young man came up and spat at me. Thirty years ago I might have got a bad beating. Looking back, I have done my bit for 'Billy'. Looking forward, when 'Billy' feels fully secure, my grandchildren might meet 'Henry' too.

So far, so very good.

Notes

1. Maureen Wall, 'Partition: the Ulster Question (1916–26) in T. D. Williams (ed.), *The Irish Struggle 1916–1926* (London: Routledge and Kegan Paul 1966), 87.
2. For a comprehensive critique of anti-partitionism see Clare O' Halloran, *Partition and the Limits of Irish Nationalism* (Dublin: Gill and Macmillan, 1987).
3. O' Halloran, *Partition*, 131–56.
4. Peter Hart, *The IRA and its Enemies* (Oxford: Oxford University Press, 1998).
5. Conor Cruise O' Brien, *Irish Times*, 7 April 1966.
6. Patrick Bishop and Eamonn Mallie, *The Provisional IRA* (London: Corgi, 1988).
7. Garret Fitzgerald, *Towards a New Ireland* (Dublin: Gill and Macmillan 1973), 14.
8. Dermot Nally quoted in *Haughey* (miniseries) (Mint Productions), RTÉ 1, broadcast July 2005.
9. Roy Johnston, 'Tomas Mac Giolla at Carrickmore July 1972', *Century of Endeavour* [website] (1999), <http://www.rjtechne.org/century130703/1970s/carkmore.htm> [accessed 1 May 2014].
10. Eoghan Harris, *The Irish Industrial Revolution* (Dublin: Repsol, 1977).
11. Jack Jones interview, *Frontline Special* (Straightforward Productions) Channel 4 (transmitted 1 June 1996).
12. John Hume, Seamus Deane and Barré Fitzpatrick, 'Interview with John Hume', *The Crane Bag* 4 (2) 'The Northern Issue' (1980/1981): 39–43.
13. O'Halloran, *Partition*, 210.
14. Eoghan Harris, 'Television and Terrorism' (RTÉ, 1987). Published as a Photostat document and distributed by the author.
15. F. Pyle, 'MacGiolla Gets a Unionist Tribute', *Irish Times*, 18 April 1988.
16. Joseph Lee, *Ireland 1912–85: Politics and Society* (Cambridge: Cambridge University Press, 1989), 79.
17. Arthur Aughey, *Under Siege* (London: Blackstaff, 1989).
18. Eoghan Harris, 'The Necessity of Social Democracy', in R. English and J. M. Skelly (eds), *Essays in Honour of Conor Cruise O'Brien* (Dublin: Poolbeg, 1998), pp. 333–45.
19. Gearóid Ó Crualaoich, 'Responding to the Rising', in M. Ní Dhonnchadha and T. Dorgan (eds), *Revising the Rising* (Derry: Field Day, 1991), 50–71.
20. Mary Robinson, *Everybody Matters* (London: Walker and Company, 2012).
21. Eoghan Harris, 'Why the Protestants Won', *Sunday Times*, 4 September 1994.
22. See Eoghan Harris, 'Selling Unionism', in T. Dunne and L. Geary (eds), *History and the Public Sphere: Essays in Honour of John A. Murphy* (Cork, 2005).

23. See Brian McIlroy, *Shooting to Kill: Filmmaking and the Troubles in Northern Ireland* (London: Steveson Press, 2001); also Padraic Coffey, 'Cinema, Northern Ireland and the Representations of Protestants' (UCD unpublished thesis, 2010).
24. Interviewed by Michael Dwyer, *Irish Times*, 7 January 1995.
25. *Irish Times*, 26 October 1996.
26. *Belfast Telegraph*, 14 November 2008.
27. Tim Pat Coogan, *Memoir* (London: Hachette UK, 2008).
28. Full text – *Sunday Independent*, 18 September 2011.

2

Investigating the Protestant 'Kaleidoscope'

Henry McDonald

At the recent Doolin Writers' Festival in May 2013 an 'alien' landed in this bucolic corner of Co. Clare. His presence inside the eco-friendly Hotel Doolin divided opinion in the hall. This 'creature from another planet' outraged and shocked as much as he entertained and amused. To those in the former camp he was described as 'something crawling from under a rock' or as a malignant force that had blown into the peninsula from a darker, stranger climate.

This 'alien' was Terri Hooley, hippy rebel, punk impresario, record shop owner, raconteur and libertine.

Hooley was the opening speaker at the festival, organised in conjunction with the Irish Writers' Centre, who regaled those attending with tales of wild nights with rock stars like Thin Lizzy frontman Phil Lynott, and physical confrontations with John Lennon over the latter's support for the IRA. Perhaps the sharpest intakes of breath among the audience – and a mini-walkout – were provoked by Hooley's protest about the attitude of the South to the North during and even after the Troubles.

'You in Dublin were living in heaven while we were living in hell', Hooley boomed, before pointing out that 75 per cent of the Republic's population under the age of 40 had never been to Northern Ireland. His mild accusations and anti-nationalism (as virulent as his loathing for the unionist establishment) did not go down well with a small section of those at the event although the majority appeared to have been wooed by his anarchic, turbo-charged diatribes and anecdotes.

If a radical socialist, secular Protestant from Belfast, who has stood up to the baseball-bat-wielding thugs of loyalism, could encounter enmity among some southerners, just imagine therefore what their reaction might have been to a mainstream unionist outlining the case for the union in the far south-west of Ireland!

24

Of course, the attitude, the 'vision' of unionism, unionists, loyalists and Ulster Protestants within nationalist Ireland very much depends on which end of the island that perception is taking place. South of the border the overwhelming image of the 'Ulster Prod' is one of bewilderment. The unionists of the north-east of Ireland are, in the main, as unknown an entity as the Bosnian Serbs or the Algerian Berbers. Outside of the caravan of North–South community relations groups and the political classes in Belfast and Dublin, 'Middle Ireland', while not overtly hostile to the unionist population, has little understanding of, or social interaction with them.

Herein, then, lies a paradox. 'Middle Ireland's' indifference to matters north of the border has played an important part in the social shift within the Republic away from revanchist, reclaim-the-Fourth-Green-Field nationalism to support for a political settlement, which in the short-to-medium term accepts partition and an Assembly at Stormont still wholly dependent on the UK Treasury.

There is a minority (dwindling?) in the South, who maintain a historic hostility towards those they regard (at its most benign) as 'misguided Irishmen and women'. Yet most people in the Republic take the attitude that as long as the North is peaceful, settled and stable, it and its people can continue taking the high road while we take the low road. Partition in mind, as well as geopolitical reality, continues. This is in complete contrast to the way northern nationalists view unionists. Because the one thing Northern Irish Catholics share with Northern Irish Protestants is that they are obsessed with one another.

Northern nationalists have basically two highly generalised reactions to unionists: fear and amused contempt. Take the latter first, which is linked to another paradox thrown up by the peace process years. It is best summed up by a football chant, or rather taunt, that some fans of Cliftonville (this author's beloved team by the way!) direct at the supporters of Belfast Linfield and Glentoran. Since the Good Friday Agreement was signed in 1998, Cliftonville fans have chanted 'You're not British anymore' to the Linfield and Glentoran support. The taunting implies that the mainly unionist supporters of Belfast's so called 'Big Two' are living in a kind of constitutional departure lounge; destination – a United Ireland.

In reality of course, the Agreement actually strengthens partition given that it left the constitutional question within the confines of the Northern Ireland electorate ... or as republicans used to call it, 'the unionist veto'. In other words, as former Deputy First Minister Seamus Mallon so correctly pointed out 15 years ago, we are back with

'Sunningdale for Slow Learners'. Indeed it could be argued that the Good Friday settlement is in fact 'Sunningdale minus one' given that the 1974 power-sharing arrangement (which both the Provisionals and hard-line unionists sought to destroy) contained far greater Dublin influence over Northern Irish affairs than the 1998 and subsequent St Andrews settlements brought about. None the less, this kind of relatively harmless football banter reflects a deeper attitude towards unionists, which dismisses their politics and culture as arcane, outmoded and destined to go out of existence shortly. In effect this kind of amused contempt actually acts as a comfort blanket for many republicans (outside of the dissident ranks) who try to convince themselves that they really are on the road to reunification in their lifetime. This patronising image of the Ulster Prod reflects back in the mirror, revealing the hidden, deeply buried fear amongst republicans in particular that the Provisional project, since the republican movement divided in 1969–70, has failed in terms of its core objective.

The irony is that when unionists, particularly working-class loyalists, appear exercised over symbolic issues like the Union flag policy at Belfast City Council, it actually helps many republicans forget about the bigger picture – that the coins in their pockets still have the Queen's head on them, that their public services, jobs, welfare and education are all 100 per cent reliant on the subvention from London. Prod anger over peripheral issues acts as a lightning rod for northern nationalists to redirect their own fears about where the peace process has actually taken the republican project, especially given that we are now only just over two years away from the magic target date of 2016.

There are of course real and genuine fears within the Catholic nationalist republican community in the north of Ireland about unionists and unionism. The old collective nightmare of 'being murdered in our beds', conjured up during the pogroms of the 1920s as both states in Ireland came into being, still invades the sleep of many Catholics and nationalists, particularly east of the Bann. The virtually random sectarian targeting of Catholics (remember ACWD 'Any Catholic Will Do') during the Troubles by loyalist paramilitaries kept this nightmarish vision alive well into the 1990s. Even non-republican Catholics witness events such as the brutal gang violence against a young Catholic woman and her Protestant friends by loyalists in a south Belfast drinking den as evidence that, given the chance, a small but innately bigoted, violent section of the Protestant working class would happily slit the throat of any Catholic they came across and think nothing of it. The incidents of visceral torture killings from John White's murder squads in north Belfast in the early '70s, to the throat slicers who murdered young Catholic women like Anne Marie Smyth two decades later, have provided enough evidence to stoke that collective fear even into the era of the peace process and power-sharing.

As an aside, it is worth pointing out that loyalist politicians have said little in the recent past about the northern Catholic population's willingness to swallow hard when it came to the early release of para-military prisoners. One of the hardest issues for pro-Agreement union-ists like David Trimble to sell in 1998 was that part of the accord which granted early release and a de facto amnesty to IRA and loyalist prison-ers from the Maze and other jails. Generally, the opponents of a Yes vote and, at least up until 2006, power-sharing itself, highlighted almost exclusively the sight of notorious IRA figures like Shankill bomber/mass murderer Sean Kelly walking free out of the turnstiles of the Maze car park in the years after the Agreement. What these unionist politicians failed to acknowledge was that many of those who enjoyed early release while their victims were left with a lifetime of sorrow and torment were prisoners who had cut the throats of their Catholic victims or sprayed betting shops with automatic gunfire in random sectarian acts. The early release of prisoners generated hurt on both sides of the communal divide; hurt that many Catholics felt was not appreciated by unionist political leaders.

Strangely, the perception of fear compared to amused contempt is an easier one for unionism and unionists to address. Or to be more specific, the Ulster loyalists. Take the case of the assault on that young Catholic woman and her Protestant friends by a mob in the Village area in south Belfast, which ended with all of them being driven out of the district, or rather being exfiltrated out of it by armed police officers. To be fair, Jackie McDonald, the leader of the Ulster Defence Association in the area, did condemn the incident. However, some loyalists in the Village responded to media reports about this incident by printing up and distributing posters accusing the women attacked of telling lies about their ordeal. Loyalists, particularly the rival UVF, some of whose members were accused of taking part in the assaults and intimidation, could have instead urged witnesses to come forward to the police with information instead of demonising the victims further.

Yet it has to be stressed that it is still a violent, but politically discon-nected minority who continue the machismo cult of paramilitarism in Protestant communities ... much to the disgust and frustration of the very people they think they are defending. Just as unionists and unionist politicians never appreciated how hard it was for the Catholic community to accept early freedom for murderers from the loyalist wings of the Maze prison, nationalists hardly ever acknowledge that most Protestants and unionists don't support the loyalist paramilitaries. Witness the paltry votes UDA- and UVF-linked parties received before and after the Troubles as evidence of this.

In addition, in some of the most dangerous zones in Northern Ireland for Protestants to live, the local unionist communities have consistently refused to turn to the UDA and UVF to help them. When this writer was co-authoring a history of the UVF in conjunction with Jim Cusack we came across an interesting phenomenon in Co. Fermanagh. During the 1970s and '80s the Provisional IRA's armed campaign was at its most nakedly sectarian in this region. PIRA units targeted the fathers and eldest sons of Protestant farmers who lived along the border, some of whom were part-time members of the security forces, some of whom were not. They fired on school buses to kill part-time soldiers, almost murdering schoolchildren in the process, including the future Stormont Industry Minister Arlene Foster. And their border campaign culminated in the Enniskillen Poppy Day massacre in 1987, with the death of 11 Protestant civilians.

A decade later the then second-in-command of the UVF and one of the key architects/supporters of the peace process reflected on this embattled Protestant border community. He revealed that the UVF's Belfast leadership went down to Fermanagh in the aftermath of the Enniskillen atrocity. They offered to set up and arm rural UVF units to strike back at the nationalist community in revenge, just as they and the UDA were doing with ruthless randomness in Belfast. This key UVF leader, who was a close adviser to the late David Ervine, admitted that local Protestants they met were outraged over their 'offer'. They (the UVF) were, in effect, given a flea in the ear and dispatched back to Belfast with the message that border Protestants/unionists wanted nothing to do with terrorism; that they preferred to support the legitimate security forces; they would stick by the forces of law and order.[1]

Of course the attitude of Fermanagh/border Protestant communities contrasts sharply with that of those in neighbouring counties, particularly Tyrone and Armagh where the UVF ran a number of units, including one led by the notorious Portadown loyalist Billy 'King Rat' Wright. None the less, the message from the most dangerous part of the 'Union' for Protestants was and still is that this community across the north of Ireland is more heterogeneous and complex than it is often painted, not only in the Irish media (in nationalist Ireland) but in the British press and broadcasting as well.

Herein lies a problem of perception, when the media seeks to use televisual shorthand to explain complex stories in increasingly short periods of time. Images of young men in hoodies using flagpoles with Union Jacks on them to bash police Land Rovers, amid Pentecostal-like flames from smashed Molotov cocktails, make for great TV pictures. Sour-faced angry men, some of them in bowler hats, scowling into the camera and the microphone make for great sectarian sound-bites.

This selective cast list, this guaranteed 'picture rich' backcloth reminds you of the way the Israeli-Palestinian conflict is often played out for Western viewers. (Leave aside the heavily loaded bias and often barely veiled anti-Semitism in the Arab and Islamic media.)

The cast list here are normally dispossessed Palestinians and wild-eyed bearded Jewish settlers, more often than not with Brooklyn accents. We rarely see the clubbers and the surfers of Tel Aviv, just as we hardly ever see the aspects of normal life that also go on across the Green Line in the Palestinian Authority, whose economy, incidentally, has been picking up of late.

Complexity is the enemy of all fundamentalist thinking whether that be Islamism, the ultra-nationalism of the Jewish Settler groups, the Taigs-Burn-in-Hell evangelicalism of the far right loyalist fringe or the nihilistic addiction to armed struggle of the republican dissidents. Complexity is also, of course, anathema to the increasingly 24/7 nature of 'churnalism' within the media worldwide.

Perhaps that is why a small but bewildered minority just 'didn't get' a gesticulating marionette of anarchy and energy from Protestant east Belfast, who had come down to Clare armed with anecdotes of drug taking, all-night drinking, financial chaos, daydream record business projects as well as a decent, utopian ideal. Here was someone who confounded all the usual stereotypes held even within sections of moderate, conservative Middle Ireland about northern Protestants, who was still 'lost in translation' once he went south of the border.

One of the most instructive and important novels to come out of Northern Ireland in this decade gives a more rounded, kaleidoscopic vision of the Protestant community there. David Park's *The Light of Amsterdam*[2] involves three sets of characters from loyalist east Belfast: a single mother, struggling financially, who reluctantly joins her daughter's hen party to the Dutch city; a middle-aged, well-off couple taking a break in Holland from their garden centre business; and the main character, a university art teacher who as a divorced, lonely father, accompanies his teenage son there for a weekend holiday he hopes will reconnect the bond between them. The centrepiece event that starts the novel off is the funeral of George Best and the main character's melancholic sense of loss, his alienation from his son Jack, and his sensing in the soccer star's death his own ultimate decline. There are sparse references to the Troubles and sectarian division; Park's book instead deals with the aftermath of divorce, isolation, frustration, the desire to break free, all existential, universal themes.

Yet Park succeeds in bringing to life a section of the Northern Irish population rarely seen in novels, films, plays or documentaries. The main cast are essentially decent but flawed human beings who are not driven by a 24/7 sectarian *raison d'être* or an impending sense of political doom. They have more important things to worry about!

Perhaps it is no accident that Park created the relatively well-heeled Marion and Richard, who live in the leafier suburban end of east Belfast and own a garden centre business. Back in 1998 when a progressive section of unionism was trying to persuade a sceptical unionist electorate to back the Good Friday Agreement, Professor of Politics at Queen's University and renowned Irish historian Paul Bew coined the phrase 'the Prod in the garden centre'.[3] Professor Bew noted the indifference of an important section of the Protestant middle class – moderate and relatively liberal – towards the feral politics of Ulster. Instead they switched off, or they 'internally emigrated' as millions of East Germans used to do by escaping from the strictures of the regime via ordinary life. In the Northern Ireland context these local émigrés escaped to the 'garden centre' rather than bother with a polling station.

Those interested in establishing real reconciliation on this side of the border and a proper understanding of those 'alien beings' that sometimes fall to southern earth, should be arguing for a shift in southern perceptions and a challenge to lazy stereotypes. The place to start this is in schools and colleges. The works to be studied could include the likes of *The Light of Amsterdam*; to allow authors, playwrights, filmmakers, musicians and even anarchist-hippy-punk-mod-dressed impresarios to shine light themselves into a community where for too long, especially for those of us who grew up with nationalist and republican backgrounds, there were only the shadows of stereotype and gross generalisation.

Notes

1. See also Jim Cusack and Henry McDonald, *UVF: the Endgame* (Dublin: Poolbeg Press, 1997).
2. David Park, *The Light of Amsterdam* (London: Bloomsbury, 2012).
3. See Dean Godson, 'A Tribute to Ulster's A. J. P. Taylor', *The Spectator*, 21 February 2007, <http://www.spectator.co.uk/features/28076/a-tribute-to-ulsters-ajp-taylor/> [accessed March 2014].

3
Lost in Translation: Loyalism and the Media

Malachi O'Doherty

Over the last four years I have been invited on about twenty occasions to meet with groups of Belfast loyalists and to provide them with training in presentation and interaction with the media. Sometimes my role has been simply to give them a talk about how the media functions; more often I have workshopped them in mock interviews and press release writing.

Some of these groups have been mixed, with members of different loyalist groups and occasionally even republicans present. Mostly they have been groups from one or other of the distinct loyalist factions, either UDA or UVF. Usually the group has consisted of between four and eight people, more men than women and across a wide range of ages from about 30 to over 80.

The experience of meeting and interacting with these groups has led me into a better understanding of Belfast loyalists than I might otherwise have had.

Some of the people I have met have been in other groups that have interacted with professionals and members of other communities. They have invariably always been brought together by a funded community group or charity or local government scheme.

Some of the meetings I have had have coincided closely with eruptions of protest or violence which people attending the groups have been helping to plan or have been engaging in.

One of the consistent impressions made by these groups, across all of them, is a sense of grievance. These loyalists feel that they have been cheated. They believe that republicans are more favoured by the political establishment and the media.

They believe that the main unionist parties have deserted them.

They distrust the media, which they believe is only ever interested in belittling them.

Though they hold these convictions strongly they are not often persuasive or even well-reasoned in the arguments they make in support of them.

Further, they are suspicious of those who do make strong reasoned arguments and often react as if some trickery is at work in the use of language which contradicts them.

They speak often like people who know they have been disadvantaged but don't quite know how or by whom.

I was not surprised, then, by the reaction to the decision by Belfast City Council to limit the flying of the Union flag over City Hall and other public buildings. Loyalists rallied in ardent protest around an issue which was coherent and simple.

They argued that they were represented as British people by the Union flag and demanded that it be restored permanently.

The weakness in this argument, as a political move, was that it could not be met with the concession they demanded. A more politically astute movement would have sought an attainable goal.

Still, hundreds of people came out on winter nights to block traffic in Belfast, to confront the police and to risk ill health, injury and imprisonment. Many in the city responded with a sense that these protesters were stupid, committing themselves to a cause of no material value to themselves. They could not, however, dismiss them as lacking in energy and resolve.

It may be that loyalists have been outflanked by the peace process. Having endorsed it they find that they have no role within it. All that is required of them is that they be silent. Republicans who, like themselves, killed and bombed to make themselves heard, and thereby indispensable to a process for ending killing and bombing, now have partnership with Unionists in the Northern Ireland Executive.

Loyalists see a huge disparity of outcome here. That disparity arises primarily from the fact that republicans attract votes while loyalists do not. An irony for them to confront is that many of them do not vote at all and of those who do, most vote for parties other than those which represent loyalism.

Indeed, only one political party currently does represent loyalism and that is the Progressive Unionist Party, an offshoot of the paramilitary Ulster Volunteer Force. The Ulster Democratic Party which advanced the interests of the Ulster Defence Association has died for want of support.

The histories of the parties which sought to represent loyalism are fractious, tensions often having strained relations between the political activists and the militants.

I will try to represent the broader experience of meeting many groups with examples of things I have heard more than once. That way I hope I will be describing fairly representative behaviour and attitudes.

In no group, for instance, did I encounter any sectarian abuse directed at me or even voiced as contempt for Catholics in general. I did encounter comments about foreigners 'taking our jobs' but I also often heard thoughtful comments about the need to foster community relations.

It may be that the groups I met are not representative of loyalist community attitudes in that many of them will have been through the grant application processes for support from the state and public bodies. They will have been well exposed to more liberal cultural values that would not tolerate sectarianism or racism. But how then did any of us learn to be more accommodating of difference other than by contact and discussion?

There is Billy. Billy is about 30 and he's skinny.[1] He gives the impression of being more naturally angry than playful. Presumably he wants to be here, but maybe someone has told him to come. When I ask the group for their opinions about the media he tells me this story.

'The Sunday World says I am a drug dealer and I can do nothing about it. I've spoken to my solicitor and he says he can do nothing about it.'

I ask him if he is a drug dealer and he says he isn't.

I tell him that if a paper said I was a drug dealer I would sue. I could lose work through allegations like that being made against me.

'But you need money to sue and they've got bigger lawyers.'

No matter how long we discuss it he will not accept that the situation is other than that he is innocent and helpless. And what do I know? This may be how things are.

More likely, I suspect, he does have a place in the drugs business, though perhaps smaller than that attributed to him by the newspaper.

A similar issue arises during an exercise with Frank.

We have discussed a possible news story of interest to the group and I have set out the elements of it on a flip chart.

The story is that a fictional character, John K, has been arrested. His arrest has prompted press speculation that a supergrass trial may be under preparation. John K is a community worker. He served 15 years in prison for a double murder in the early 1980s.

'How do they know that?' says Frank.

'Know what?'

'That he done time.' They don't, of course. This is a fictional exercise.

'Well, newspapers and broadcasters keep files. Or maybe they just googled his name and it came up.'

'You see, that's the bit I can't stand', says Frank. 'They rake it all up on us but there's no one saying what Gerry Adams did.'

'They might if Gerry Adams was arrested.'

But his main point is this: 'They – the media – shouldn't have the right to go back into your past. That's private.'

'It's hardly private', I say, 'if the past includes a prison sentence for murder.'

'But now he hasn't got a chance when his case comes up.'

I tell him the case is not *sub judice* until John K is charged.

I talk the group through different possible media responses to the arrest of John K and ask them to consider whether they want to contact the media and try to contribute to the unfolding story.

I ask them to imagine an editorial team in a newspaper discussing how they might follow up the report of the arrest of John K.

Perhaps an editor will ask a security correspondent to write an analytical or speculative piece about the history of supergrass trials and their limited success rate. A reporter might phone round people in the UVF and ask them if people are going into hiding to evade arrest. A political correspondent might write a piece asking how this might or might not affect the peace process.

'Fuck them', says Frank. 'They are just making it up. And they twist everything.'

Then there is Keith. Keith is about 25. He might have been to university. He is comfortable in the company of Frank and Billy but he speaks better than they do and nothing in his manner is brusque or unnerving.

What would Keith do if he wanted to influence this unfolding story about John K and the possible supergrass trial?

'My big concern here is that we are getting trial by media and I want nothing to do with it.'

Well, I suggest, you might say that you don't want people tried by the media. You might say that in a press release or letter to the media.

'Why would they listen to me?'

'Because they don't have anything at all yet except speculation. Any quote from a concerned party might fill out a story.'

'Then the best thing for me to do is make it harder for them to have a credible story by staying out of it.'

This is a more reasoned approach than Frank's but arrives at the same conclusion: have nothing to do with the media because no good can come of it.

This is the point at which I get them to write a press release. Some of them don't see the point. Keith takes my side however and reminds them that this is a training exercise. He explains to me: 'If it came to it, we would never be the ones to write a press release anyway. It would come from further up.'

The press release we devise is a statement from an imaginary loyalist group calling on the media to be more restrained in its coverage of the arrest of John K. He has not been charged with anything, yet his past is being raked over and this has the potential to jeopardise his prospects of a fair trial. Besides, he is a respected member of the community and this is distressing for his family.

I get Diane to read it over. 'Shouldn't we say that this is internment?'

I say, 'That depends on how you want to pitch it. Do you want people to read you as political campaigners for reform of the justice system or do you want to focus on the media. I would keep it simple and focus on the media.'

They agree to this.

Now we imagine that the press release has arrived on a news desk and a reporter phones you for further information. What are you going to say to him?

'I'm going to tell him to fuck off', says Frank. 'You've got the press release; that's all you're getting.'

What do others think?

Keith says: 'We pooled our thinking on the press release. We made tactical decisions about how to pitch it. We don't want to get drawn into other discussions or say any more. So Frank's right. We don't talk to the reporter.'

Diane?

'If you say anything more they will just twist it.'

My plan is that they should talk to the reporter politely, using first names the way reporters always do.

I role-play it for them: 'Thanks very much for calling, Jean. We appreciate your interest in this story. What can I do for you? Our big concern is trial by media. If John K is going to be charged then let him have his trial in court by due process. It isn't right that some of the papers have him damned already, is it?'

I'm asking them if it would hurt to be civil to the reporter and at the same time to stick to the line of the press release.

'I get it', says Frank. 'They twist it their way; we twist it ours.'

I say it is all about strategy and that appeals to the part of him that imagines he is a soldier.

Even though they have to be careful, in this approach, not to feed the reporter's suggestions of other angles on the story, they don't have to shut down the interview rudely.

But they also have to learn to anticipate what angles the journalist might find if they leave the agreed script. This requires them to think like a reporter and to do this they have to break out of their assumption that a prime objective of the media is to make loyalists look stupid.

They also have to recognise that every story fits into the context of the wider news agenda. The reporters will be asking themselves how this story fits into others.

We act out the conversation with the reporter and I show them where things can go wrong for them.

> Reporter: Do you think these arrests are unsettling the loyalist paramilitaries?
> Wrong answer 1: Yes, some people are getting very annoyed and who knows what they'll do?
> Possible headline: 'Increased Threat from Loyalists Following Supergrass Arrest.'
> Wrong answer 2: Well it's made a lot of people nervous and they're lying low.
> Possible headline: 'Old Killers Back On the Run.'
> Right answer: My primary concern is that the media shouldn't presume John K is guilty and should know better than to risk prejudicing his trial.
> Possible headline 1: 'Touchy Loyalists Lecture Media on Justice: Look Who's Talking!'
> Possible headline 2: Let Law Take Its Course, Say Loyalists.

In all of these exercises it is emphasised that these tips on how to interact with the media do not guarantee fair coverage or predictable outcomes. However a long-term relationship developed with the media through being civil and tactical builds up credit for those who engage, as reasonable people.

My sense is that even after some effort to persuade loyalists of this some were still resistant. The understanding within loyalist communities is that the media will always undermine them.

A corollary of that is that other groups, particularly Sinn Féin, get treated more gently by the media.

Could it be, I ask, that Sinn Féin are just better at this stuff than you are? In which case the better image within the media is a reward for their persistent endeavours.

Some of these sessions were conducted during the flag protests. Several incidents in the media response to these protests were cited against me as evidence that the media is always unsympathetic to loyalists.

Inexperienced spokespeople were mauled in aggressive interviews.

So I suggested another exercise in which I would play – indeed overplay – the role of a radio presenter mocking and haranguing each of them in turn.

I advised them to agree and rehearse the line they would take in the interview and resolve not to be deflected from it. 'If I say, "What gives you thugs the right to block the road?" you will say, "The important thing here is the sense of insult felt in our communities." If I say, "Who the hell are you to complain about police brutality when you are only brutes yourselves?" you will reply, "Our main concern is for the free expression of British identity in the institutions of government and the removal of any sense that one community here has scored over another."'

We played out these roles with me, at times, shouting at them and twisting their words, in some sessions dealing with the fear of supergrass trials, in some with the apprehensions about republican dissidents, in some with the flag protests. In all cases the issues we worked on were suggested by the loyalists themselves. My role was to show them what angles a journalist might take on these questions, and how they might direct the discussion back to their perspective when the only other alternatives were to disengage or get angry and lose the argument.

This exercise introduced a heightened level of drama and playfulness into the sessions. These exposed a division between those who could enter into the game with confidence and those who could not. I am always struck in these sessions by how rarely one can anticipate who will be good players.

Sometimes the more bullish men – the Frank types – were good at this, sometimes they were not. Sometimes the Diane type was adept or thought she was but simply couldn't play well enough not to be deflected. But this comes out in a lot of media training, the discovery that the people in a group best able to defend its interests may not be easy to identify and may often be the ones least inclined to take on the job.

There is a danger in these exercises that participants will conclude that they were right all along to fear and suspect the media.

As one put it: 'The only thing that makes a story for them is us cocking up. We organise a street festival and bring in Catholic kids or whatever and they ignore us. Ten thousand people enjoy a parade and the media focuses on one incident of trouble.'

But their understanding of how the media comes to find the trouble at a parade is often naive. They speak as if they think the media may have flooded a parade with reporters looking for negative incidents to report. They overestimate the resources of the media. They tend to view it as a managed conspiracy against them and they make little or no distinction between the various outlets. Media, I tell them, is a plural noun.

Actually, I tell them, the media is also under-resourced and, being human like you, often is as incompetent as you are.

Frank says: 'How did they find out about that incident or this other incident?'

'Someone told them.'

'Who told them?'

'A man with a camera in one case. Maybe the police in another. Sometimes the reporter doesn't even leave the office, just phones the police and asks if there was trouble and then just reports what the police say.'

'This is corrupt', says Frank. 'It is loaded against us.'

He thinks anyone can phone a reporter and tell any lie about loyalists and get into the media.

What I want him to see is that he could have a relationship with the media himself, if only to be called on occasionally to offer his own perspective.

I say, 'Sinn Féin faced the media for decades being asked only about bombings and shooting and they developed a thick skin and a winning smile. You could have done the same. You still could.'

Afterthought: some journalists might fear that work like this with loyalists encourages them to manipulate the media and evade awkward questions. That's true, but it would only be bringing them a little closer to the level of competence in evasion and manipulation that is evinced by all other political groupings. It is the job of the journalist to work back through that to get at the story. An open society relies on their ability to do that. But in a milieu in which it is necessary for political groups to tool themselves up with the skills to defend themselves in the media, little is served by one faction being conspicuously inept.

Note

1. The workshop participants remain anonymous, and the names used for these typical exchanges do not refer to any actual person.

4

Typical Unionists? The Politicians and their People, Past and Present

James Greer

The actions and personas of Ulster unionist politicians have been the key factor in forming perceptions of Northern Ireland's Protestants. If nationalist Ireland, the largely disinterested Great British public or, by some accident, the outside world ever hear an Ulster Protestant perspective articulated it will likely be from the lips of a unionist politician. For generations unionist representatives have advocated their cause through adaptations of familiar language and predictable political strategies. This familiarity has created easily identifiable archetypal unionist politicians. The leading members of this cast list are such stock unionist characters as: the dour rejectionist; the emotional fatalist; the triumphalist bigot; the big house paternalist; the deposed leader; the marginal liberal; and the unelectable loyalist. The origins of these varied 'typical unionists', and the contradictions evident between them, have much to tell us about the complexities of the broader Ulster Protestant experience.

With a public image dominated by these archetypes, Ulster unionist party politics has consistently proven singularly unattractive to the majority of those looking in from outside, and in recent years falling voter turnout suggests it has increasingly lost traction within Protestant-unionist communities themselves. Yet, both as stereotypes imposed upon unionists by political opponents, and as default settings the political leaders themselves return to during the perpetual crisis that is the Northern Ireland political process, it seems these archetypes are here to stay. This chapter will explore how and why these 'typical unionists' developed and have been sustained across the sweep of twentieth-century history and contemporary politics.

Defined by circumstances

There are many evolving cultural factors relevant to a discussion of Northern Ireland's Protestants' political behaviour, but it is the structural position of Ulster unionism within Britain and Ireland that primarily shapes their conduct. Support for the union has defined the politics of an overwhelming majority of Northern Protestants throughout the democratic era – across the significant fault lines of social class, denomination, and the rural–urban divide. A blend of insecurity, defensiveness and triumphalism is not innate to Ulster Protestants. The oft-cited unionist siege mentality is a result of the priorities and choices made by generations of Protestants, but it has also been a consequence of very real threats to the political settlement and cultural identities that a vast majority of Northern Protestants have sought to sustain.

One consequence of unionism's reputation for dour intransigence has been the frequent surprise of journalists, negotiators and others when the Orange bogeymen turn out to be personally convivial, humorous and downright polite.[1] A prime example of this phenomenon was shown when Tony Blair – an *An Phoblacht* reader as an Oxford undergraduate – was, like many before him, swayed by Ian Paisley's personal charm.[2] The apparent spiritual dialogue and friendship between the Catholic convert Blair and the founder of the Free Presbyterian Church is one of the more surreal episodes of the peace process but it highlights the otherwise mostly obscured ability of unionist politicians to build unlikely partnerships when they have the political space, and capital, to do so. However, stuck between nationalist Ireland, a distrusted British establishment and disinterested British populace, and the ever-present threat of internal schism, successive unionist leaders have mostly faced political suffocation rather than the luxury of such space.

The belief that their place in the United Kingdom is precarious has ensured that reasonable co-operation has not been the standard unionist approach to domestic politics and constitutional talks. Furthermore, a political creed often united only through opposition to the objectives of nationalists, and divided on possible remedies for a better society, all too often has had little to say beyond holding the line and reacting to pressures from external forces. The qualities required for advocating such an instinctively defensive platform favours politicians either defined by inflexible caution or by fatalistic despair. The popularity of the caution of dour rejectionists at times of broader political paralysis is best exhibited by the leadership of Jim Molyneaux – when 'minimalism' passed for a political strategy. At times of political crisis the

Doomsday analysis best utilised by pre-Chuckle-Brother Ian Paisley comes to the fore.

Despite their differences, these two styles can be complimentary. Of the Molyneaux era Graham Walker notes:

> There was a certain sense in playing the quiet man to Paisley's raucous political gunslinger during opposition to the Anglo-Irish Agreement; this produced a blend of styles which held the alliance together. Yet this was an ambiguous achievement. Unionist unity was bought at a price of serious estrangement from the British government and British political life more generally, and it probably hindered ideological development and the formation of sharper policies.[3]

As a snapshot of unionist strategising, the uneasy Molyneaux–Paisley duet captures much of the broader unionist dilemma – stuck between the competing necessities of unionist unity and engagement with other forces. The contrasts in the character between the Quiet Man and the Big Man can be seen to represent the competing, but not necessarily contradictory, emotional responses to this dilemma.

The 'Triple Minority' model of defining Northern Ireland is a fruitful method for approaching the psychology of unionism.[4] This model builds upon the recognised Double Minority problem within Ireland – namely unionists as the minority on the island and nationalists as the outnumbered in Northern Ireland. The third strand is the place of Ulster unionists as a tiny minority within their preferred framework of the United Kingdom – where they find themselves on the periphery of the UK's culture and politics, with a status often shifting on the spectrum between unacknowledged and unwanted. One unionist response to this uncertain position, between the 'imagined communities' of the UK and Ireland, is succinctly described in the Tom Paulin poem 'An Ulster Unionist Walks the Streets of London', in which the protagonist, reeling from the Anglo-Irish Agreement, feels 'like a half-foreigner/ among the London Irish'.[5]

The tendency of unionists to portray their intrinsic political position as uniquely precarious can, of course, be disputed. For example, unionists tend to ignore the parallels between their dysfunctional relationship with the rest of the UK and the similar sense of betrayal and separation many northern nationalists feel with regard to the Republic of Ireland: '26-county Irish nationalism' excludes in a similar way to 'mainland' Britishness. Furthermore, presenting Great British opinion, especially that of Whitehall, as uniformly agnostic or antagonistic ignores the very survival of the union – a settlement initially in large part dependent upon machinations within the British elite and subsequently long sustained by the London Exchequer.

Nonetheless, despite these qualifications, the Triple Minority model is insightful when considering the foundations of unionist political behaviour. The importance of insecurity is of course markedly more important in those areas where unionists are in an actual minority, or where demographic changes appear to threaten their position. In particular, as Henry Patterson has detailed, unionists living in border communities have been scarred by the vicious cycle of long-established sectarian tensions over land ownership, demographic change and republican violence.[6] Variations of this Frontier Unionism may most obviously be located in North Belfast or the Fountain in Londonderry but something of its political culture resonates much wider.

A paradox of the unionist experience is the status of being an isolated community whose core political strength remains in being a majority within its jurisdiction. This paradox helps to explain how unionism can veer wildly: between expressions of isolated impotence and majoritarian complacency; between self-pity and triumphalism. Sarah Nelson notes how forms of insecurity and majoritarian hubris running in parallel are common to both nationalism and unionism.[7] Nelson argues that both movements have historically shared a limited definition of democracy centred upon majority rule at the expense of minority rights, with both sides disagreeing on where the boundaries of this majority-governed democratic unit should be set.

During the era of the old Stormont a secure majority within Northern Ireland was often presented by unionism as sufficient evidence to support its overall legitimacy and the moral force of individual governments. Frequently this rationale promoted political complacency and facilitated 'democratic' justifications for anti-Catholic discrimination. This toxic blend was most evident in local government. While unionists governed many local authorities with surprising equity, when unionism held power in areas where its local majority-status was under threat, especially west of the Bann, it was willing to engage in systemic anti-Catholic discrimination in order to maintain the local balance of power.[8] Therefore, while many discriminatory practices by unionists were undoubtedly fuelled by prejudice and self-interest, structurally discrimination was deemed necessary due to insecurity about losing political control rather than assumptions about Protestant supremacy.

Any remaining unionist superiority complex has been dramatically eroded in recent years. Changing demographics and secularisation have narrowed the in-built majority of traditional Protestant-unionists; the old heavy industries and their culture of skilled, socially cohesive, intergenerational employment have long gone; and the hegemony of the old Stormont was replaced first by the disempowerment of Direct Rule and then the mutual veto of power-sharing with nationalism. As Richard Bourke powerfully argues, in the context of Northern Ireland democratic competition is not in itself a solution to the problems of competing national aspirations and paralysed political cultures.[9] Indeed in a consociationalist political settlement the 'typical' unionists and nationalists of old may be encouraged to thrive.

The era of Carson and Craig

The character of unionist politics has also been significantly influenced by the inspiration politicians and voters alike have taken from unionist history. Of most importance in this regard have been the achievements of Edward Carson and James Craig. Interpretations of the personalities, tactics and strategies of the founding fathers of modern Ulster unionism have been the basis for many of its archetypes, and continue to subtly influence contemporary politics. A broader analysis of this pivotal period highlights the positive and negative legacies of Carson and Craig as templates for unionists, and incorporates other aspects of life in their era that challenge established stereotypes about Ulster Protestants.

During the period of the Third Home Rule Bill Crisis, 1912–14, Edward Carson and James Craig defined unionist political action and public image in the new environment of mass-electorates and broad participation in politics. The complementary differences between the two men, and their dynamic but complex relationship, created a leadership style successive generations of unionists have yearned to recreate. The aforementioned Molyneaux–Paisley axis can be seen as the most prominent attempt at a tribute act.

The template offered by Carson to future generations of unionists is one based primarily on charismatic oratory and an ability to galvanise audiences. In recent years all wings of unionism have used the memory of Carson to argue their corner in contemporary politics. John McCallister, on the liberal margins, has told a republican audience that 'unionism failed to address Edward Carson's warning that a Catholic minority should have nothing to fear from a Protestant majority in a new Northern Ireland'.[10] Ian Paisley used the one hundredth anniversary of the signing of the Ulster Covenant to present Carson as a – familiar-sounding – principled anti-establishment 'man of the masses'.[11] Peter Robinson's analysis of Carson as a pragmatist 'who was prepared to compromise and alter direction when the situation demanded it' signalled his own struggles.[12]

All three of these appeals to Carson reflect important aspects of the man's complex legacy, but it is Robinson's acknowledgement of Carson's compromises and failures that contemporary unionism perhaps most needs to hear. By moving beyond the image of Carson as merely an unbending militant, who stood his ground and won, unionists can also take from the era the importance of strategic retreat and adaption. After all, a Home Rule Parliament and partition had not been Carson's political objectives.

The thesis that as a consequence of Calvinist and other cultural influences unionism has an overly contractarian understanding of politics,[13] which seeks legalistic certainty and a full-stop to the political process rather than engaging with the ongoing uncertainties of politics, remains potent; further acknowledgement by unionist leaders of the historical necessity for accepting change and modifying core goals could go some way towards challenging this political culture. However, memory of 1912–14 is dominated by the ultimate example of contractarian unionism, the Ulster Covenant, and by the mobilisation of the UVF. The unionist achievement of partition has obscured the dangers of this militancy and how the First World War pressed pause on a political process in Ulster that had moved beyond Carson's control. That fate, more than political calculation, helped unionists avoid a hopeless confrontation with the British state has left a dangerous legacy for unionism – namely, an exaggerated sense of the utility of militant refusals to compromise and the elevation of dour rejection as a political strategy.

With regard to Carson's personality, the image of a steadfast conviction politician appears to have obscured a man frequently riddled by self-doubt. In correspondence with friend Lady Londonderry, Carson and his wife reveal how the political crisis had left him exhausted and in one case seeking 'electrical treatment'.[14] Alvin Jackson details that by the summer of 1914: 'Bed-ridden and exhausted by a neurotic anxiety, he passively awaited civil war.'[15] This makes Carson all the more human, considering what was at stake, and does not detract from his other exceptional qualities, but the disconnect between the legend and this cowed figure is remarkable. How has the legend remained in place? It has primarily done so because it has suited unionists and nationalists alike to present Carson as: 'a lantern-jawed Ubermensch ... whether as the Bismarckian creator of Northern Ireland, or the Hitlerian demagogue of the 1912–14 era'.[16] Representations of Carson are one example of a wider factor in the creation of unionist stereotypes – namely that Irish nationalist and Ulster unionist narratives of 'typical' unionist characteristics can be mutually reenforcing and self-fulfilling.

While Carson, the Dublin Episcopalian outsider, provided the political flair and inspired devotion from Ulster unionist crowds, James Craig emerged as the definitive tough uncharismatic Ulster Presbyterian administrator. It is telling that despite Craig's much larger contribution to the nuts and bolts of unionist leadership he has received respect rather than Carsonite adulation. Craig's personality and Protestant populism – forever associated with his oft-misquoted 'Protestant Parliament and a Protestant state' retort to de Valera – make him an archetype for much of what remains exclusivist, dry and uncommunicative about unionism. But his achievements as a practical man of government, capable of successfully leading the construction of the state's apparatus against the extremely unpromising backdrop of the 1920s, offer a role model for unionist achievement and action not easily found elsewhere.

The Craig–Carson axis and the high politics of Westminster dominate the historiography of unionism in this pivotal era, and as a result wider social and political forces that counter visions of unionism as elitist, uniform and reactionary are often marginalised or half-forgotten. This is most striking with regard to the active role of unionist women in Ulster society. When the extraordinary growth of the Ulster Women's Unionist Council[17] is viewed together with the activism of women in the suffrage movement, the churches, temperance associations and the fledgling trade unions, the prominence in public life of northern Protestant women in this era is comparable with that of women in any European or North American community. The number of women mobilised by the UWUC during the crisis of 1912–14 remains unprecedented in Irish history, and contrasts notably with their Redmondite nationalist opponents.[18]

Women's entrance into participatory politics was vividly illustrated, in September 1912, when the signatories to the 'Women's Declaration' against Home Rule outnumbered the names on the male Covenant.[19] Male recognition of the changing roles of women unionists was evident in the Ulster Unionist Council's September 1913 announcement of a planned 'Ulster Provisional Government', to be formed if Home Rule became a reality. The Unionist leadership informed the UWUC that the final document would proclaim the enfranchisement of Ulster women within its articles, resulting in women 'taking their proper share in the affairs of Ulster … in which matters we fully realise that their interests are as much at stake as those of men'.[20] A stated objective four years prior to the passing of UK franchise reform in the House of Commons, the franchise announcement ensured Ulster unionism rare plaudits from British radical circles – but political intrigue and Carson's continued opposition to votes for women were to make this an all-too-brief progressive moment. Despite James Craig's personal support for women's suffrage, the Unionist leadership quietly retreated from the enfranchisement commitment the following year, justifiably enraging suffragists and returning the Unionists to the fold of the often ambiguous positions on this issue exhibited by the Liberal, Tory and Irish nationalist parties. However, the radical moment of 1913 had symbolised a broader, quiet revolution that had been conducted by Edwardian unionist women. Within the confines of a deeply engrained patriarchy, women's activism had earned them a significant voice in shaping unionist discourse and in the functioning of unionist institutions during the crucial period of modern unionist history.

The relative liberation of Ulster women's public lives, in the context of this period, was not to be sustained in the new Northern Ireland state, or in the other new conservative state on the island. Nonetheless, the role of unionist women in public life was remarkable for the time and hugely significant in the modernisation and survival of unionism. Despite this rich history the public image of unionism has remained almost uniformly male. Why is the pioneering suffragist Isabella Tod not celebrated alongside other leading unionists? Why are the local women who campaigned for the Ulster unionist cause in Britain, the women of Unionist Associations, and the thousands of UVF auxiliary nurses not central to how unionists commemorate the creation of Northern Ireland? Why is the remarkable history of women's social activism not more prominent in the Ulster Protestant story? In order to counter many of the damaging clichés regarding the community they represent, political unionism could begin by incorporating these stories into their narratives of the past.

The journey to direct rule

The Northern Ireland state built by Craig and Carson stifled many of the radical strands of Ulster Protestant society, and the 50 years of unionist hegemony that followed were to cement perceptions of a uniform and rigidly conservative community. The absolute priority of Protestant political unity was an accepted fact of life for the majority, but behind this unity were a diversity of worldviews defined by differences in social class, religious domination, local cultural norms, political geography and other factors. The Unionist Party's ever-present concern about schism reflected the potential fragility of this alliance.

Rather than a people whose political loyalties simply represent a form of elite-manufactured false-consciousness, as the republicanism of Connolly and his heirs argues, even under the old Stormont the Protestant population displayed a repeated willingness to challenge established hierarchies and forces. From the Independent Unionist tradition prior to the Second World War,[21] to the Northern Ireland Labour Party, through to the rise of Ian Paisley, Protestant voters exhibited strong strands of anti-elitism and employed the language of social class. The growth of Paisleyism in the 1960s and 1970s provides a telling example of a Protestant mobilisation that sought to maintain perceived traditional unionist values but which did so by challenging the established hierarchies and institutions of the Unionist Party, the Orange Order, the unionist press and the Protestant Churches.[22]

That prior to the era of the civil rights crisis and Paisley the Protestant political alliance was able to withstand these challenges owes most to the unifying threat of Irish republican irredentism and the safety valve provided by British social reforms. The Northern Ireland party system and political culture was encouraged to remain static through the depoliticising of much of government by the formula of largely following British social and economic policy 'step-by-step'.[23] Instinctively conservative and suspicious of the developing Welfare State, Unionist Party leaders nonetheless accepted its application in Ulster in order to maintain the cross-class basis of their electoral success. As Peter Brooke has neatly summarised, 'Northern Ireland legislation followed British legislation without sharing in the political struggles which produced it.'[24] This solution did not kill off Protestant working-class disaffection – as witnessed by the frequent surges in NILP support and consistently high levels of industrial action – but it did allow the function of local politics to remain largely rooted in the constitutional question.

The core objective of maintaining the constitution whilst benefiting from reforms originating from Britain points to why unionist electors have placed a premium on those who play it safe. The missed opportunities that can flow from such a position defined the Brookeborough Premiership (1943–63). Under Brookeborough unionism failed to adapt to a changing world despite the uniquely favourable circumstances of a weak and divided northern nationalism, successive sympathetic UK governments (following the North's contribution to the war), and the unchallenged position of the leader as a unionist icon. Brookeborough was the archetypal Big House paternalist: liberal by inclination (and education) but shameless in employing sectarian rhetoric as part of his populist appeal. He possessed undoubted political skills, and cross-class appeal throughout Protestant Ulster, but he utilised these skills only in defence of short-term unionist unity.[25]

The failure of Brookeborough, and his colleagues, to begin a dialogue with the nationalist minority, or to address the storm of deindustrialisation that was beginning to engulf the Protestant working class, was to leave a bitter legacy for his successor Terence O'Neill. The gap between O'Neill's rhetoric and his actions, and the competing strands of his vision for Northern Ireland, makes him an elusive figure. The journey from Eton and the army to a safe unionist seat in the mid-Antrim constituency of his family estate make him a classic Big House unionist, but O'Neill lacked the personal charm and paternalistic empathy for Protestant heartland opinion that Brookeborough possessed.

O'Neill's rhetorical embrace of modernisation in his economic programme and his later piecemeal attempts at dialogue with Catholics ensured he broke the mould of unionist leaders. O'Neill symbolises two adaptations of 'typical unionists': the deposed leader, and the marginalised liberal. For all their differences O'Neill, Brian Faulkner and David Trimble have become grouped together as flawed leaders who sacrificed their personal standing for peace and were rejected by their parties and electorates. All three made a journey from traditional or hard-line unionist beginnings to become leaders who offered more pluralist visions of the Union, and unionist opponents of all three were later to quietly accept much of their platform. Of course for many Protestants O'Neill, Faulkner, Trimble, and even Paisley, don't represent deposed, or wronged, leaders but rather an even older archetype – Lundys.[26]

The ambiguities and contradictions in the progressive credentials of a figure like O'Neill can be seen more broadly within those who become defined as marginal liberal unionists. For a section of liberal unionist opinion, with a disproportionate voice in the local media and academia, there is a desire to impose upon complex or cautious politicians their hopes for a more open unionism. Variations of this process have occurred with figures as diverse as Brian Maginnis, Robert McCartney, Sylvia Hermon and the NI21 Party of Basil McCrea and John McCallister. All of these figures undoubtedly provide different challenges to traditional unionism, but there has also been an element of wish fulfilment on the part of commentators when describing their transformative potential, the coherence of their alternative unionism and their wider appeal.

The unionist divisions of the O'Neill era pale into significance when measured against the traumas and violence of what was to follow. The abolition of Stormont and the splintering of the old Unionist Party left Ulster Protestants politically disempowered and fragmented, and culturally dislocated by the speed with which the old certainties disappeared between the quiet summer of 1968 and the bloody year of 1972. The UWC Strike temporarily brought back memories of 1912 and the collective assertion of Protestant power. Bill Craig and Paisley fought it out for the mantle of Carson, but it is telling that the origins of the strike lay with power-station shop stewards, not political leaders.[27] Despite the possibility that Doomsday, a British withdrawal, really was on the table this time, unionist unity could not be maintained in the 1970s as it had been at the formation of the state.

Contemporary unionism

Disunity continues to define unionist politics. Insights into this continuing fracturing can be gained by considering how rhetoric surrounding 'loyalism' has changed in recent years. While once unionist leaders on Orange platforms and in the media frequently proclaimed themselves as loyalists, now the term has become marginalised. In everyday use 'loyalist' now signifies working-class communities, or indeed conceptions of a Protestant underclass, and paramilitarism. As a consequence, now when issues such as low educational attainment, unemployment and cuts to public spending are discussed with reference to Protestants they have become marginalised as issues for 'loyalist communities' – rather than topics pivotal for a wide section of society. The DUP is led by figures such as Peter Robinson and Sammy Wilson with roots in these very same communities, and the party continues to win a comfortable majority of those working-class Protestant ballots that are cast. However, the disconnect between working-class Protestants and their erstwhile political representatives is such that the DUP are now widely caricatured as social-climbing Big House unionists for a new generation.

The reflex to push the term 'loyalist' to the margins is, however, most clearly felt due to unionist discomfort with dealing with the legacy of their own communities' paramilitaries. This discomfort is in itself linked to social class, given the overwhelmingly working-class character of the paramilitaries, but it spreads well beyond the suburbs. Core unionist narratives about the Troubles are weakened by acknowledging such factors as the mass membership of the early 1970s paramilitaries,[28] the sneaking regard many held for paramilitary activity, the complex and varied roles paramilitaries played in some Protestant communities, and the brutality of much of their campaigns. When those associated with the paramilitaries have stood for election the response of union- ist electorates has been one of almost uniform rejection. This was the case even at the high watermark for the paramilitaries in the aftermath of the UWC Strike. Although the flag protests of 2012–13 have given a renewed focus to the Progressive Unionist Party, it remains to be seen if they can move beyond the paradigm of the unelectable loyalist, espe- cially given the persistence of UVF organisation and activity.

The electoral failure of loyalism shouldn't, however, mask the impor- tance loyalist political thought has historically played in advancing debate within unionism. Documents such as the UDA's *Beyond the Religious Divide* (1979) and *Common Sense* (1987) highlighted the ability of loyalists to re-evaluate their politics, and the overall position of the Protestant community, in a reflective and critical manner. The continu- ation of the PUP as a left-of-centre alternative unionist voice, and the emergence of a new generation of activists with progressive views on issues such as same-sex marriage, suggests loyalism will continue to promote fresh thinking not evident within the unionist mainstream.

The caricature of the DUP as Big House Unionism was at play in the defeat of Peter Robinson in the 2010 East Belfast election to Westminster. The circumstances of this defeat were extraordinary, given the swirl of media coverage surrounding the Robinson family, but the MP of over 30 years, First Minister and man widely judged to be the most capable unionist politician of his generation could not count on loyalty, sentiment or personal standing to hold the seat. The contrast with West Belfast was telling, where Gerry Adams, facing family scandal of a much more serious nature,[29] was returned as MP with 71.1 per cent of the vote. East Belfast perceptions of the Robinson family, and the DUP more broadly, as out of touch contrasted with perceptions of Sinn Féin in nationalist West Belfast.

The 2010 electoral fortunes of Robinson and Adams point to the underlying lack of confidence unionists have in their leadership com- pared with that of republicanism. Equally, however, Robinson's 2010 defeat can also be interpreted as signifying elements of a healthy democratic culture within unionism. The relationship between unionist politicians and their people is certainly not one defined by deference or blind party loyalty. The alphabet soup of unionist parties in the modern era and the swing in the fortunes of the parties point to the eagerness with which unionist electors have held their leaders to account and, for better or for worse, changed political direction.

While accountability to a sceptical electorate and political competitors is clearly democratically preferable to one-party dominance within unionism, fear of the electorate and the constant electoral cycle has contributed to the paralysis of the political process. Political gridlock has had the effect of further weakening confidence in the current political settlement. Although the 2011 Assembly Results confirmed the DUP's leadership of unionism, subsequent months of flag protests and other unionist discord finally led to public debate about an anger and disengagement within Protestant communities that had long been evident but considered outside the bounds of polite conversation. The response of the DUP to this anger has been to retreat into rhetoric designed to shore up its base. The proposed dialogue with Catholic unionists and the new Northern Irish identity, much discussed prior to the flag protests, has largely been superseded by the old archetypes. But in the context of joint office with Sinn Féin and a changing population, such appeals offer only a short-term fix rather than a viable long-term strategy for unionism.

While unionism is in the midst of another cycle of its particular form of pessimism it is important to note it is not alone in struggling to articulate a vision for the future, or an honest reckoning with the past. Across all communities in Northern Ireland economic peace dividends have been sporadic or insecure, and Irish nationalism and republicanism have many unanswered questions about their own Troubles narratives. The current political landscape may have secured an uneasy peace, and may be supported by an ethnic-bloc style of power-sharing, but recognition of its inadequacies is spreading. Further afield, the constitutional reconfiguration of the UK and the political and economic crises in the EU point to broader uncertainties and challenges. How unionism responds to these evolving local, British and European circumstances will dictate its future. A re-engagement with unionist history highlights the continuity and strong structural roots of old mindsets, but it also points to the potential for Ulster Protestants to move beyond the default settings when facing the challenges of a rapidly changing world.

Notes

1. See Ruth Dudley Edwards, *The Faithful Tribe* for an example of the revelation of Orange conviviality (London: HarperCollins, 2000).
2. *Belfast Telegraph*, 4 September 2010.
3. Graham Walker, *A History of the Ulster Unionist Party: Protest, Pragmatism and Pessimism* (Manchester: Manchester OP, 2004), 248–9.
4. John Whyte, *Interpreting Northern Ireland* (Oxford: Clarendon, 1990), 100–2.

5. Tom Paulin, 'An Ulster Unionist Walks the Streets of London', in *Fivemiletown* (London: Faber and Faber, 1987), 67.

6. Henry Patterson, *Ireland's Violent Frontier: the Border and Anglo-Irish Relations During the Troubles* (Palgrave Macmillan: Basingstoke, 2013).

7. Sarah Nelson, *Ulster's Uncertain Defenders – Loyalists and the Northern Ireland Conflict* (Belfast: Appletree Press, 1984), 36.

8. John Whyte, 'How Much Discrimination Was There Under the Unionist Regime, 1921–68?', in Tom Gallagher and James O'Connell (eds), *Contemporary Irish Studies* (Manchester University Press: Manchester, 1983).

9. Richard Bourke, *Peace in Ireland: the War of Ideas* (London: Pimlico, 2003).

10. 'All Must Confront Our Painful Past Says UUP Man John McCallister', *BBC News* [website] 20 November 2011, <http://www.bbc.co.uk/news/uk-northern-ireland-15806918>.

11. *Newsletter*, 28 September 2012.

12. CAIN, Peter Robinson, 'The Edward Carson Lecture', Iveagh House, Dublin, 29 March 2012, <http://cain.ulst.ac.uk/issues/politics/docs/dup/pr290312.htm>.

13. David Miller, *Queen's Rebels: Ulster Loyalism in Historical Perspective* (Dublin: Barnes and Noble, 1978).

14. PRONI, D2846/1/1/135. Private Correspondence, Lady Carson to Lady Londonderry.

15. Alvin Jackson, *Sir Edward Carson* (Dublin: The Historical Society of Ireland, 1993), 41.

16. Jackson, *Carson*, 4.

17. Formed in January 1911, the Ulster Women's Unionist Council (UWUC) had a membership of over 115,000 by early 1913. Diane Urquhart, *Women in Ulster Politics, 1890–1940* (Dublin: Irish Academic Press, 2000), 61. Some estimates put its peak membership at 200,000 in the build-up to the First World War.

18. Senia Paseta, *Irish Nationalist Women, 1900–1918* (Cambridge: Cambridge University Press, 2013).

19. Initial announcement of total signatories: *News Letter*, 23 November 1912. The final figures were: 234,046 women, 218,206 men.

20. *News Letter*, 13 September 1913, 7.

21. Colin Reid, 'Protestant Challenges to the "Protestant State": Ulster Unionism and Independent Unionism in Northern Ireland, 1921–39', *Twentieth Century British History* 19 (4) (2008): 419–55.

22. James Greer, 'Paisley and his Heartland: a Case Study of Political Change', in Coimhe Nic Dhaibheid and Colin Reid (eds), *From Parnell to Paisley* (Dublin: Irish Academic Press, 2010).

23. Paul Bew, Peter Gibbon and Henry Patterson, *Northern Ireland 1921–2001: Political Forces and Social Classes* (London: Serif, 2002), 86–99.

24. Peter Brooke, *Ulster Presbyterianism: the Historical Perspective 1610–1970* (Belfast: Athol Books, 1994), 170–1.

25. For the legacy of Brookeborough's Premiership see Walker, *History of the Ulster Unionist Party*, 147–50.

26. Derogatory term, used to describe those who have been perceived to have betrayed the Protestant, unionist or loyalist cause. The word 'Lundy' itself derives from the name of Robert Lundy, the Governor of Londonderry and Culmore during the Siege of Derry in 1689. Lundy was on the verge of

surrendering Derry to the forces of King James. Once this was discovered his treachery became an historical byword for 'sell-out' and 'surrender'.
27. Gordon Gillespie, 'Loyalist Politics and the Ulster Workers' Strike of 1974'. PhD Thesis, Queen's University of Belfast, 1994.
28. Henry McDonald and Jim Cusack *UDA: Inside the Heart of Loyalist Terror* (Dublin: Penguin Ireland, 2004), 5, suggests that the figure for UDA 'supporters' was 40,000. A similar figure is given by Gordon Gillespie, 'Loyalist Politics and the Ulster Workers' Council Strike of 1974', 8.
29. In October 2013 Gerry Adams' brother Liam was convicted of raping and abusing his daughter. *BBC News* [website], 1 October 2013, <http://www.bbc.co.uk/news/uk-northern-ireland-24348798>.

References

Primary sources
BBC News Online
Belfast Telegraph
Newsletter
CAIN: Conflict Archive on the Internet, <http://cain.ulst.ac.uk/>.
Correspondence of Lady Londonderry; Public Records Office of Northern Ireland (PRONI), D2846/1/3.

Secondary sources
Bew, Paul, Peter Gibbon and Henry Patterson, *Northern Ireland 1921–2001: Political Forces and Social Classes* (Serif: London, 2002), 86–99.
Bourke, Richard, *Peace in Ireland: the War of Ideas* (Pimlico: London, 2003).
Brooke, Peter, *Ulster Presbyterianism: the Historical Perspective 1610–1970* (Athol Books: Belfast, 1994), 170–1.
Dudley Edwards, Ruth, *The Faithful Tribe* (Harper Collins: London, 2000).
Gillespie, Gordon, 'Loyalist Politics and the Ulster Workers' Strike of 1974' (Unpublished PhD thesis, Queen's University of Belfast, 1994).
Greer, James, 'Paisley and his Heartland: a Case Study of Political Change', in Caoimhe Nic Dhaibheid and Colin Reid (eds), *From Parnell to Paisley* (Dublin: Irish Academic Press, 2010).
Jackson, Alvin, *Sir Edward Carson* (Dublin: The Historical Society of Ireland, 1993), 41.
McDonald, Henry and Jim Cusack, *UDA: Inside the Heart of Loyalist Terror* (Dublin: Penguin Ireland, 2004).
Miller, David, *Queen's Rebels: Ulster Loyalism in Historical Perspective* (Dublin: Barnes and Noble, 1978).
Nelson, Sarah, *Ulster's Uncertain Defenders: Loyalists and the Northern Ireland Conflict* (Belfast: Appletree Press, 1984).
Paseta, Senia, *Irish Nationalist Women, 1900–1918* (Cambridge: Cambridge University Press, 2013).
Patterson, Henry, *Ireland's Violent Frontier: the Border and Anglo-Irish Relations During the Troubles* (Palgrave Macmillan: Basingstoke, 2013).
Paulin, Tom, 'An Ulster Unionist Walks the Streets of London', in *Fivemiletown* (London: Faber and Faber, 1987).

Reid, Colin, 'Protestant Challenges to the "Protestant State": Ulster Unionism and Independent Unionism in Northern Ireland, 1921–39', *Twentieth Century British History* 19 (4) (2008).

Urquhart, Diane, *Women in Ulster Politics, 1890–1940* (Dublin: Irish Academic Press, 2000).

Walker, Graham, *A History of the Ulster Unionist Party* (Manchester University Press: Manchester, 2005).

Whyte, John, 'How Much Discrimination Was There Under the Unionist Regime, 1921–68?', in Tom Gallagher and James O'Connell (eds), *Contemporary Irish Studies* (Manchester: Manchester University Press, 1983).

Whyte, John, *Interpreting Northern Ireland* (Oxford: Clarendon, 1990).

5
'Doing Their Bit': Gendering the Constitution of Protestant, Unionist and Loyalist Identities

Fidelma Ashe and Caireen McCluskey

Explorations of Protestant, unionist and loyalist (PUL) women's identities during the conflict suggested that they were less politically active than their Irish nationalist and republican counterparts. Throughout the conflict, they appeared to be suspicious of feminism and content to 'do their bit' to defend the Union within the regulatory gender structures of male dominated unionist politics and culture. Generally, unionism has been viewed as providing limited space for feminist reconstructions of PUL women's identities. Certainly, in comparison to Irish nationalist and republican women, PUL women were less visible during the conflict. However, recent feminist research has illustrated that their political agency and gendered transgressions are diverse and shifting. This chapter employs a radical constructionist framework to explore the complex processes through which PUL gendered identities are constituted, disciplined and transgressed. This volume's division of pro-unionist identities into the categories of Protestant, unionist and loyalist already recognises the necessity of mapping the effects of intra-communal differences on seemingly homogeneous groups. This chapter explores the concept of difference in the unionist community further by foregrounding the intersection of Protestantism, unionism and loyalism with gender. Throughout, it illustrates how extant feminist research exposes the challenges for PUL women in a context not only marked by contested political histories and processes of conflict transformation/management, but also the historical relationships of gender that have impacted women in both ethno-nationalist communities.

Regulatory ethno-nationalisms

In recent times there has been much debate about how Northern Ireland deals with the legacies of armed conflict, but less discussion about how it deals with the legacies of a culture that regulated and disciplined women's identities through ethno-nationalist narratives that were saturated with 'patriarchal' moralities. Much feminist work in the area has exposed how both ethno-nationalisms constituted gender and sexual difference in ways that served the ideals of the broader ethno-nationalist struggle (see for example Ashe 2006b; 2007; Conrad 2004; Roulston and Davis 2000; Morgan 1995). Ethno-nationalism called on men to protect the nation politically or militarily from attack by the 'enemy', while women's roles were constituted as primarily domestic (see Ashe 2006a: 151–4). Northern Ireland's 'ethno-gendered regime', as Racioppi and O'Sullivan See (2001) term it, constituted a gendered public/private divide during the period of conflict. Both Irish nationalism and unionism structured women's roles around the ideals of motherhood, domesticity and sexual purity (Ashe 2006a and 2008). These ideals of 'womanhood' supported the maintenance of the heterosexual family, which was a central area of concern for both ethno-nationalist groups. Historically, both groups have viewed it as a vital mechanism for the socialisation and biological reproduction of the ethnic group (Conrad 2004). During the conflict the formal political arena reflected these ideals as women were virtually excluded from political decision-making (see Brown et al. 2002).

In contrast, unionist and loyalist men were called upon to serve the interests of the ethno-nationalist community through maintaining the region's constitutional position and protecting the institutions, culture and religious freedoms of the unionist people in the context of ethno-nationalist antagonism. Subsequently, normative masculinities became associated with the defence of the ethno-nationalist group which entrenched male power politically, culturally and also in militarised arenas. Unionist commemoration valorises male heroes who defended the Union with Britain. The figure of Ian Paisley most clearly expressed the ideals of unionist masculinity in the formal political arena during the conflict. As Lysaght (2005: 119) notes Paisley utilised a rhetoric which is 'highly attuned to the masculinity of defence'. He came to epitomise the intransigence of a wider political culture marked by the stance of not giving 'an inch' to the 'enemy'. This heavily masculinised political culture marginalised women (see Roulston and Davis 2000). More broadly, the political climate ensured that women's political representation remained low during the conflict (see Brown et al. 2002). PUL women tended to be active in the community sector or engaged in activities designed to support the campaigns of male politicians (Urquhart 2000: 77–84). 'Throughout the conflict "Ulster's daughters" appeared to serve as helpmates to the male defenders of the Union' (Racioppi and O'Sullivan See 2001: 94). As women tended to express political agency through community work which was a 'much safer arena of activism' and through their involvement in supporting men's electoral campaigns, two gendered spheres of political activity emerged in Northern Ireland and women became located in civil society organisations while men dominated formal politics (Roulston and Davis 2000; Racioppi and O'Sullivan See 2001: 99).

Culturally, the core institutions of unionism such as the Orange Order reinforced a strict gendered divide. Racioppi and O'Sullivan See explain the gender dynamics of Orange Order marches as follows:

> Most women participate by bringing children to the march, by providing lunches, and by cheering on their menfolk. Some teenage girls attend with their families, but others, especially in urban areas, attach themselves to particular bands and follow them along the march route. Some girls wear shirts with band logos on them; others wear team sport shirts that identify them as supporters of Ulster or British teams or of neighborhood bands associated with particular teams. For all these women – mothers, wives, daughters, band supporters – the dominant femininity is to be supportive of their men's political and cultural leadership and their expressions of Ulster Protestantism: women are there to cheer on the brethren and/or the bands. The ritual formula to these long-practiced marches reinforces a gendered ethnic order that appears highly dichotomous; simultaneously, this formula reinforces a sense of the continuity of traditions and of the historical significance of the parades. (Racioppi and O'Sullivan See 2000: 13)

The intertwining of ethnic and religious identity in Northern Ireland also strengthened the traditional gendered binary. Brady (2013: 231) notes that: 'The key to the relationship between Unionist politics and the Protestant churches is, and has always been, the Orange Order.' Additionally, the church's influence on PUL culture has been bolstered through its influence in matters of political and social import. Both Protestant and Catholic churches played important roles in the strict regulation of gender and sexual identity (Conrad 2004; Jeffery-Poulter 1991). Paisley once remarked that 'the bible states clearly that man is the head of the woman' (cited in Racioppi and O'Sullivan See 2001: 98). Galligan and Knight (2011: 588) write that: 'Protestant clerics emphasised male authority ... and submission to a husband's moral guidance in

home and worldly matters were extolled as desirable womanly virtues.'
In effect, religion and ethno-nationalism created a culture marked by
a heavily regulated sexual terrain and pronounced sexual conservatism
(see Ashe 2009b; Conrad 2004; Side 2006).

The position of unionist men in formal politics, cultural arenas and
religious institutions was reflected at the local level in the ideal of men
as defenders of the community. Militarised cultures invariably produce
militarised forms of masculinities (see Ashe 2009a). The security forces
in Northern Ireland provided legitimate arenas for men to take up
militarised roles, but some men who were unable or unwilling to join
organisations such as the Royal Ulster Constabulary, defended unionist
culture through paramilitary organisations. Loyalist men's participation
in low intensity conflict during what became known colloquially as the
'troubles' combined with continual outbreaks of ghetto warfare in urban,
working-class communities during this period to reinforce men's status
and power at local levels. In effect, loyalist militarism was constituted as
the preserve of 'Ulster's loyal sons' (Racioppi and O'Sullivan See 2001:
94). This was not simply power that was accrued through mechanisms
designed to exert control over loyalist communities. Potentially, membership of a paramilitary organisation also provided mechanisms to control
intimate partners (McWilliams 1997); an aspect of the conflict that led
to the feminist claim that women in the region were living in an 'armed
patriarchy' (Eileen Evason, cited in Aretxaga 1995). The association of
loyalism with men and more specifically with men involved in physical force violence meant that increasingly, throughout the period of the
conflict, loyalism became represented through the hyper-masculinities
of a few high-profile male paramilitaries, and loyalist women received
little public or academic attention (see Ashe and Harland forthcoming;
McEvoy 2009; Stapleton and Wilson 2013).

Regulation and resistance

As already noted, individual PUL women challenged the gender order
during the conflict by working through cross-community groups to
challenge gender inequalities (see Roulston and Davis 2000). Moreover,
groups of unionist and loyalist women also attempted to meet and
address the needs of women in their 'own' communities through civil
society involvement (Cockburn 1998). Yet, in relation to Irish nationalist/
republican women's activism, activities that challenged or troubled
normative gender roles were less visible and appear to have been more
circumscribed in the PUL community. Higher levels of political activity

by Irish nationalist/republican women have been viewed as an outcome of their politicisation through participation in struggles around ethno-nationalist concerns during the conflict (see Alison 2004; Aretxaga 1997; McWilliams 1995).

Open conflict often disturbs the traditional fabric of society and can promote the disruption of normative gender identities. During the conflict, as Aretxaga (1997) notes, the boundaries between the public and the private sphere were disrupted in Irish nationalist communities and traditional gendered roles become disturbed. Sectarian attacks on homes and neighbourhoods were commonplace. The boundary between the home and the street became increasingly fluid during times of high sectarian street violence and women were impacted directly by the conflict at local levels (Aretxaga 1997). The shape of the conflict and its localised expressions meant that in the Northern Ireland case women's utility for the nationalist struggle extended beyond the socialisation of the young into the values of the nation and the biological production of the nationalist group (Yuval-Davis and Anthias 1989). Sharoni (1998) highlighted the disruptions to gender in west Belfast during the early years of the conflict. She notes how women established an alarm system designed to alert the community to the presence of the British Army during the night and she assessed the effects of their participation in sounding the alarm as follows:

> Unlike anywhere in the world, where the streets at night are considered unsafe for women, during the period of heightened conflict discussed here, women in West Belfast not only felt safe on the streets at night. They protected the men in their communities while celebrating their power to frighten the young British soldiers who were unable to comprehend, let alone deal with, the gender role reversal they encountered. (Sharoni 1997)

While unionist women appeared to occupy a marginal position in the context of Orange Order parades and other expressions of unionism, Irish nationalist women were active in organising these kinds of 'popular forms of resistance' during the conflict (see e.g. Aretxaga 1997; McWilliams 1995). Potter and MacMillan (2008) argue that the differential levels of popular protest between Irish nationalist and unionist women were a product of Irish nationalism's ideological base. They suggest that republicans were fighting a 'war', whereas loyalism was defensive. 'Logically, whole communities can be mobilised for a war, including women, but "normal" societies not operating on a war footing could afford to maintain a more traditional social structure, sending the men out to fight and leaving the women to attend to the domestic sphere' (Potter and MacMillan 2008: 27). Historically, militaristic forms of Irish nationalism anchored political resistance in claims that the Irish people must defend themselves and Ireland against a colonial power, which justifies the recruitment of women as activists within this community (Alison 2004: 448). Alison (2004: 448) therefore explains these differential rates of women's activism as follows: 'Theoretical analysis suggests that anti-state (working against the existing state authority) so-called "liberatory" nationalisms often provide a greater degree of ideological and practical space for women to participate as combatants than do institutionalized state or pro-state nationalisms.' In contrast unionist politics has not been involved in contesting the constitutional status quo, so there have been fewer opportunities during the conflict for women to transgress traditional roles through, for example, becoming combatants; an activity that raises a set of complex issues for feminism (see Alison 2004; Ashe 2006b for further analysis). Official figures record 2368 women imprisoned between 1969 and 2007, 128 of whom had paramilitary affiliations and 20 per cent of these were affiliated to loyalist organisations (Potter and MacMillan 2008: 9).

Moreover, feminist studies have suggested that anti-state nationalist movements can more easily absorb feminist claims about women's equality into their ideological narrative. However, such claims have been debated in the international literature (see for example West 1997 for discussion). In the Northern Ireland case, contextual factors certainly led to a stronger association between feminism and Irish nationalism, and PUL women have been less likely to identify with it. 'Protestant women in particular found it difficult to support feminism, since this was seen to represent a left-wing and/or anti-state agenda. It was therefore associated with republicanism and perceived as antithetical to the unionist cause' (Stapleton and Wilson 2013: 4). The fusion of feminist ideas about women's equality and nationalist challenges to the treatment of women prisoners in Armagh Gaol reinforced perceptions that feminism was being utilised for Irish nationalist ends (see Loughran 1986). Monica McWilliams noted that 'the dominant voice within the feminist movement in Northern Ireland has been that of the various shades of [Irish] nationalism. Giving top priority to the [Irish] nationalist questions served to silence the voices of Protestant women' (1995: 27). What is clear is that during the conflict 'feminism couldn't exist outside of prevailing power structures inescapably defined by the ethno-nationalist framework' (Loughran 1986: 15). The intersectional nature of identities meant that feminist standpoints and discourses became intertwined with ethno-nationalist politics.

During the conflict the gendered dimensions of PUL culture combined with the more visible activism of Irish nationalist women led Carol Coulter (1998) to comment that unionism is inimical to women's progress. Subsequently, feminist framings of these women have had a distinctive, domestic quality. Cockburn (1998: 59) remarked that unionist women's involvement in political campaigns was limited to 'making the sandwiches', which reflects the 'tea-maker' stereotype articulated by other writers (Coulter 1998: 164). Viewed as more actively involved in political struggle and as ideologically closer to feminism, nationalist women received much more analytical attention than PUL women for much of the period of the conflict and the identities of PUL women were under-theorised. McGlynn and McAuley (2011) contend that: 'In research terms, this group is doubly marginalized in relation to both male loyalists and republican women' (cited in Stapleton and Wilson 2013: 6). The conservative and patriarchal ideology of unionism meant that for much of the conflict PUL women were unrecognised or at times misrecognised and research produced in the conflict transformational period has led to a more informed and complex picture of PUL women's political agency.

For example, Ward (2006) challenged the tea-maker stereotype at the level of formal politics. She found that unionist women were engaged in a range of activities within the political parties (see also Urquhart 2000 for a historical analysis of unionist women's political agency). Recent studies also suggest that the level of loyalist women's conflict-related activities has been underestimated. McEvoy's (2009) study estimated much higher levels of involvement by women in paramilitary/conflict-related activities compared to previous work in the area. Her (2009: 269) study 'documented approximately two dozen active women's units at various times throughout the conflict with a combined membership as high as three thousand women'. However, according to Alison, 'Only a very few loyalist paramilitary women were involved in the full range of the paramilitaries' violent activities; put crudely, in general loyalist women carried the guns and loyalist men used them' (Alison 2004: 456). However, like Alison (2004) and Potter and MacMillan (2008), McEvoy (2009: 267) found denials by men of women's paramilitary involvement: 'In the early stages of the fieldwork I was told by men affiliated with LPOs (Loyalist Paramilitary Organisations) that "the women were never there"'. As Alison (2004: 456) notes: 'In the hyper-masculine world of Loyalist paramilitary organizations, military women create a fundamental unease' (see also McEvoy 2009; Potter and MacMillan 2008).

McEvoy's study suggests that PUL women were more active in paramilitary-related activities than once thought, but the complexity of women's agency during conflict makes any simplistic analysis of transgressions of gender by PUL women difficult. Potter and MacMillan (2008: 22–3) capture this complexity well when they observe that:

> The difficulty lies in the reality of women's lives during conflict. Some women may wish to be actively involved and be recognised as being so as much as the men. Some women may be coerced into becoming involved in opposition to their own wishes and the traditional societal position that insists they should be left out of the conflict. Others may wish to rebel against being held up as an excuse for men to 'defend' them by pursuing a conflict with which they do not agree. Women are individuals that encompass a range of characters and identities that might not fit into an assumed societal or community structure.

Furthermore, it is important to note that while militarism transgresses traditional gendered norms, there is no guarantee that it improves the power and positioning of women within ethno-nationalist groups. Rick Wilford (1998: 3) notes, 'fighting alongside men to achieve independence does not provide a guarantee of women's inclusion as equal citizens'; they are invariably 'left holding the wrong end of the citizenship stick' when the fighting ends (15) (see also Gilmartin 2013, for recent research on Irish republican women, and Dowler 1998). Yet, the disruptive potential of women's conflict-related activities is reflected in the attempts to deny it discussed above.

However, the displacement of PUL women's transgressions of normative femininity was more easily maintained during the period of conflict. In the conflict transformational period more light has been thrown on PUL women's disruptions of their traditional gender roles and the different standpoints of women in this community on a whole range of social issues. Moreover, the dimensions of the conflict transformational context have made the agency of PUL women in political arenas more visible.

Changing times

After the Agreement the discourses surrounding women's participation were reshaped by the main unionist parties. Empirical data has suggested

Table 5.1 Northern Ireland Assembly election results, 2011

Party	Seats	Male	Female	% Female
APNI	8	6	2	25
DUP	38	33	5	13.2
SF	29	21	8	27.6
SDLP	14	11	3	21.4
UUP	16	14	2	12.5
Other	3	0	0	0
Total	108	87	20	18.5

Source: Centre for the Advancement of Women in Politics.

that the two unionist parties have recently acknowledged the importance of encouraging more women to seek political office. For example, one male member of a unionist party stated when interviewed by Matthews (2012: 19): 'there is an attitude that we need to encourage more women to become members of the party, to become elected representatives of the party, to hold positions in the party at all levels'. However, the proof of change lies in the size of unionist women's slice of the representational 'pudding'. Matthews (2012: 5) notes the 'neat ethno-national split, with the two Unionist parties, the DUP and UUP, trailing behind their nationalist counterparts, Sinn Fein and the SDLP' (see Table 5.1).

However, high-profile women have emerged in the unionist parties. McGlynn and McAuley (2011: 141) note the appointment of Arlene Foster as caretaker leader of the DUP in 2010. Yet, Galligan and Knight (2011: 589) observe that: 'Only from 2010, though, were there early signs of unionist political willingness to accord a place to women in the public sphere.'

The involvement of the former leader of the Progressive Unionist Party Dawn Purvis in recent challenges to the bio-politics of ethno-nationalism has also raised the profile of loyalist women in feminist struggles in the public sphere. Purvis not only defied conventions of gendered leadership in the loyalist community; in 2012 she was involved in setting up a Marie Stopes Clinic in Victoria Square, in the heart of Belfast City Centre. She was hauled before the Assembly's Committee for Justice in January 2013 to be questioned with colleagues from the Clinic on how the facility was complying with criminal law. The day after that committee session the journalist Fionola Meredith commented on the tone of the questioning.

From the start, they [the women] were confronted with suspicion and barely veiled hostility from members of the almost exclusively male committee. What with all the hectoring, the moralising and the finger-pointing, it seemed as though this was Stormont's answer to the Salem witch-trails. I half-expected someone to stand up and shout, 'I saw Goody Hawkins with the Devil'. (2013: 2)

Yet, the opening of the Stopes Clinic and the confidence of Purvis in the face of intensive questioning by members of the Committee for Justice suggested that traditional sites of authority were going to be increasingly challenged. For example, during the committee session Purvis was asked about the siting of the clinic near transport links to the Republic of Ireland. Committee member, Jim Wells asked: 'Is one of your roles to encourage women to come up from the Irish Republic for terminations to be carried out in Northern Ireland?' (Hansard 2013: 18). Purvis replied coolly that: 'The location was paramount when I was looking at sites in Belfast because, yes, I was thinking of clients from all over the island coming to avail themselves of our services. I wanted to ensure good transport links to the clinic ...' (Hansard 2013: 18).

The Agreement failed to reshape gendered power-relationships in the region in any meaningful way and the gains for women in the new Northern Ireland have been limited. Yet, gender politics remains an arena of struggle, and issues concerning women's social positioning, access to abortion and LGBT civil rights have been forced on to political agendas by civil society groups. PUL women have not only been involved in those struggles but as Purvis, May Blood, Pearl Sagar and others have illustrated, at times, they have been on the frontline of those struggles (see Fearon 1999).

Protest

Changing times have also increased the potential for PUL women to come into direct confrontation with state institutions, making them much more visible in political protests and their transgressions of normative gender identities more exposed to analysis. Additionally, feminist conceptual frameworks have been reframed locally and internationally in ways that have opened more space for considering women's more active participation in ethno-nationalist conflict (see Alison 2004; Ashe 2006a). In the past, strands of feminism tended to explain these transgressions as an outcome of 'masculinist' movements that ideologically regulated women into participation in ethno-nationalist struggles that often did little to address the position of women within the broader ethnic community (see Ashe 2006b). This kind of framing recognises the gendered hierarchies within nationalist movements and highlights how nationalism utilises women's agency during conflict but fails to address gender equality when the conflict ends, but it also places women outside of the contextual processes that construct women's culturally mediated experiences of ethnicity. This runs the risk of placing women's identities outside of the complex social conditions that constitute them. Aretxaga (1995) puts the point eloquently when she states: 'The pervasive idea that women are mere victims of the war and naturally oppose it has obscured the complex processes by which women take sides, take risks, take arms and wage war. This idea obscured the complex dynamic through which women become subjects and not mere objects of social transformation.' The analysis of women's involvement in protests can make visible their role in contesting ethno-gendered regimes even if that resistance emerges from the adoption of highly gendered understandings of women's familial and social roles.

The Agreement (1998) caused a number of anxieties for the unionist community (Aughey 2005). Patterson (2012: 248) states that there was 'a general hardening of Unionist opinion against the peace process which by the early part of the new century was seen to be a one-way street of concessions to Sinn Fein'. These perceptions generated protests and clashes with the security forces over matters relating to rulings on the flying of flags on government buildings and the routing of parades. Conflict with the institutions of governance led to women's increased visibility in political protests. One night during the 2012 Union flag protests, loyalist protesters gathered on the grounds of Belfast City Hall and tried to force their way into the monthly meeting being held inside the building. One woman pushed her head through the glass doors of City Hall and shouted 'no surrender'. The incident was lampooned across the internet. The philosopher James Beattie (2013) argued that laughter is caused by 'two or more inconsistent, unsuitable, or incongruous parts or circumstances, considered as united in one complex object or assemblage ...' The fusion of 'the feminine' with behaviours more associated with men was therefore ridiculed. The few studies of loyalist women who were involved in more recent ethno-nationalist protests expose how gender is disciplined, deployed, contested and reconfigured through this agency. Moreover, they highlight how concrete political cultures impact on women's perceptions of their ethno-nationalist and gendered identities.

Stapleton and Wilson's (2013) study exposed that while loyalist women's involvement in protest was generated by a more general perception of the erosion of unionist identity, gender identity was utilised in the protest by the women involved for strategic purposes. They (2013: 5) conducted focus groups in 2005–6 with women who had experienced marching conflicts within the greater Belfast area to examine the 'complex and contested' positions women occupy when located in conflicts. Using data from focus groups with loyalist women, they found that the women explained their role in the protests through narratives that invoked prevailing gendered expectations. The women claimed that they 'were keen to keep their own protest as an "all-female" event since this allowed them to maintain the moral high ground by virtue of particular "female" characteristics for example, the idea that women are less violent than men; are more "reputable" or respectable; and are more vulnerable to physical attack' (Stapleton and Wilson 2013: 17). This deployment of femininity reproduced traditional gendered stereotypes but when combined with protest in public arenas appeared to disturb the historical relationships of gender within loyalist communities. 'Thus they [the women] claim that through the strength and success of their "female-only" protest, the men have come to accept them as co-players within the community structures who have particular (gendered) strengths to offer' (Stapleton and Wilson 2013: 17).

Byrne's recent study of women who participated in the City Hall flag protests in 2012 and 2013 also suggested that women's involvement in the protest had disrupted traditional gendered narratives in that community. One participant noted, 'women are more passionate', they are 'more committed to the protests' (Byrne 2014: 12). Several went further and concluded: 'some women have felt let down by the men in their community. They have stood on the line, taking abuse from the other community and the police, and the men just hover in the background' (Byrne 2014: 12). The continued analysis of gendered protests by unionist and loyalist women has the potential to draw out further insights about the impact of women's political resistances on gendered-power relationships in the PUL community.

Conclusions

PUL politics and culture has reinforced, and at times, valorised traditional gendered identities. The cultural reiteration of normative ideas about gender and the concrete conditions of their reproduction means that gender remains a site of political and social inequality. Women participated in PUL politics and culture during the conflict, but their roles have been configured as mainly supportive of a political agenda constructed and dominated by men. The period of conflict transformation has made PUL women and their transgressions of normative gendered identities more visible across a number of arenas. Broader societal shifts have challenged aspects of the traditional 'ethno-gendered' regime. The further dismantling of that regime is not simply a matter for PUL women, but a pressing challenge for the whole PUL community. Moreover, the task for mainstream researchers is to acknowledge gender as a site of inequality within the PUL community and to make visible the various manifestations of that inequality across mainstream research agendas.

Bibliography

Alison, M. (2004), 'Women as Agents of Political Violence: Gendering Security', *Security Dialogue* 35 (4): 447–63.

Aretxaga, B. (1995), 'Ruffling a Few Patriarchal Hairs: Women's Experiences of War in Northern Ireland', *Cultural Survival Quarterly* 19 (1). Online: available at <http://www.culturalsurvival.org/publications/cultural-survival-quarterly/ireland/ruffling-few-patriarchal-hairs-womens-experiences-w#sthash.gfAlk6tv.dpuf> [accessed 14 October 2013].

—— (1997), *Shattering Silence: Women, Nationalism and Political Subjectivity in Northern Ireland* (Princeton and Chichester: Princeton University Press).

Ashe, F. (2006a), 'Gendering the Holy Cross School Dispute: Women and Nationalism in Northern Ireland', *Political Studies* 54 (3): 147–64.

—— (2006b), 'The Virgin Mary Complex: Feminism and Northern Ireland Politics', *Critical Review of International Social and Political Philosophy* 9 (4): 573–88.

—— (2007), 'Gendering Ethno-nationalist Conflict in Northern Ireland', *Ethnic and Racial Studies* 30 (5): 766–86.

—— (2008), 'Gender and Ethno-nationalist Politics in Northern Ireland', in C. Coulter and M. Murray (eds), *Northern Ireland after the Troubles* (Manchester: Manchester University Press), 45–60.

—— (2009a), 'From Paramilitaries to Peacemakers: the Gender Dynamics of Community-based Restorative Justice in Northern Ireland', *British Journal of Politics and International Relations* 11 (2): 298–314.

—— (2009b), 'Iris Robinson's Excitable Speech: Sexuality and Conflict Transformation in Northern Ireland', *Politics* 29 (1): 20–7.

Ashe, F. and K. Harland (forthcoming), 'Troubling Masculinities: Changing Patterns of Violent Masculinities in a Society Emerging from Political Conflict', *Studies in Conflict and Terrorism*.

Aughey, A. (2005), *The Agreement* (London and New York: Routledge).

Beattie, J. (2013), *Essays: On Poetry and Music, As They Affect the Mind: On Laughter, and Ludicrous Composition; on the Utility of Classical Learning*. Online: available at <http://archive.org/details/essaysonpoetrymu00beat> [accessed 14 October 2013].

Brady, S. (2013), 'Why Examine Men, Masculinities and Religion in Northern Ireland?', in L. Delap and S. Morgan (eds), *Men, Masculinities and Religious Change in Twentieth-Century Britain* (Basingstoke: Palgrave Macmillan), 197–218.

Brown, A., Donaghy, T., Mackay, F. and Meehan, E. (2002), 'Women and Constitutional Change in Scotland and Northern Ireland', *Parliamentary Affairs* 55: 71–84.

Byrne, J. (2014), *Flags and Protests: Exploring the Views, Perceptions and Experiences of People Directly and Indirectly Affected by the Flag Protests* (Belfast: Intercomm).

Centre for the Advancement of Women in Politics, 'Elections', available at <http://www.qub.ac.uk/cawp/election.html> [accessed 14 October 2013].

Cockburn, C. (1998), *The Space Between Us: Negotiating Gender and National Identities in Conflict* (London and New York: Zed Books).

Conrad, K. A. (2004), *Locked in the Family Cell: Gender, Sexuality and Political Agency in Irish National Discourse* (Madison, WI: University of Wisconsin Press).

Coulter, C. (1998), 'Feminism and Nationalism in Ireland', in D. Miller (ed.), *Rethinking Northern Ireland: Culture, Ideology and Colonialism* (Essex: Addison Wesley Longman), 160–17.

Dowler, L. (1998), '"And They Think I'm a Nice Old Lady": Women and War in Belfast, Northern Ireland', *Gender, Place and Culture* 5 (2): 159–76.

Evason, E. (1991), *Against the Grain: the Contemporary Women's Movement in Northern Ireland* (Dublin: Attic Press).

Fearon, K. (ed.) (1999), *The Story of the Northern Ireland Women's Coalition* (Belfast: Blackstaff).

Galligan, Y. and K. Knight (2011), 'Attitudes towards Women in Politics: Gender, Generation and Party Identification in Ireland', *Parliamentary Affairs* 64 (4): 585–611.

Gilmartin, N. (2013), 'Negotiating New Roles: Irish Republican Women and the Politics of Conflict Transformation', *International Feminist Journal of Politics*. Online, available at <http://www.tandfonline.com/doi/pdf/10.1080/14616742.2013.806060> [accessed 14 October 2013].

Hansard (2013), Official Report: Committee for Justice, Marie Stopes International: Compliance with Criminal Law on Abortion in Northern Ireland, Thursday, 10 January. Online, available at <http://www.niassembly.gov.uk/Assembly-Business/Official-Report/Committee-Minutes-of-Evidence/Session-2012-2013/January-2013/Marie-Stopes-International-Compliance-with-Criminal-Law-on-Abortion-in-Northern-Ireland/> [accessed 14 October 2013].

Jeffery-Poulter, S. (1991), *Peers, Queers and Commons* (London: Routledge).

Lysaght, K. (2005), 'Mobilising the Rhetoric of Defence: Exploring Working-Class Masculinities in a Divided City', in B. Van Hoven and K. Horschelmann (eds), *Spaces of Masculinities* (London: Routledge), 115–27.

Loughran, C. (1986), 'Armagh and Feminist Strategy', *Feminist Review* 23: 59–79.

Matthews, N. (2012), 'Gendered Candidate Selection and the Representation of Women in Northern Ireland', *Parliamentary Affairs* 11: 1–30.

McGlynn, C. and J. W. McAuley (2011), 'Auxiliaries in the Cause?: Loyalist Women in Conflict and Post Conflict', in J. W. McAuley and G. Spencer (eds), *Ulster Loyalism after the Good Friday Agreement* (Oxford: Palgrave Macmillan), 132–46.

McDowell, S. (2008), 'Commemorating Dead "Men": Gendering the Past and Present in Post-Conflict Northern Ireland', *Gender, Place and Culture* 15 (4): 335–54.

McEvoy, S. (2009), 'Loyalist Women Paramilitaries in Northern Ireland: Beginning a Feminist Conversation about Conflict Resolution', *Security Studies* 18 (2): 262–86.

McWilliams, M. (1995), 'Struggling for Peace and Justice: Reflections on Women's Activism in Northern Ireland', *Journal of Women's History* 6 (4): 13–39.

——— (1997), 'Violence against Women and Political Conflict: the Northern Ireland Experience', *Critical Criminology* 8 (1): 78–92.

Meredith, F. (2013), 'We Need Brave Leaders Who Place Truth Above Tribalism', *Belfast Telegraph*, 16 January. Online, available at <http://www.belfasttele graph.co.uk/opinion/columnists/fionola-meredith/we-need-brave-leaders-who-place-truth-above-tribalism-29015229.html> [accessed 14 October 2013].

Morgan, V. (1995), 'Women and Conflict in Northern Ireland', in A. O'Day (ed.), *Terrorism's Laboratory: the Case of Northern Ireland* (Aldershot: Dartmouth), 59–73.

Patterson, H. (2012), 'Unionism after Good Friday and St Andrews', *Political Quarterly* 83: 247–55.

Potter, M. and A. MacMillan (2008), 'Unionist Women Active in the Conflict in Northern Ireland'. Online, available at <http://www.twnonline.com/twn_docs/Research/uniWomActConNI.pdf> [accessed 14 October 2013].

Racioppi, L. and K. O'Sullivan See (2000), 'Ulstermen and Loyalist Ladies on Parade: Gendering Unionism in Northern Ireland', *International Feminist Journal of Politics* 2 (1): 1–29.

Racioppi, L. and K. O'Sullivan See (2001), '"This We Will Maintain": Gender, Ethno-nationalism and the Politics of Unionism in Northern Ireland', *Nations and Nationalism* 7 (1): 93–112.

Roulston, R. and C. Davis (eds) (2000), *Gender, Democracy and Inclusion in Northern Ireland* (Basingstoke: Palgrave).

Sharoni, S. (1998) 'Gendering Conflict and Peace in Israel/Palestine and the North of Ireland', *Millennium: Journal of International Studies* 27 (4): 1061–89.

Side, K. (2006), 'Contract, Charity, and Honourable Entitlement: Social Citizenship and the 1967 Abortion Act in Northern Ireland after the Good Friday Agreement', *Social Politics* 13 (1): 89–116.

Stapleton, K. and J. Wilson, J. (2013), 'Conflicting Categories? Women, Conflict and Identity in Northern Ireland', *Ethnic and Racial Studies*, Early View. Online, available at <http://www.tandfonline.com/doi/abs/10.1080/01419870.2013.80 0570> [accessed 12 October 2013].

Urquhart, D. (2000) *Women in Ulster Politics, 1890–1940: a History Not Yet Told* (Portland, Oregon: Irish Academic Press).

Ward, R. (2006) *Women, Unionism and Loyalism in Northern Ireland: From 'Tea-Maker' to Political Actors* (Dublin: Irish Academic Press).

West, L. A. (1997) *Feminist Nationalism* (New York: Routledge).

Wilford, R. (1998) 'Women, Ethnicity and Nationalism: Surveying the Ground', in R. Wilford and R. L. Miller (eds), *Women, Ethnicity and Nationalism: the Politics of Transition* (New York: Routledge).

Yuval-Davis, N. and F. Anthias (eds) (1989), *Women-Nation-State* (London: Macmillan).

6
The Re-invention of the Orange Order: Triumphalism or Orangefest?

Reverend Brian Kennaway

The present challenges facing the Orange Institution have their immediate origins in what has become generally known as the 'Drumcree Debacle'.

One of the oldest, if not the oldest, annual Orange Parade to a church for a service of worship, commenced in 1807 to Drumcree Parish Church, outside Portadown, in County Armagh. Major conflict arose in the 1970s over the route via Obins Street and after a stand-off in 1987, the Royal Ulster Constabulary and Portadown District Loyal Orange Lodge agreed to return by the Garvaghy Road, following the service. However with the change in the religious and political allegiances of those who lived on the Garvaghy Road, conflict arose again in 1995.

The result of this conflict is well documented in terms of widespread opposition to Orange Order parades throughout Northern Ireland. However Gerry Adams's speech at a Sinn Féin Conference in Athboy, County Meath, in November 1996, is often forgotten:

> Ask any activist in the north 'Did Drumcree happen by accident?' They will tell you 'No'. Three years of work in Lower Ormeau, Portadown, and parts of Fermanagh, Newry, Armagh, Bellaghy and up in Derry. Three years' work into creating that situation and fair play to those people who put the work in ... they are the type of scene changes that we have to focus in on and develop and exploit.[1]

Some years later a letter appeared in the *Irish News* in which John McCabe from Newry confirmed the Athboy assertion:

> In 1996 Sinn Fein covertly set up 'Newry Coalition Against Sectarian Parades' of which I was chairman. This was part of its overall strategy

which was replicated throughout the six counties to confront loyalist parades against the backdrop of the then Drumcree dispute.[2]

The immediate effect of this conflict was the North Report, which led to the establishment of the Parades Commission. The bad publicity surrounding the conflict over parades in the 1990s led the Grand Orange Lodge of Ireland to engage the public relations company 'Reputation Matters', in an attempt to deal with the ever-increasing dysfunction of the leadership in relation to the media.

In an attempt to present a new image to the world the leadership of the Orange Institution came up with two new ideas. Whether this was a repositioning, rebranding or reinvention is open to question. Whether this was a genuine attempt to improve the image of the Order or an attempt to make the Order more acceptable for funding, particularly lottery funding, is also open to question. No attempt was made to deal with the extensive issues of discipline, particularly in relation to the engagement and behaviour of paramilitary-style bands.

The first attempt at repositioning was to earmark particular Twelfth parades as 'Flagships'. This initiative is explained on the Grand Lodge website as follows:

> Each year since 2006, the Grand Lodge of Ireland has bestowed a small number of the 18 Twelfth demonstrations with flagship status.
>
> Working closely with the Northern Ireland Tourist Board, organisers of the chosen parades will ensure each venue offers a unique programme of events leading up to the big day itself.
>
> Director of Services of the Grand Orange Lodge of Ireland, Dr. David Hume, insisted the flagship initiative has led to a higher profile for the Twelfth.
>
> 'The flagship programme has increased confidence, developed capacity and assisted in international marketing of the Twelfth as well as giving obvious pride to the flagship venues over the years', he said.[3]

As this repositioning continued, the second attempt was the creation of Orangefest as a cultural expression of the Orange tradition. This exercise to persuade a sceptical world that the Institution was genuinely interested in political change was accompanied by an attempt to make the Orange Order more acceptable to the non-religious Orangeman by emphasising the importance of its *culture* rather than its *faith*.

Orangefest appears to have been the brainchild of the Committee for Educational Affairs, and was reported to the Grand Lodge in March

2005 as 'a method of delivering "Education through Celebration"'.[4] It was taken up by Belfast County Grand Lodge, where they attempted to give a more family-oriented feel to the now quite belligerent parade through Belfast, where even at this stage the numbers of bandsmen on parade exceeded the number of Orangemen on parade. Orangefest is, strictly speaking, a Belfast phenomenon, though it was originally designed to apply throughout the Institution. As the Report of the Committee for Educational Affairs stated – 'the ownership of OrangeFest is firmly of a localised nature – County, District and Private Lodges'.[5] Understandably, many associate this title with the overall attempt to make the Twelfth more acceptable.

As Orangefest is now purely a Belfast County Grand Lodge occurrence, my comments are therefore directed to the expression of Orangeism as displayed by Belfast Orangemen. Orangemen in rural Ulster tend to express their Orangeism in a much more benign way.

Orangefest has introduced 'floats' in the Belfast parade as well as the provision of children's activities, at what appears as the new demonstration field at Barnett's Demesne at the top of the Malone Road in South Belfast. The most surprising aspect of this Orangefest is its relationship with the Belfast business community, and Belfast City Council. The Council supply some 200 portable toilets out of ratepayers' money. Businesses in Belfast were encouraged to open for business on what is a public holiday. The writer can well recall some years ago when it was rumoured among Belfast Orangemen that the British Home Stores were going to open for business on that 'sacred day'. The Orangemen of the Belfast County Grand Lodge discussed the possibility of organising a boycott!

The Orangefest concept has not been universally acceptable among Orangemen. Not just because it is not 'traditional' but also because it has not addressed the core issue of the behaviour of bands, which has brought such discredit to the public image of the Institution.

Early in 2006 the Grand Lodge website revealed that:

> Drew Nelson, Grand Secretary of the Orange Order, said that over the last two years senior Orangemen had visited both London's Notting Hill Carnival and the Alarde Parade in Hondarribia in the Basque region of Spain. 'These study tours flagged up important issues about the organisation of large street festivals in the 21st century. The most important lesson we learned is that civic involvement is vital at a time when all public events throughout Europe are subject to increasing regulation', said Mr Nelson.[6]

The word 'Orangefest' did not appear on this statement on the website but its substance was clearly evident. It was an attempt to make parades more acceptable by inculcating a carnival atmosphere, an Orange Festival or Orangefest. Will Glendenning, the former Chief Executive of the Community Relations Council who, as a private consultant, was engaged to advise the leadership, arranged these trips.

In an in-depth interview with Chris Thornton, published in the *Belfast Telegraph* on 28 April 2006, the Grand Secretary, Drew Nelson, attempted to present a positive image of the Institution, but also displayed a naive lack of understanding of the situation on the ground, particularly in Belfast. Thornton said that:

> Recent years have seen the parades dispute become the Orange institution's main distraction, but Nelson says the Order is quietly rebuilding and returning to its roots. 'The Orange Order's got two core values', the Grand Secretary says. 'The first one is the Protestant religion – the preservation and propagation of the Protestant religion. The other core value is as a mutual support organisation. And in that one, I think we made a very significant contribution – unnoticed – in the last ten years in two fields.'[7]

In this interview Chris Thornton went on to make reference to the *two fields* in which Nelson believed the Institution had made a 'very significant contribution'. These were 'building up more than 60 credit unions, many in Orange halls, and hundreds of community groups in Protestant areas'.[8]

In many interviews of this type it is what is not said which is important, rather than what is. No reference is made to the first core value – 'the Protestant religion – the preservation and propagation of the Protestant religion', by way of example. No evidence was presented to support the statement that the Institution was 'returning to its roots'. Was this further evidence that *faith* was being replaced by *culture*?

As the interview progressed Drew Nelson was quoted as saying:

> We understand there's influence from loyalist paramilitaries in those areas in Belfast, but I mean we're not working with them, so we're not . . . In fact, I want to say and put this on the record that loyalist paramilitary activity is incompatible with membership of the Orange institution.[9]

Nelson is further questioned about paramilitary connections to the Institution:

> Orangemen do sit on the North and West Belfast Parades Forum with paramilitary representatives, but Nelson says he doesn't know about that. 'I should know about it, but I don't', he says. 'That's the one that comes up all the time'.[10]

For someone in the leadership of the Orange Institution to make such statements and present them to the wider public, reveals the parallel universe which the leadership inhabited.

A further interview with the Grand Secretary appeared in the *Irish Times* on 17 June 2006. In this interview, in which the word 'Orangefest' again does not appear, Nelson is quoted as saying that he wants to see annual Orange parades, 'celebrated the way Brazilians celebrate Mardi Gras'. Such a statement was astounding and only served to isolate the religious body politic within the Orange Institution.

Was Drew Nelson unaware that Mardi Gras (French for 'Fat Tuesday') is a Roman Catholic celebration held just before the beginning of Lent? How would this highly decorative spectacle of half-naked men and women contribute to what he had previously described as the first 'core value' of the Institution – 'the preservation and propagation of the Protestant religion'?[11]

An 'Orangefest', or Orange Festival, cannot get the Institution out of its present predicament. A 'Mardi Gras' is not the answer to the protection of cultural identity. Any intelligent assessment of the present state of the Institution will recognise that there is a foundation within Protestant culture beyond which it cannot go and without which it loses its *raison d'être*. That foundation is the authority of Scripture. This is reflected in the *Qualifications of an Orangeman*, which every Orangeman is required to assent to on initiation:

> An Orangeman should have a sincere love and veneration for his Heavenly Father; a humble and steadfast faith in Jesus Christ, the Saviour of mankind, believing in Him as the only Mediator between God and man. He should cultivate truth and justice, brotherly kindness and charity, devotion and piety, concord and unity, and obedience to the laws; his deportment should be gentle and compassionate, kind and courteous; he should seek the society of the virtuous, and avoid that of the evil; he should honour and diligently study the Holy Scriptures, and make them the rule of his faith and

practice; ... he should remember to keep holy the Sabbath day, and attend the public worship of God, and diligently train up his offspring, and all under his control, in the fear of God, and in the Protestant faith; he should never take the name of God in vain, but abstain from all cursing and profane language, and use every opportunity of discouraging those, and all other sinful practices, in others; his conduct should be guided by wisdom and prudence, and marked by honesty, temperance, and sobriety; the glory of God and the welfare of man, the honour of his Sovereign, and the good of his country, should be the motives of his actions.[12]

If the Orange Order is, as it claims, 'a Christian organisation', if it is 'Christ-centred, Bible-based, Church-grounded', if religion plays a significant role rather than a merely symbolic role, then that dynamic must be to the fore in its cultural expression.

The Deputy Grand Master of the Grand Orange Lodge of Ireland, the Rev. Stephen Dickinson, appeared initially to get sucked into this Orangefest celebration, by comparing it to the Chinese New Year celebrations:

> Mr Dickinson said the Order had much to offer as a 'family day out'. 'We have pageantry, spectacle, music, banners, spirituality, celebration', he said. The Twelfth has many similarities to Chinese New Year celebrations, Mr Dickinson said. 'We are cultural, historic, popular and we are colourful. And, contrary to popular opinion, we are even fun', he said.[13]

However he soon recognised the danger of moving the Orange Order from a 'faith' organisation to a 'cultural' organisation, when, in the presence of the Grand Master Robert Saulters, he addressed the 2006 Twelfth demonstration at Ballycastle in County Antrim:

> The Orange Order is first and foremost a Protestant organisation whose focus is on the Lord and upon the Scriptures and the faith once handed down to the saints – and from that we must not move!

> Some are trying to move us on and turn us into a culture club – or a community club – but we are first and foremost a Protestant organisation out for the defence of Protestantism – and from that we must not move ... Those who want to take part in a fancy dress parade should join the Women's Institute and not the Orange Institution![14]

Dickinson continued his opposition to the Orangefest concept. Speaking at the Ballyclare Twelfth in 2008 he told his hearers:

> I notice that Peter Robinson and others have been saying in recent days we're about cultural tourism. This is about Protestantism, this is about Britishness – it's not about cultural tourism, Mr Robinson.[15]

As the Orangefest vision took hold it continued to provoke internal opposition. Many Christian people within the Institution recognised the not-so-subtle shift from *faith* to *culture*. Dickinson and others were to set up an internal Orange organisation called 'Orange Reformation', which it claimed aimed to 'put Protestantism back into the order'. It was launched in July 2009, when Dickinson addressed the Twelfth demonstration in Coagh, County Tyrone. In his address he denounced the leadership of the Institution as 'modernisers' and 'compromisers'.[16]

Rallies organised by 'Orange Reformation' received little support, as there was no stomach on the part of many for another fight. Inevitably, the Rev. Stephen Dickinson resigned from the Orange Institution in September 2011,[17] having previously indicated in a letter to the *Belfast News Letter*:

> I am another Orangeman thinking about walking away – not because I have lost interest in religion but because the Orange Order has.[18]

The summer of 2006 saw traditional Orange demonstrations being repackaged as cultural festivals, with 'Flagship Twelfths' in rural Ulster and Orangefest in Belfast. It is little surprise that Liam Clarke perceptively observed:

> One wonders if the Orange Order realises the extensive remodelling it will have to undergo to make itself widely acceptable after years of contested marches, sporadic violence and refusal to talk.[19]

The response of the wider media was equally less than positive. The leadership had attempted to present the Orangefest logo as a tourist attraction for Europe's 'largest community festival'. In a strongly worded piece in the *Belfast Telegraph*, Lindy McDowell revealed the financial incentive of £100,000 of taxpayer's money in order to promote 'Orangefest' as a tourist attraction. She seriously questioned the wisdom of such public expenditure:

> But is it wise for the Government to give £100,000 of public money towards promoting the Orange festival as a tourist attraction? ... So

let's not kid ourselves that this handout is anything other than a Blair bribe. Money given for compliance later expected.[20]

The *Sunday World* followed with the declaration that 'Orangefest is a tourist flop!'[21] Reporter Stephen Moore highlighted some of the negative images of the demonstration in Belfast held four days previously. These included a picture of a bandswoman who had publicy urinated outside the *Sunday World* offices and police in riot gear attending an Orange parade. The caption posed the question 'Can the Twelfth attract tourists with a heavy police presence?'[22]

The substance of the *Sunday World* article was to challenge the view widely presented by the Institution that the Twelfth in Belfast generated major income for the city. Lord Laird of Artigarvan (formerly John Laird), a member of Royal York LOL 145, had claimed that visitors generated £6 million during the Twelfth celebrations. A survey conducted by Steven Moore revealed that, contrary to Orangefest attracting tourists, there were almost 200 empty hotel rooms in seven major hotels in Belfast.

The response of the Orange leadership to these negative press reports may well have been – 'NO ONE LIKES US ... WE DON'T CARE'. However the real issue concerning the use of public money for the promotion of Orangefest is this – does it produce any visible, positive and measurable end product? This Orangefest explosion began in 2006 with the input of £100,000, now seven years later it is impossible to see any product. The same problems exist today as in 2006. There is the same confrontation over parades, the same aggressive playing of music whilst passing places of worship, the same complaints of public urination and the same complaints of paramilitary involvement. Lindy McDowell's comment may well have been wishful thinking, but as has been the case of so much public funding in recent years it has been conveniently forgotten:

> As for the £100,000 and what it achieves, the Order will know that this will, rightly, be closely monitored and analysed by the public.[23]

It will be evident to any observer that Orangefest is an attempt to move the Orange Institution from a place where *faith* is central to the place where *culture* becomes sacred. The tragedy of the events of recent years with the introduction of Orangefest is that it is being used to compensate for the demise of the religious aspect of Orange culture. Any visitor to Twelfth demonstration fields cannot help but notice that in spite of thousands parading, only a relative few attend the religious service.

An unnamed Orangeman is quoted by Glenn Jordan in *Not of This World? Evangelical Protestants in Northern Ireland*, as saying:

> Within the city [of Belfast] a lot of them aren't churchgoers, the vast majority aren't, so we can't call it a solely religious organisation. There is a religious dimension to it, but that doesn't make it a religious organisation.[24]

It is therefore understandable that those in leadership, particularly those who themselves are not religious, would want to see the demise of the religious aspect in order to keep an ever-increasing non-religious membership on board. However the honesty of such a project remains questionable when the foundation documents of the Orange Institution are clearly religious, in the Reformed Protestant sense.

There is of course an Orange culture, even though the word culture does not appear in any of the foundation documents of the Institution.

The United Nations Economic, Social and Cultural Organization (UNESCO) described culture as follows:

> ... culture should be regarded as the set of distinctive **spiritual**, material, intellectual and emotional features of society or a social group, and that it encompasses, in addition to art and literature, lifestyles, ways of living together, **value systems, traditions and beliefs** ...[25]

On the basis of that definition, religion therefore plays a significant role in culture. Orange culture, which forms part of that wider tapestry of culture, has every right to be recognised and celebrated as part of Irish culture. But Orange culture is a culture based on the Christian Reformed faith and is not the exclusive domain of those who are or were members of the Loyal Orange Institution of Ireland.

The Rev. William Bingham, addressing a New Dialogue Labour Party fringe meeting in Brighton on 30 September 1997, stated:

> The Orange Order is merely the manifestation of Orangeism which is not a rigid belief system peculiar to Ireland but is a set of core values accepted and appreciated by many throughout the five continents.[26]

The Loyal Orange Institution in Ireland is therefore not the sole custodian of Orangeism or of Orange culture. Even a cursory view reveals that given there are circa 30,000 members of the Orange Order in Ireland, that only represents circa 5 per cent of the membership of the main Protestant denominations. Culture, from the Reformed Evangelical theological perspective, develops from the religious and philosophical views of its participants. It is the tangible expression of religious thought seen as individuals live out their lives in society.

The traditional values which are to be the objective of all Orangemen are presented to members following initiation:

> We must all endeavour to disarm suspicion and antagonism. This can best be done by setting a good example in our daily lives, by living up to the high principles of the Order so that every section of the community will be compelled to admit that there is something in the Orange Society that elevates a man and raises him above the average of humanity. Something that makes him a better man morally, socially and intellectually.[27]

If the Orange Order is – 'a Christian Organisation' – which 'is Christ-centred, Bible-based, Church grounded', then this is the dynamic which must be to the fore in its cultural expression. The real danger for the Institution is that *culture* becomes the substitute for *faith*.

Cultures are worth protecting and preserving so long as they are authentic. That is, a culture which has an authentic, historic past, even though it is *evolving*, taking into account the dynamics of the changing society within which it functions.

A culture is worth protecting and preserving which adds to the value of society as a whole, making it a richer and more diverse society. An authentic Orange cultural identity, as expressed in the Qualifications and Values of the Institution, is therefore worth protecting and preserving.

A culture which *evolves* without losing its core values is worth protecting and preserving, but not a culture which is *artificially* created. In terms of the *faith-based* Orange culture to which I belong, the problem lies not so much in the culture itself, but some of the expressions of that culture which at times give the greatest cause for concern.

The bottom line is you cannot present a positive image under the guise of Orangefest and not take steps to deal with the negative image constantly publicly displayed year after year. The negative image, all too public in recent years, of members appearing in court charged with a variety of criminal offences, and the constant provocation by the engagement of bands with perceived or real paramilitary connections, negates any positive impact.

Orangefest came to its most violent manifestation on the Woodvale Road in Belfast following the Parades Commission restriction on three Lodges returning to Ligioniel on the evening of 12 July 2013. Subsequently many appeared in court, including 30-year-old Mark Blaney of Alliance Close. He was charged with attempting to murder a PSNI officer, possession of an offensive weapon, and riotous behaviour in the Woodvale Road area. He had allegedly attacked a police officer with a ceremonial sword. He was remanded in custody by District Judge Fiona Bagnall.[28] When he later appeared in the High Court on 16 September he was again refused bail:

> Police came under sustained attack as they enforced the marching prohibition on July 12. Photographs of the incident shown in court allegedly depict Blaney wearing a sash and wielding the ceremonial sword. He has emphatically denied intending to harm or kill anyone. But a prosecution barrister opposed his bid to be released on bail due to the risk of re-offending. Mr Justice Stephens was told police believe tensions remain high in the area, with ongoing protests being staged at Twaddell Avenue. Bail was refused due to the risk of any further offences being committed.[29]

Orangefest it would appear is not so much a reinvention, repositioning or rebranding but the creation of a new alternative culture. A culture which is acceptable to the modern secular world in general, and the modern non-religious Orange world in particular.

Seven years after its introduction, there is no evidence that Orangefest has been used by the leadership of the Institution to justify the statement that: 'the Order is quietly rebuilding and returning to its roots'.[30] In fact, given the events of 12 July 2013 and the subsequent protests since, Orangefest has become a byword for violence and lawbreaking.

Because of the continuous confrontation over parades in Belfast, with the new area of Donegall Street being added following the Twelfth 2012, the Belfast City Centre Management produced a damning report in September 2013. Referring to the Twelfth 2013, they said that 81 per cent of shops that opened reported trade below expectations, and that 65 per cent of shops said they were thinking twice about opening next year.[31] One wonders how long Orangefest can continue, considering that it is a relationship between Belfast City Council, the Belfast City Centre Management and the County Grand Lodge, given the continued confrontation and violence since the Twelfth of 2013.

Notes

1. Gerry Adams, speech at a Sinn Féin conference in Athboy, County Meath, in November 1996. (Reported on RTÉ *Prime Time* 4 March 1997 and quoted in the *Irish Times* 5 March 1997.)
2. 'Letters', *Irish News*, 30 April 2013.
3. 'Twelfth Tourism', *The Orange Order* [website] <http://www.grandorange lodge.co.uk/tourism>.
4. *Report of the Committee for Educational Affairs* (Belfast: Grand Lodge Report March 2005), 6.
5. Ibid.
6. The Orange Order [website] <http://www.grandorangelodge.co.uk/>.
7. Chris Thornton, 'Shades of Orange Identity', *Belfast Telegraph*, 28 April 2006.
8. Ibid.
9. Ibid.
10. Ibid.
11. Ibid.
12. *Qualifications of an Orangemen* (Belfast: GOLI Education Committee, 1998).
13. William Scholes, 'Twelfth "Is a Day Out for All the Family"', *Irish News*, 16 February 2005.
14. 'We Shall Not Be Moved', *Coleraine Chronicle*, 12 July 2006, 22.
15. 'Orangeman Slams Cultural Tourism', *BBC News* [website], 12 July 2008, <http://news.bbc.co.uk/1/hi/northern_ireland/7503644.stm>.
16. 'Top Orangeman Quits Order Over "Protestant Betrayal"', *Belfast News Letter*, 10 September 2011.
17. Ibid.
18. 'Letters', *Belfast News Letter*, 2 July 2009, 16.
19. Liam Clarke, 'History is the Key for Orangemen to Draw a Road Map For Change', *Sunday Times*, 9 July 2006.
20. Lindy McDowell, 'The Sash the Tourist Wore', *Belfast Telegraph*, 12 July 2006, 7.
21. Stephen Moore, 'Orangefest an Attraction for Tourists … So How Come Lots of Hotel Rooms Were Empty?', *Sunday World*, 16 July 2006, 14.
22. Ibid.
23. McDowell, 'The Sash the Tourist Wore', 7.
24. Glenn Jordon, *Not of This World? Evangelical Protestants in Northern Ireland* (Belfast 2001), 117, 118.
25. *Universal Declaration on Cultural Diversity* (UNESCO, 2002), <http://unesdoc.unesco.org/images/0012/001271/127162e.pdf>, 4. Bold type is the author's own emphasis.
26. Rev. William Bingham (Deputy Grand Chaplain of the Grand Orange Lodge of Ireland), *Making Sense of Northern Ireland: an Orange Perspective* (Belfast: GOLI Education Committee, 1997).
27. *The Order on Parade* (Belfast: GOLI Education Committee, 1996).
28. 'Man Who Attacked Police with Ceremonial Sword "Committed" to Violence, Court Hears', *Belfast News Letter* [website], 8 August 2013, <http://www.newsletter.co.uk/news/regional/man-who-attacked-police-with-ceremonial-sword-committed-to-violence-court-hears-1-5368727>.

29. 'Orange Sword Accused Refused Bail', *UTV* [website], 16 September 2013, <http://www.u.tv/News/Orange-sword-accused-refused-bail/ee7dc 709-a5a4-4e72-b21f-da3224e30ffc>.
30. Thornton, 'Shades of Orange Identity'.
31. Julian O'Neill, 'Belfast Stores Hit by Twelfth Tensions', *BBC News Northern Ireland* [website], 3 September 2013, <http://www.bbc.co.uk/news/uk-northern-ireland-23944856>.

7
Loyalism On Film and Out of Context

Stephen Baker

Introduction

> We knew full well that the media were short-changing
> us when it came to representing 'our' side of the story,
> but what *was* our side of the story? We couldn't even
> explain it properly ourselves. And it's still the same.
> There's plenty of times people around here have refused
> to take part in cross-community meetings, not because
> we don't want to sit down with Catholics, but because
> we don't have the self-confidence to do so. Few of us
> can articulate our case the way they can theirs.[1]

Northern Ireland's loyalists frequently lament what they perceive as
their misrepresentation in the media, and in doing so they join the
chorus of marginalised and oppressed sections in society that complain
of being caricatured or ignored by the press, broadcasters and filmmakers.
As Stuart Hall has pointed out with regards cultural representation generally, some people are

> always in a position to define, to set the agenda, to establish the
> terms of the conversation. Some others [are] ... always on the mar-
> gin, always responding to a question whose terms and conditions
> have been defined elsewhere: never 'centred'. (1995: 5)

Whether loyalism can count itself among the beleaguered and marginalised is a moot point, given its historic association with Britain's
imperial mission and its former relatively privileged position in Ireland.
But certainly in recent times loyalism's predominantly working-class

composition and cultural complexion have come into sharper focus, as any privileges it enjoyed have been eroded. The industries that once provided employment to the Protestant working class have largely disappeared, while the state to which that community gave its allegiance is disintegrating. Stormont, of course, was prorogued in 1972 but now the United Kingdom, more broadly, is undergoing a radical transformation with the contraction of the welfare state and the gradual break-up of Britain.

While loyalism has been vociferous in its defence of Northern Ireland's place within the UK, it has been relatively silent on the broader economic challenges and political context that face it. Most recently it has made its stand on questions of cultural expression and identity, where it has been confronted by its old antagonist, Irish republicanism, over the display of the Union flag and parade routes. However loyalism also faces a more insidious challenge in the determination of Northern Ireland's political and economic leaders to establish the region as a fully-signed-up member of the global free market. Loyalism's stout allegiances and noisy public manifestations make it anathema in this new dispensation, where the preferred form of cultural expression is that of individual, consumer lifestyle choices. It is within this context of cultural estrangement, economic impoverishment and political homelessness, that loyalism's dreadful media image and reputation is perhaps best understood.

In this chapter I want to consider film as a means by which to understand loyalism's alienation from the good opinion of others. But I want to argue that film also has the potential to offer a means by which working-class Protestants can begin to articulate alternatives to their derogatory representation. This requires a critical cultural practice that demonstrates an understanding of film form and history; an appreciation of the social context in which the practice is formed; and a willingness to see cultural practice as an aid to social transformation and not merely a means by which to achieve 'affirmative' cultural representations, which can be anodyne and trivialising. In any case audiences will have seen few affirmative representations of loyalism on film. More typically it is captured in the image of a gunman, as a monstrous outsider in cinematic Ireland, or alternatively viewed through the lens of generic conventions – horror and gangster films – where it provides an image of delinquent masculinity to trouble and thrill contemporary cinema audiences. Seldom is loyalism presented in any historical or social context that would help illuminate its politics or its actions; nor is it afforded any sense of political idealism, and as a consequence it is reduced to a form of psychopathology.

Of course loyalism is not alone in suffering such treatment on screen. Republicans, while occasionally allowed a degree of political romanticism, have also had their fair share of mad, bad and dangerous gunmen. Indeed as John Hill has pointed out, there is a historic tendency in cinema to portray the conflict in Ireland as a consequence of an inherent flaw in the national character that dooms its combatants to a violent and tragic fate (1987: 147). These representations of Ireland as 'dark and strife-torn maelstrom', and a site of primordial violence are mostly found in British films, so providing an ideological alibi for Britain's history of military and political involvement in Ireland. If the Irish can be presented as predisposed to violence then Britain appears to stand above the conflict, intervening only as a civilising influence. North American cinema, on the other hand, has provided the other dominant image of Ireland as a 'generally blissful, rural idyll' (147), playing to the fond remembrances of the large immigrant Irish population that make up a significant section of its domestic audience. John Hill argues that even early indigenous film production in Northern Ireland tended to pander to the expectations of North American audiences, producing romanticised images that pleased the local tourist industry but failed to satisfy unionism's aspiration for a distinctive 'Ulster' character, differentiating the North from the South of Ireland. More particularly, visions of 'nostalgic pastoralism' (147) provided no place within the film-frame for the North's urban Protestant working class, let alone the Catholic working class.

Illiberal and violent loyalism in the reimagined Ireland

If Ireland on film has largely been the imaginative work of British and North American cinemas, their predilections have not gone unchallenged. By the 1980s a generation of indigenous filmmakers in Ireland had begun to defy the stereotypes associated with Ireland on screen, but they also took aim at the shibboleths and essentialist myths of Irish identity. Martin McLoone refers to their films as constituting 'in embryo a cinema of national questioning, an attempt to reimagine Ireland in new ways beyond the confines of traditional nationalism', and as 'explorations of the many-layered and contradictory nature of identity' (1994: 168). Although radical in form and content, these films nevertheless tended to either ignore the existence of loyalism or present it as a threatening, violent interloper. For instance, in Pat Murphy's experimental, feminist feature *Maeve* (1984), loyalism appears inherently malevolent and perverse. The film is a feminist critique of

Irish patriarchy, in which Maeve, a young Belfast woman, returns home from London to an environment that she finds stifling and alienating. Through a series of conversations with her republican boyfriend and her more conventional sister, she begins to question the male-dominated version of Irish republican history and the gendered myths of nationhood. But despite the challenge that Maeve's feminism presents to traditional ideas of Irishness, the film never explores any possible alliance with loyalist women. Indeed it seems to deliberately disavow the idea in a scene that offers an excoriating representation of what is presumably Maeve's Protestant counterpart in the film. Passing through a barricade into Belfast's city centre, Maeve encounters a young woman caught in an act of loveless, passionless sex with a British soldier in uniform. Standing upright, the woman stares impassively over the soldier's shoulder at Maeve, as he, in an automated fashion, rhythmically humps her in the dark. The scene acts as an allegory for a deficient, dispassionate union between Ulster loyalism and Britain, the apparent progeny of which is encountered, briefly, earlier in the film when Maeve's sister is attacked by a loyalist boy, who then threatens Maeve with stream of bigoted invective. There is no attempt to place the assault in any historical or social context of sectarian antagonism in Belfast. Indeed, attributing such violent prejudice to a child seems to reject any contextualisation. It is as if little loyalist bigots spring fully formed from the womb.

Loyalists are similarly decontextualised and malevolent in Joe Comerford's *High Boot Benny* (1993), where they have a walk-on part as murderous automatons, activated at the behest of their 'official' handlers. Like previous Comerford films, it is peopled with apparent nonconformists and the socially marginalised, whose inclusion in the film-frame challenges and contradicts conventional notions of Irish community. In *High Boot Benny*, the eponymous protagonist is a teenage delinquent who flees Northern Ireland and seeks refuge in a small, rural school just over the border, run by a Protestant matron who is cohabiting with a defrocked priest. When an RUC informant is found dead in the school, a joint British army and RUC patrol make incursions over the border in pursuit of the killers. They suspect the residents of the school of being involved in the murder. Consequently, the matron, the ex-priest and Benny find themselves drawn into the conflict between the IRA and security forces. When a gang of loyalist gunmen enter the school under the watchful eyes of the RUC and assassinate the matron and the priest, they are quickly apprehended at gunpoint. Then they lie prostrate, passively and silently at the feet of their British Army captors. This mute, relatively anonymous depiction paints the loyalists as little more than lackeys carrying out the murderous work of their British masters. Their Otherness in the context of the film is further emphasised by the way in which their very clothes look out of place in the film's rural *mise en scène* and Comerford's primitivist aesthetic. Dressed in shell suits, they appear alien against the often harsh, bleak landscape provided by the Inishowen peninsula of Donegal where the film was shot. They also contrast sharply with Benny, who seems to be coded in the film as a 'native', sporting a Mohawk hairstyle and punk attire that draws inspiration from 'Red Indian' styles of dress. In effect, Benny and many of the other central characters in Comerford's film may be offered as dissenters and exiles from Irish society, but loyalists are presented as social ciphers and trespassers.

This is not the case in Thaddeus O'Sullivan's *December Bride* (1990), with its engaging depiction of a rural Presbyterian community in the early twentieth century that appears thoroughly integrated into the landscape around Strangford Lough in Co. Down. Based on the novel of the same name by Sam Hanna Bell, the film's central character is Sarah Gomartin, a young woman who establishes a *ménage à trois* with two landowning brothers, Hamilton and Frank Echlin. As a consequence, the three are ostracised by their conservative neighbours, and when Sarah has a child, the local minister intervenes and tries to persuade her to marry one of the brothers for respectability's sake. However, Sarah refuses, determined to preserve the matriarchal relations that she has established on the farm.

December Bride, like *Maeve* and *High Boot Benny*, focuses on dissenters and non-conformists and once again loyalism is represented as a largely illiberal and violent force. It manifests itself in the film in the shape of an Orange parade and the beating of a Lambeg drum, and as a constituent of the broader puritan community from which Sarah and the Echlin brothers stand apart. As such it is implicated in the vicious assault on the younger brother, Frank, whose attempt to reintegrate himself into the communal life of his neighbours is violently rejected, leaving him a cripple. Nevertheless the film is an important milestone in the cinematic representation of northern Protestants generally. As Martin McLoone (1999) argues, its strength lies in the way it takes a rural landscape usually associated with Catholic, nationalist Ireland, and peoples it differently with Protestants, whose belonging there is emphasised by the film's sustained attention to that community's labour in that landscape. There is barely a scene in the film in which its characters are not engaged in some work or other, which runs contrary to the long-held association of the Irish rural scenery with leisure and romanticism.

In this way *December Bride* not only strives to 're-imagine the cultural map of Ireland and the Irish differently', it also invites reflection upon northern Protestant identity and its relationship to the landscape (53).

It is precisely the cultural relationship between landscape and people that Brian Graham draws attention to in his discussion about the crisis in Protestant identity. He argues that Ulster Protestants in general and unionists in particular suffer from 'the lack of an agreed representation – or imaginary – of a place to legitimate and validate their domicile in the island of Ireland' (1997: 34). 'Ulster', in Graham's phrase, is 'a place yet to be imagined' in a way that would culturally link people to territory (36). He argues that this is because of unionism's reliance on sectarian discourses, which has resulted in it being unable to confer upon Northern Ireland an agreed and inclusive representation of place. It is perhaps the absence of an imaginary homeland that allowed subsequent filmmakers to easily appropriate loyalism's image and disassociate it from its proper historical and social context, relocating it to the generic cinematic landscapes of gangsterism and horror.

Generic loyalists in ceasefire cinema

The peace process that began in the 1990s might have provided the cultural environment for the inclusive and 'integrative place consciousness' that Brian Graham argues is necessary if Northern Ireland is to achieve legitimacy and integrity (1997: 52). Indeed the peace process saw a significant shift in the cinematic representation of Northern Ireland, as film sought to contribute to the mood of determined optimism at the time. Where Belfast had previously been imagined on screen as a maelstrom of primeval violence, in the new dispensation it became the backdrop to a number of romantic comedies that offered an upbeat and sometimes gentrified vision of the city. Cinema audiences also saw less of the monstrous or tragic Irish gunman, whose apparent predisposition to violence left him ostracised from civilised society and domestic life, and doomed to a brutal and premature death. In his place appeared a new 'housetrained' republican, presented in films such as *The Boxer* (1997) and *The Mighty Celt* (2005) as a family man striving to put his violent past behind him (McLaughlin and Baker 2010).

Two films that are striking in their contrast to these largely affirmative and upbeat representations of the period are Thaddeus O'Sullivan's *Nothing Personal* (1996) and Marc Evans's *Resurrection Man* (1998). Both bring loyalism to the centre of the big screen for the first time and present it as the image of unconscionable violence in Ireland, in effect stepping into the gap left on screen by the newly domesticated republicans. Both films include graphic scenes of torture and sectarian assassination that evoke some of the most barbarous murders in Northern Ireland's history. In particular they deliberately recall the notorious loyalist gang known as the Shankill Butchers that terrorised Belfast in the mid-1970s and derived its name because of a preference for torturing its victims with knives and axes before murdering them. However, *Nothing Personal* (1996) and *Resurrection Man* (1997) are not in any way histories of the period. Instead both appropriate the images of 1970s Belfast and loyalism as means by which to explore violent masculinity as viewed through the lens of cinema genres.

At its core *Nothing Personal* is a gangster film, although in its credits it acknowledges a debt to Gillo Pontecorvo's film *The Battle of Algiers* (1965), which recreated the struggle for Algerian independence. However where Pontecorvo's film employed the style and techniques of *cinéma-vérité* in its depiction of political insurrection, *Nothing Personal* owes more to Martin Scorsese's *Mean Streets* (1973) and its gritty urban drama of male fealty. It uses contemporary Dublin to recreate the terraced streets, waste ground and drinking dens of 1970s Belfast. This is the stamping ground of Kenny, the suave leader of a loyalist gang and his evidently psychotic friend, Ginger. The gang are ordered to observe a ceasefire by their commander, but Ginger flagrantly disobeys and Kenny seems at best ambivalent about the peace. As Ginger's insubordination grows, Kenny is ordered by his superior to kill his friend but he prevaricates, reminded of the oath of loyalty they swore to one another when Kenny initiated Ginger into the gang. The depth of their relationship is hinted at during the swearing-in of a young recruit who is clearly infatuated with Kenny and gang membership. The enigmatic gang leader takes the eager boy's hand as they pledge that their first loyalty is to one another. The solemn, ceremonial nature of the occasion appears almost matrimonial, which gives a clue to Ginger's jealous reaction to the inclusion of the young newcomer in the gang. It is as if Ginger sees him as a rival for Kenny's attention and affection, hinting that beneath the violent male camaraderie of the gang lie more libidinous tensions.

Kenny's reluctance to discipline Ginger ends tragically when after a night of rioting in the city and tit-for-tat violence, the gang seeks vengeance. They pick up Liam, a Catholic father who leaves his children at home while he goes out to join his neighbours in defending the district from loyalist rioters. But he gets injured and then stranded on the wrong side of the peace line, where he is rescued by Anne. She is coincidentally Kenny's estranged wife, and as she tends to Liam's wounds there is a growing intimacy between the couple that holds out the possibility of some form of romantic restoration among the sectarian violence of Belfast. But shortly after Liam resumes his journey home he is bundled into a car by Kenny and his gang. They drive him to a loyalist bar after closing time where he is subjected to an interrogation and vicious beating. During this the gang engage in misogynistic banter, designed to demonstrate their sexual prowess but which in the end only confirms their estrangement from legitimate heterosexuality.

Liam looks doomed (another victim for the uncontrollably violent Ginger), but Kenny recognises the Catholic father as a childhood friend and resolves to see him safely home, much to Ginger's consternation. Once Liam is reunited with his children in the street, Ginger threatens to kill him but Kenny intervenes, wounding his comrade by shooting him in the leg. Even at this stage Kenny is incapable of carrying out the order to kill Ginger. Less hesitant is a Catholic teenager, who in a fit of manly bravado, tries to extract revenge from the loyalist gang but ends up accidentally shooting Liam's daughter. Wracked with remorse, and disgusted at Ginger's obvious delight at the girl's death, Kenny finally squares up to his friend and comrade in their broken-down getaway car. In this scene they are shown in close up, nose to nose, looking directly into one another's eyes, while they wrestle over a pistol. It looks like a bizarre reinterpretation of the lovers' embrace at the end of a romantic film. However Kenny and Ginger's relationship is not consummated with a kiss. Rather Kenny pulls the trigger just before a British Army patrol, which has belatedly arrived on the scene, opens fire on the stranded car killing everyone inside.

The film's message is a humanist one: violence begets violence, and the desire for revenge leads to tragedy; worthy enough sentiments but far too general to illuminate the Northern Ireland conflict in any significant or specific way. Neither does the film add anything of substance to our understanding of loyalism, which it presents as a form of madness in the case of Ginger, and misguided masculinity in the case of men like Kenny, who forgo domestic life and romantic attachments for the violent homosociality of gang membership.

A similar shortfall in legitimate heterosexuality seems to underscore the violence in *Resurrection Man*, which, like *Nothing Personal*, also tries to recreate the mean streets of 1970s Belfast, although this time filmed in Warrington, Manchester and Liverpool. In it Victor Kelly is a rising star in the loyalist firmament who builds a terrifying reputation on account of his savagery, mortally butchering his victims with a knife. He is clearly a man in the grip of an Oedipal crisis, too enamoured of his overbearing and indulgent mother, and apparently disinterested in consummating his relationship with his promiscuous girlfriend, Heather. The only thing that Victor seems to derive sexual gratification from is killing, taking libidinous pleasure in the sanguinary imagery of his homicidal work. It is this psychosexual perversion that lies at the root of Victor's violent behaviour, not political conviction. Yet *Resurrection Man* shows no sociological curiosity in the erotic appeal of violence; rather its coupling of sex and violence is viewed through the accumulated history of film genres.

Resurrection Man is in part a gangster film, with its urban *mise en scène* of narrow streets, backyards and smoky dive bars, coupled with an iconography of guns, cars and chic '70s clothing. It even opens with a scene of Victor as a boy watching *Public Enemy* (1930) from the projection booth of a cinema, an experience which seems formative in Victor's later attempts to project his own Jimmy-Cagney-gangster-style image into the public sphere. On the other hand, *Resurrection Man* draws inspiration from the horror genre, indicated immediately by its title that conjures up the notion of the undead. Victor is even presented as almost vampiric in his lust for blood and also in the way he confines himself to nocturnal hours and murky interiors, avoiding sunlight. His horrific credentials are further emphasised by the way in which the film references Alfred Hitchcock's *Psycho* (1960), the pioneer of slasher movies, with its Oedipal drama and knife attacks. It even has its own shower-scene-writ-large, when towards the end of the film Victor holes up in the appropriately named Tomb Street bathhouse, with its milieu of ceramic tiles, bloodstained shower curtains, gurgling water pipes and taps, and Victor's final victim lying lacerated in a bathtub. Seen in these terms *Resurrection Man* is less a film about loyalism and substantially a film about other films. As John Hill argues, its 'aspiration to represent the actual past [...] gives way to a simulation of the past based on a reworking of earlier [film] representations and styles' (2006: 207).

Loyalist in entrepreneurial Northern Ireland

One film stands out as an attempt to understand loyalism within the contemporary social environment – *As the Beast Sleeps*. Although made for television, the film was premiered at the Belfast Film Festival in 2001 and later broadcast on BBC2 in February 2002. Based on the stage play by Belfast playwright Gary Mitchell, it is the story of a loyalist 'team' who find themselves marginalised by the peace process, and struggling in the wake left behind by their politically aspiring leaders and entrepreneurial associates. At the centre of the drama is Kyle, his wife Sandra and his intemperate friend and comrade, Freddie. Freddie is to all intents and purposes one of the family; the godfather of Kyle and Sandra's young son and frequently referred to as 'uncle'. At the same time, Kyle acts as a father-figure to his more immature and impetuous buddy. Yet despite Kyle's attempts to counsel him, Freddie's impulsiveness and alienation from the new realities of the peace process bring him into conflict with his commanders, eventually leading to the disintegration of Kyle's loyalist 'family'.

The film opens against the backdrop of the ceasefire called by the Combined Loyalist Military Command in 1994, which far from being greeted with joy and relief by Kyle, Freddie and the other 'footsoldiers', is viewed with scepticism. This turns to resentment when it becomes clear that an end to all paramilitary and criminal activities means that the gang are faced with a loss of status and illicit earnings. Kyle considers this a temporary hiatus in their fortunes but is confronted by Sandra's resentment at the drop in household income and Freddie's growing disaffection and dissent. A humiliating trip to the job centre reveals just how grave the situation is for Kyle and his men. They learn that their lack of formal qualifications means that only the most menial, low-paid jobs are open to them. To add insult to injury they are excluded from the local loyalist bar that they once supplied with stolen cigarettes and alcohol. Now the bar is a legitimate business, its profits funding the political ambitions of the loyalist leadership, and in this new political economy, Kyle and Freddie are considered liabilities. As the bar manager tells his loyalist employers: 'Every time these fucking Comanches come in here it pegs us back. People are feeling uncomfortable and intimidated. That's not an atmosphere that I want to create here and it's not an atmosphere that's good for business.'

Eventually Freddie's provocative behaviour in the bar results in him being banned from the premises. Angry and frustrated he robs the place. When the loyalist leadership find out, they order Kyle to punish him and reclaim the stolen money, a command he reluctantly carries out. In the process he discovers that his wife, Sandra, has been Freddie's accomplice. She is disgusted at Kyle's betrayal of his friend, and she leaves him despite his protestations that he had no choice but to punish Freddie.

The limited options available to Kyle and his comrades, and their lack of agency in the new political and economic environment emerging around them, lie at the heart of *As the Beast Sleeps*. As Kyle tries to explain to the disconsolate Freddie, 'this is the way things are going to go no matter what we do.' And so even Freddie's robbery of the bar appears less an exercise in free will than a futile, nihilistic act of protest against a new dispensation he cannot come to terms with and scarcely understands. Kyle, on the other hand, sounds fatalistic in his view of the future but the film invites the audience to see something more than the hand of providence at work in the lives of its loyalist family. It is doomed, not merely because of a misguided commitment to violence – a common enough trope in films about political conflict in Ireland – they are actively pushed out by the newfound legitimate entrepreneurship of the bar manager who excludes them from his premises and the loyalist leaders who can find no place for their subordinates in the new dispensation. As one loyalist leader tells another in stark terms: 'these violent young men have no place [...] in our future'.

Kyle, Sandra and Freddie's place is given figurative and literal expression through the film's social realist aesthetic. The housing estate on which they live looks dismal and bleakly rendered, and the characters frequently appear confined in the film's claustrophobic interiors. This aesthetic strategy owes something to the work of British director, Ken Loach, whose naturalism emphasises the social environment within which his working-class characters live. *As the Beast Sleeps* even opens with a football match, reprising the amateur game in Loach's *My Name is Joe* (1998) that offers a symbol of working-class male camaraderie and a fleeting relief from the otherwise grim world around the men. But just as Loach's characters struggle to ever transcend their social environment, so the loyalist gang in *As the Beast Sleeps* appear trapped by their class, their lack of qualifications and the new political and economic realities emerging around them. In mapping out this contemporary terrain the film seems to presage some of the problems and controversies that have beset loyalism more recently.

For instance, in December 2012 the Belfast City Council voted to restrict the number of days the Union flag would fly over city hall. Loyalists were incensed and engaged in a series of street demonstrations that disrupted the commercial life of the city in the run-up to Christmas. For this they attracted the ire of the business community, concerned about the loss of customers and profits during the busiest retail period of the year. A campaign encouraging conspicuous consumption in support of the city centre's retailers, restaurateurs and pub owners was organised through social media using the Twitter hashtag #takebackthecity. Whatever one's views of the rights and wrongs of the flag protests, there is surely an irony in proposing to 'take back' Belfast from people who are among its residents, especially when the city has become increasingly privatised. But what this reveals is not only the level of disenchantment among loyalists at what they perceive as their increasing social marginalisation; it also highlights their growing alienation from the good opinion of their more affluent neighbours. Indeed, at least one commentator noted the sneering condescension of 'middle Ulster' for the largely working-class Protestants involved in loyalist demonstrations (McCann 2013).

As Conor McCabe (2013) points out, Northern Ireland has undergone a 'double transition', from conflict to political accord, and from a broadly social democratic settlement to neoliberalism. Indeed the much-lauded 'peace dividend' is better understood as the region's incorporation into global capitalism, a world where old political allegiances are a burden and where all are expected to succumb to the atomising, enterprising and commercial demands of the market. As Eric Hobsbawm has argued 'Free-market theory effectively claims that there is no need for politics because the sovereignty of the consumer should prevail over everything else' (2000: 113). Similarly David Harvey describes the environment in which we find ourselves as 'a world in which the neoliberal ethic of intense, possessive individualism, and its political withdrawal from collective forms of action, becomes the template for human socialization' (Harvey 2008: 31). This new dispensation is no place for loyalism as it is presently constituted. Loyalism's predilection for rowdy public demonstrations (and street confrontations) and its ardent political convictions make it a liability in the eyes of those who see the future of Northern Ireland as a mere brand in the global marketplace. The enterprising new bar manager in *As the Beast Sleeps* speaks for these people when he complains about how Kyle and Freddie's presence in the bar 'pegs us back'.

As the Beast Sleeps is a bleak representation of loyalism, but it is not without empathy for the predicament that its characters find themselves in – with little choice and no place. It distinguishes itself from other representations of loyalism by engaging with the contemporary political and economic milieu, rather than portraying loyalists as trespassers and depraved individuals in a reimagined Ireland, or as pathological killers in a generic landscape. And yet despite the drama's conscientious look at loyalism its writer, Gary Mitchell, and his family were intimidated into leaving their Belfast home in November 2005 by loyalists, who it is said were angered by his depiction of them. In an interview the playwright offered a rather different rationale for the intimidation, saying that he was '99 per cent sure' that his assailants had never seen any of his plays, and that their animosity was rooted in their opinion of him as being 'a fellow who's got above himself' (Jury 2005). The Ulster Defence

Association (UDA), the organisation widely considered to have been behind the intimidation, denied responsibility, blaming instead 'rogue elements'. But whoever was behind it and whatever their reasons, it added credence to the perception that loyalism is ignorant of, or hostile towards anything that falls under the rubric of 'culture'. Indeed as one broadsheet journalist saw it, what had up until then 'protected' Gary Mitchell from loyalism's violent attention was 'the paramilitaries' prejudice that culture was something only for "taigs and faggots"' (Chrisafis 2005). The notion that loyalists are cultureless may be tedious, ignoring the fact that they have access to broadly the same popular consumer culture as others and a political lexicon of their own that is rich in symbolism, narrative and ritual. But the accusation highlights another aspect of the loyalism image problem: that perception that it stands apart from and contributes nothing to the broader cultural life beyond its own narrow constituency.

Conclusion

Loyalism needs to be the subject of a politically informed cinema and it needs to be a participant in a critically engaged film culture if it is to challenge and change its lamentable image and reputation on screen. In short, if loyalism feels it has been misrepresented and misplaced in the films made by others, then the obvious solution is for loyalists to make their own! Yet that is a lot to ask of a community that is economically straitened and, as the quote at the top of this chapter suggests, lacks the confidence to articulate itself through anything other than its own exclusive idioms. However there are ways and means and precedents. Filmmaking does not necessarily have to subscribe to the big-budget, high production values of Hollywood features. To this end Colin McArthur has argued that there is virtue in a cinema that works with limited resources, what he describes in the Scottish context as a 'poor Celtic cinema'. He argues that 'the more your films are consciously aimed at an international market, the more their conditions of intelligibility will be bound up with regressive discourses about your own culture' (1994: 119–20). Alternatively, low-budget filmmaking has the potential to free filmmakers from the commercial imperatives that can lead to shorthand generalisations and lazy stereotypes.

McArthur takes as inspiration the Italian *arte povera* movement of the 1950s that produced art out of what resources and materials were available, forgoing the need to compete with the 'glitzy and financially inflated world of the gallery circuit' (121). But he also traces the cinematic lineages of his proposed 'poor cinema', back to what he describes as the 'quasi-artisanal' practices of the British documentary movement of the 1930s; post-war Italian neorealism and the French *nouvelle vague*; as well as Third World cinematic practices. In all these instances, he argues, 'the films were low-budget not just for economic reasons, but in order to be able to say things which remained unsaid in more orthodox structures and practices' (121).

Similarly Third Cinema, a film movement with its roots in 1960s Latin America, also attempts to 'speak a socially pertinent discourse' that articulates a set of aspirations that dominant mainstream cinema excludes or marginalises (Willemen 1994: 184). Paul Willemen highlights how Third Cinema's pioneers advocated an intellectual cinema; a cinema that was aesthetically non-prescriptive; a cinema that while conditioned and tailored by its own social situation was not limited to Latin America in its appeal; and above all a cinema committed to social transformation (1994: 179–82). This is film as a critical cultural practice, aesthetically strategic and conscious of the social processes and context of its production.

For many the idea of loyalism's association with Third Cinema or a 'poor Celtic cinema' will seem incongruous given its historical defence of monarchy and imperial power. Indeed its attempts to appropriate the language of the oppressed have been treated with incredulity and have, at times, looked absurd. Yet no community is impervious to change and transformation, and the 'double transition' that Northern Ireland is undergoing at the moment demands a response from working-class Protestants whose economic status has been undermined and whose political place seems uncertain. So far loyalism has mobilised in defence of its residual cultural forms – parades, flags and emblems. These are important to a community that feels beleaguered and excluded from social life, but surely what is called for are emergent critical cultural practices, one of which is potentially film. That cultural practice must be neither myopic in its attention to local culture and tradition nor 'evasively cosmopolitan' (Willemen 1994: 177); and it must also coherently engage with questions of economic redistribution and political power in an era when austerity is being imposed ruthlessly from above.

Note

1. Anonymous contributor to a community discussion about working-class Protestants in Northern Ireland, quoted in Hall (1994).

References

Chrisafis, A. (2005), 'Loyalist Paramilitaries Drive Playwright from His Home', *The Guardian* [website], 21 December, <http://www.theguardian.com/uk/2005/dec/21/arts.northernireland> [accessed 9 August 2013].

Graham, Brian (1997), 'Ulster: a Representation of a Place Yet To Be Imagined', in Peter Shirlow and Mark McGovern (eds), *Who Are 'the People': Unionism, Protestantism and Loyalism in Northern Ireland* (London: Pluto Press), 34–54.

Hall, Michael (ed.) (1994), *Ulster's Protestant Working Class* (Belfast: Island Pamphlet), 8.

Hall, S. (1995), 'Negotiating Caribbean Identities', *New Left Review* 209: 3–14.

Hill, J. (1987), 'Images of Violence', in K. Rockett, L. Gibbons and J. Hill (eds), *Cinema and Ireland* (London: Croom Helm), 147–93.

Hill, J. (2006), *Cinema and Northern Ireland – Film, Culture and Politics* (London: British Film Institute).

Jury, L. (2005), 'Belfast Playwright Forced into Hiding after Loyalist Threats', *Independent*, 23 December.

McArthur, Colin (1994), 'The Cultural Necessity of a Poor Celtic Cinema', in J. Hill, M. McLoone and P. Hainsworth (eds), *Border Crossings: Film in Ireland, Britain and Europe* (Belfast: Institute of Irish Studies/British Film Institute), 112–25.

McCabe, Conor (2013), *The Double Transition: the Economic and Political Transition of Peace* (Belfast: Irish Congress of Trade Unions and Labour After Conflict).

McCann, E. (2013), 'No Unilateral Fix to Hardship which Spawned Loyalist Rage', *Belfast Telegraph*, 11 January.

McLoone, M. (1994), 'National Cinema and Cultural Identity: Ireland and Europe', in J. Hill, M. McLoone and P. Hainsworth (eds), *Border Crossings: Film in Ireland, Britain and Europe* (Belfast: Institute of Irish Studies/British Film Institute), 146–73.

McLoone, M. (1999), 'December Bride: a Landscape Peopled Differently', in James MacKillop (ed.), *Contemporary Irish Cinema: From the Quiet Man to Dancing at Lughnasa*, (New York: Syracuse University Press), 40–53.

Willemen, Paul (1994), *Looks and Frictions: Essays in Cultural Studies and Film Theory* (London: BFI).

8

This Sporting Life: Anything to Declare? Community Allegiance, Sports and the National Question

Thomas Paul Burgess

In 2012, a young, mild-mannered, lower-middle-class, Controlled Grammar School-educated County Down man (Roman Catholic by religion for those interested in such matters), inadvertently reminded us of the depth of significance that the two jurisdictions on the island of Ireland still place on stated sporting allegiance and all that this might imply. In a wide-ranging interview with *Sportsmail*, the then 23-year-old, whose Northern Irish roots made him eligible for both British and Irish representation – had spoken candidly about this dilemma:

> Maybe it was the way I was brought up, I don't know, but I have always felt more of a connection with the UK than with Ireland. And so I have to weigh that up against the fact that I've always played for Ireland and so it is tough. Whatever I do, I know my decision is going to upset some people but I just hope the vast majority will understand.[1]

Whether his aspiration was realised is a matter for conjecture. However, for a significant number of opinion formers in the media and on social networking sites, they most assuredly did not understand.

And golfing icon Rory McIlroy learned a salutary lesson in regard to the place that sports, sporting success and allegiance hold in the collective national psyches of both traditions in Ireland, North and South.

What was perhaps most depressing about the subsequent outpouring of vitriol, jingoistic tub-thumping and rash editorial comment, was the unforgivably thoughtless filicide of a new and emerging post-conflict generation in Northern Ireland. One uncomfortable with the traditional religious-political stereotypes foisted upon them and refreshingly honest in their opinions based on their own lived experiences.

McIlroy enjoyed a largely middle-class upbringing, provided by the Herculean efforts of his working-class parents, who sought to create a non-sectarian environment for themselves and their son. Enjoying a religiously mixed social and educational setting and growing up in an area relatively free from social unrest ensured that young Rory was able to take pleasure in the interests and enthusiasm of his peers. Supporting the Ulster Rugby team, following Manchester United, representing Ireland in his chosen field – whilst declaring for team GB in the golfing Olympics – were all passions that he pursued without the encumbrance of believing that he had to belong to one side or the other. Rather than lamenting him for his political naiveté, the popular and sporting press should have been lauding him as the successful face of an emerging, post-conflict Northern Ireland. Someone who fought shy of the minefield of nation statehood and undoubtedly saw himself as first and foremost, *Northern Irish*.

But we can't allow that in Ireland ... now can we?

Having lived and worked in the Republic for some twenty years now, I was appalled at the irresponsibility of journalists, broadcasters, social commentators and casual acquaintances alike who decried McIlroy for daring to describe himself as (technically anyway) 'British' and declaring for '*them*'. Had he come from a Protestant or Loyalist tradition, then this might have been accepted or understood. There was, for example, no axe to grind regarding Darren Clarke or Graham McDowell for example. However that the youngest and most talented of them – a northern nationalist by birth – should have seemingly denied his Hibernian birthright and '... took the soup'?

For some it was nothing short of treachery.

The incident was a timely reminder of how the whole panoply of sporting life on this island remains mired within the history and perceived culture of the two main traditions; and how 'ownership' of successful sporting individuals and their achievements can be used as a celebration or affirmation of community identity. Within the Protestant/unionist/loyalist tradition, sporting devotees can be just as rabidly possessive of their sporting heroes as their nationalist counterparts. Those two icons of northern sporting culture, George Best and Alex 'Hurricane' Higgins, are revered as flawed geniuses and celebrated on many a working-class gable wall mural. That their battles with alcohol addiction (a stereotypical cliché more often associated with generic '*Irishness*') is oft-times overlooked, begins to hint at wider confusion of associations from outside this community.

Whether they like it or not, the probability is that for a majority of their fellow British citizens on the mainland, Ulster's sporting heroes are frustratingly just as likely to be designated as 'Irish' rather than '*Northern* Irish'. That both of the individuals in question rarely if ever engaged directly with the thorny issue of national identity or political allegiance – often preferring broadly to be defined in regard to their working-class roots – perhaps accounts for their largely uncritical acceptance by sports fans in ROI.[2]

Other notable sporting success from this community; Dame Mary Peters and Mike Bull (athletics); Jackie Kyle, Mike Gibson, Syd Miller and Willie John McBride (rugby); Norman Whiteside and Harry Gregg (Association football); the aforementioned Darren Clarke and Graham McDowell (golf); Joey Dunlop; Eddie Irvine (motor sports racing); Dave 'Boy' McCauley and Wayne McCullough (boxing), have in the main fought shy of overtly aligning themselves with the accepted cultural associations or political stance of the community from which they come. Indeed many have comfortably settled for the mantle of simply being 'Irish' when competing internationally or being categorised by the media.

Whilst there have been examples of sports people from the Protestant community (particularly in athletics and equestrian events) declaring for the Republic of Ireland for opportunistic reasons, this 'flag of convenience' 'belt and braces' approach is not pronounced. Often it is the history of the local and national sporting associations in each of the individual disciplines that have influenced the development (or lack of it) of cross-community ownership of sporting success in the province; and by extension, at times stymied the unfettered or liberated sporting celebration of the Protestant/unionist/loyalist communities in ways that are not automatically rejected as triumphalist or sectarian.

This is particularly evident in relation to Association football on the island of Ireland.

Association football

As with rugby football, Association football or 'soccer' was (and still is in some sections of the nationalist community) traditionally viewed and subsequently rejected as a 'garrison game' introduced to Ireland by occupying British soldiers. This stance is particularly ironic given the massive interest in the English and Scottish Premierships by millions on the island of Ireland – North and South – who would consider themselves as Irish nationalists. Furthermore, recent controversies concerning the 'poaching' of young northern players (predominantly from nationalist backgrounds) who have enjoyed the full benefits of

Irish Football Association (IFA) coaching and training, by the Football Association of Ireland (FAI), adds further irony upon irony.

Drawing from an already drastically diminished pool of eligible talent – and despite a proud history of international achievement in major competition which predates their southern neighbours – Northern Irish football and the IFA perhaps face an unprecedented crisis.

To view the relative fortunes of each association by current form and fortune, one might be excused for thinking that the 'junior' partner in this arrangement was the IFA. However, a brief review of the origins of the organised game in Ireland reveals otherwise.

Association football was originally administered from Belfast and was largely confined to Ulster in the early years. Clubs in the Belfast area came together to form the Irish Football Association in 1880 and it operated as the organising body for football across all of Ireland for 41 years. Three years had elapsed before the first club outside of Ulster affiliated, the Dublin Association Football Club, which was formed in 1883. The development of the game outside of Ulster was accelerated when the Leinster Football Association was formed in 1892. The clubs based outside of Ulster were often dissatisfied with the decisions of the administrative body. There was always the belief that the Belfast-based clubs exerted undue influence, especially when it came to selecting teams for international matches. The political events of the time and the rise of nationalism after the Easter Rising of 1916 undoubtedly exerted an influence as the southern affiliates grew more demanding in their dealings with the IFA. The Leinster Football Association was backed by the Munster Football Association in instigating the meeting at which decisions were taken that led irrevocably to a split between the Irish Football Association in Belfast and the southern football organisations who would go on to form the FAI.

As with so much else on the island, sport again mirrored wider political and religious allegiances, with the prospect of any 'reunification' of the Associations or the teams as remote today as it has ever been. On the rare occasions that the teams have met in competitive fixtures, the level of rivalry has been pronounced. Even putting aside old enmities in some unlikely manifestation of a shared proposal for one national team (along the model employed by the Irish Rugby Football Union), the purely pragmatic questions of where games would be played, who would select the team and what anthem would feature, seem insurmountable. Not to mention the clearly sectarian attitudes that still exist amongst a significant number of supporters from both camps and that are often manifest in club allegiances (particularly Rangers and Celtic), flags, emblems and party songs.

For those supporters hailing from the Protestant/unionist/loyalist communities – irrespective of current form or prospects – the continuance of the IFA and the fortunes of the Northern Ireland football team have become synonymous with those wider and deeper feelings regarding their perceived national identity and any threat to it.

Club affiliations and allegiances

Away from the national team with its historical vagaries and territorial baggage, one might assume that club affiliation – whether in Northern Ireland or in GB – could offer an opportunity of respite from purely political or sectarian allegiances by supporters. To some extent this is true in regard to the top Premiership teams in England. For example, Manchester United and Liverpool enjoy significant support from both communities in Northern Ireland, the former due perhaps to a high proportion of Northern Irish (and Republic of Ireland) players historically associated with the club. However, despite the cosmopolitan nature of the modern game, if the bigot is so inclined it is possible to dig deeply enough to find spurious reasons within a club's history and origins to designate it sympathetic to either Protestant or Roman Catholic allegiances.

I have variously heard claims that Everton are 'the "Fenian" club in Liverpool'. And that Manchester City are the 'Prod' club in Manchester. This propensity for Ulster football fans to project community allegiance – real or imagined – onto unwitting English clubs knows no bounds. Occasionally though, there appears to be some tangible credibility for these claims. In London, a section of Chelsea supporters seem to share a common fan base with some followers of Rangers FC and certainly show an active affiliation with aspects of English/British nationalism. Arsenal, largely due to a significant proportion of Irish immigrant support and their fielding of a large number of Irish players during some of their most notable triumphs, became known for some as 'London Celtic'.

In more recent times the Irish consortium who bought Sunderland FC and appointed Niall Quinn and Roy Keane obviously engendered a favourable response from Irish supporters. However, what was viewed as a benign enough development took on more serious undertones for Ulster loyalist/Protestant sports fans when Londonderry/Derry-born player – James McClean – compounded his decision to switch international allegiance from Northern Ireland to Republic of Ireland, by refusing to sport a Remembrance Poppy on his club shirt in compliance with FA and club requests.

In Scotland of course, football allegiance along sectarian lines is ingrained and well documented. Both Celtic FC and Rangers FC have had to formally address issues of sectarianism on the pitch, on the terraces and in the courts. Despite efforts to directly prohibit sectarian songs and provocative behaviour, the naked sectarian hatred that exists between elements of these clubs' fan bases remains the emotional and tribal touchstone for supporters from both communities.[3] (This can even extend to the barracking of foreign international players who have the misfortune of playing for either Glasgow club, during international games against both N. Ireland and Republic of Ireland.) Undoubtedly within the working-class Protestant/unionist/loyalist community, affiliation with Rangers FC offers a well-established expression of identity and affinity.

In a local footballing context, there are opportunities to follow clubs *not* defined by sectarian community identification. Additionally, considerable efforts have been made by the IFA (at international and club level) to introduce a robust programme of community relations/anti-sectarian initiatives. However, as one might expect, traditional loyalties are also well represented – particularly in Belfast – through support for clubs like Linfield, Cliftonville and Donegal Celtic. Linfield draw their support almost exclusively from the Protestant/unionist/loyalist community (as do East Belfast rivals, Glentoran).

There exists a chequered and ignoble history within domestic football in Northern Ireland. Belfast Celtic – a team supported predominantly by the nationalist community – withdrew from the Irish League at the end of the 1948–9 season, in protest against a mob assault on players at Windsor Park the previous December. Cliftonville and Donegal Celtic have to some degree taken up their mantle (although in the past, the former traditionally drew support from both communities).[4]

Indeed the case of Cliftonville dramatically reveals how the fortunes of a local sporting institution tellingly reflect the experience of the wider Protestant community in this particular area of north Belfast. Formerly Cliftonville Football and Cricket Club, this society founded in 1870 was to find its home premises and surrounding local area targeted for resettlement by an expanding nationalist/republican community, hostile to the traditions and culture of their sporting heritage. The so-called 'greening' of this area ultimately rendered a religious sea change in the support base for the football team and all but usurped and destroyed the cricket club, replacing its ground with a GAA facility. According to the official history of Cliftonville Cricket Club:

> The outbreak of civil disorder in August 1969 and the geographical positioning of the ground had made it increasingly difficult to travel to and from practice/games etc. with bomb scares and street

protests a regular occurring event. However, members overcame this and enjoyed the good spirit which abounded from within. By 1972 a campaign of intimidation had begun against the Club, its members and what it represented in the area. Members were verbally and physically attacked, two young Protestant men were abducted, executed and their bodies dumped within the grounds of Cliftonville Cricket club. Whilst the British Army stood idly by and watched, the club was looted and set on fire by a hostile crowd.

With no assurances coming from local or national government regards guaranteeing members safety, the Club had no alternative but to make the heart-breaking decision to abandon the ground.[5]

The introduction of the All-Ireland Setanta Cup competition offered an ambitious opportunity for clubs from both jurisdictions to meet. However, the same problems that bedevilled international and local football were of course revisited to some degree in these fixtures, with supporters often goading each other with songs, national flags and banners of a sectarian nature. Crowd trouble inevitably followed. In summary then, it would seem that affiliation and identification with specific football clubs and (to a lesser extent) the national team, remain a constant reference point when considering expressions of cultural identity from the Protestant/unionist/loyalist communities.

To support Linfield, Rangers and the Northern Ireland team is to accept one's collective cultural responsibility, even birthright. Much of the history and paraphernalia surrounding these teams remains steeped in Orange and loyalist dogma, ensuring that the triumphalist and exceptionalist aspects of this mode of cultural expression persist. The fact that Roman Catholics have been associated with these teams on the playing and coaching staff seems to do little to defuse the situation, particularly in games with their nationalist counterparts. And to some degree it might be argued that this situation will continue whilst there exists a diametrically opposed sporting/politico-cultural adversary.

Irish Rugby Football Union (IRFU)

Superficially at least, when one considers the provincial system by which the Irish Rugby Football Union operates, we might be forgiven the assumption that here is a sporting administrative model (as with hockey and cricket) under which sectarian difference can be transcended. And perhaps one where unionists and loyalists can comfortably embrace a sense of their own (Ulster) 'Irishness' in supporting a national team in competition with other home nations. In 1879 two unions representing all Irish provinces at the time agreed to amalgamate on the following terms: a union to be known as the Irish Rugby Football Union was to be formed for the whole country; branches were to be established in Leinster, Munster and Ulster; the union was to be run by a council of 18, made up of six from each province. The pre-professional era of the 1980s saw Ulster Rugby dominate the national game, culminating in the team being the first Irish province to lift the European Cup in 1999. During this period, Ulster provided a large number of players to compete for Ireland at international level and some of the legends of the Irish game have been Ulstermen.

Yet in practice, the very real issues arising from a player panel drawn from two sovereign territories, inevitably engender questions regarding allegiance and commitment to the common cause (certainly amongst supporters from the Republic of Ireland). And questions regarding favouritism in selection of players and coaches (primarily from Northern-Ireland-based fans). Take for example the thorny issue of the anthem to be played before each game. The Irish team must first stand for the anthem of the Republic, 'Amhrán na bhFiann' (The Soldier's Song), with references to '... the Saxon Foe'. In deference to those players, officials and supporters from the other jurisdiction on the island, this is followed by 'Ireland's Call', an anthem written primarily for just such an occasion and which studiously avoids partisan reference. Subsequently, 'Amhrán na bhFiann' is replaced entirely by 'Ireland's Call' for away matches. It is interesting to reflect that – when the team are performing badly – the letters pages of the *Irish Times* are awash with irate fans bemoaning the dilution of patriotic team spirit due to the national anthem's absence!

Many Ulster Protestants simply reject Irish rugby due to the IRFU decision to play its games in Dublin, under the flag and anthem of the Republic. (Although the traditional flag of the four ancient provinces is also flown, in a sop similar to the arrangement for an alternative anthem.) This sensitivity was particularly noted in August 2007, when the IRFU *did* decide to play north of the border for the first time in 50 years, against Italy. In a post-Good-Friday-Agreement Northern Ireland – sensitive to the principles of tolerance and mutual respect – the flying of the Union Flag and the playing of 'God Save the Queen' at Ravenhill were notable by their absence.[6] Significant individuals have at times directly and indirectly contributed to the debate within rugby circles. Ken Maginnis (former Unionist politician and now Baron Maginnis of Drumglass) seemingly saw little contradiction in promoting robust anti-nationalist views whilst happily travelling to Lansdowne Road to stand for Amhrán na bhFiann and heartily cheer on the Irish rugby team. (As a former Major of the Ulster Defence Regiment, this displayed considerable chutzpah at a time when the Provisional IRA was rampant.)

Trevor Ringland, MBE is a former Ulster, Ireland and British Lions player. Ringland was Vice-Chairman of the Ulster Unionist Party's East Belfast Branch and was adopted by the Ulster Unionist Party and Conservative Party as their joint candidate in East Belfast for the 2010 General Election. Significantly, in 2010 he became involved in a controversy with the then new leader of the Ulster Unionist Party, Tom Elliott. Upon Elliott's election as party leader, Ringland publicly asked him if he would be prepared to attend a Gaelic Football All-Ireland Final in Dublin if an Ulster team were to take part. Elliott said he would refuse and Ringland resigned from the Ulster Unionist Party. He continues to be involved with 'Peace Players International', an organisation devoted to promote interreligious unity in Belfast through sport.

Not all players or former players have exhibited such magnanimity toward the challenges of dealing with cultural and political identity within a shared rugby family. Munster and Ireland player Ronan O'Gara famously used the opportunity of a team photocall with the Queen to thrust his hands deep within his pockets and demur a handshake with the monarch. The gesture was widely seen as variously puerile, disrespectful or as striking a mischievous blow for republicanism. It would not have enamoured him to Ulster rugby fans or players.

Many believe that differences of opinion amongst northern Unionists regarding Irish rugby can be explained in class terms (rugby still being a primarily middle-class sport in the province, unlike say, in Munster). And indeed, deep fissures within the Ulster Protestant monolith have been pronounced in class terms since the formation of the state, with much more serious consequences than simply sporting endeavour. Despite Ulster Rugby having a number of Roman Catholic players and staff, it should also be noted that the game still recruits largely via a grammar school education system that remains divided along sectarian lines. Additionally, those Ulster counties within the Republic have tended not to be as involved in the sport as the other six counties. Ulster Rugby has recognised this and targeted these areas for particular developmental attention.

What is undeniable is that Ulster rugby is viewed differently by the supporters, players and administrators of the other three provinces and not always in a sympathetic or generous manner. Additionally, some northern nationalists offer support to other Irish provinces rather than give allegiance to their native Ulster team (and despite the inclusion of Donegal, Monaghan and Cavan within the affiliation). Of course some of this ambiguity arises from the state of Northern Ireland's insistence on making itself synonymous with the designation of the term *'Ulster'*. (BBC Radio Ulster; the University of Ulster; the Royal Ulster Constabulary; the Ulster Farmers' Union; the Ulster-American Folk Park; Ulster-Scots, etc.)

Whilst the overt sectarian mistrust evident in soccer is mercifully absent, there nevertheless persists an attitude of 'otherness' projected onto the northern rugby province that is understandably more notable at international than club level. Indeed it is fair to assume that Leinster, Munster and Connacht reserve something special for their encounters with their (British/Irish) cousins. Southern media coverage and even the comparative unavailability of Ulster shirts in Dublin, Galway or Limerick sports shops suggests that Ulster rugby is still somewhat viewed as unionism in disguise.

Gaelic Athletic Association (GAA)

It is axiomatic to suggest that Gaelic games – North and South – are almost exclusively the domain of nationalist, Catholic Ireland. The history and culture of the games are synonymous with ethnic identity and Celtic/Gaelic tradition. With more than 1 million members worldwide, assets in excess of €2.6 billion, and declared total revenues of €94.8 million in 2010, the GAA remain a formidable organisation at both national and community level. In terms of crowd attendance, GAA sports remain the best attended in ROI and Gaelic football is the largest participation sport in NI. Notably, the most prestigious trophy awarded in Gaelic football – the Sam Maguire Cup – is named after a Cork Protestant, noteworthy for recruiting Michael Collins to the republican cause.

For many well-documented reasons born of historical happenstance and perfidious manipulation, there continues to be little affinity between the legacy of previous generations of Protestant United Irishmen and the GAA. Similarly, Protestant citizens of the Republic who did not relocate after partition and contemporary northern Protestants who define themselves primarily as 'British' and 'unionists' perhaps find the Association less than welcoming.

In short then, there seems little to encourage this community to attend games or lend support to Ulster GAA teams (despite considerable success for provincial counties). To further compound matters, unofficially, the GAA has been linked to republican terrorism. In the past, there have been allegations that it secretly funded IRA operations. It is also alleged that some clubs continue to glorify IRA actions and celebrate former combatants as martyrs. Indisputably, the Association has historically been isolationist in character.

However, there have arguably been attempts to address the situation. Perhaps most notably in the repeal of the infamous Rule 21 (which precluded members of the RUC and the British Army from joining the GAA). Additionally the repeal of Rule 42, allowing for non-Gaelic games to be played at GAA headquarters, Croke Park, might also be cited as the organisation endeavouring to move away from its cultural/political exclusivity.[7]

Additionally, there exist formal guidelines within Association laws which claim an anti-sectarian stance:

Anti-Sectarian/Anti-Racist

The Association is Anti-Sectarian and Anti-Racist and committed to the principles of inclusion and diversity at all levels. Any conduct by deed, word, or gesture of sectarian or racist nature or which is contrary to the principles of inclusion and diversity against a player, official, spectator or anyone else, in the course of activities organised by the Association, shall be deemed to have discredited the Association. Gaelic Athletic Association. Official Guide – Part 1.

However, the high-profile case of Darren Graham – a Protestant playing Gaelic football for Lisnaskea Emmets (his local team in County Fermanagh) against a team from nearby Brookeborough – hinted at prejudices that are not adequately addressed by laws and guidelines. When he was called a 'black cunt', ('Black' as a reference to 'Black Protestant', a long-standing term of sectarian abuse) Graham decided to reveal a protracted and difficult history of similar sectarian intimidation and insisted on a formal apology from the GAA. His case was perhaps particularly significant as his father – a former UDR soldier – had been murdered by the IRA when Graham was a child. Depressingly, abuse within the GAA is not confined to sectarianism. The case of Crossmaglen player, Aaron Cunningham – who is of mixed race – provides a serious indictment. In an Ulster club football final between Crossmaglen and Kilcoo, players and fans alike were reported as calling Cunningham a 'nigger' throughout the game.

Perhaps the most perplexing variation on sectarian abuse within the GAA has featured sectarian insults aimed at Ulster club players purely by dint of their 'six county' location. In what seems a bewildering turn of events, it is apparently quite common for teams from the north of the country to be called 'Orange bastards', 'Brit lovers', and much worse, when playing teams from the south of the country.

Many instances of this nature are a matter of record. Notwithstanding First Minister Peter Robinson's recent lauding of the GAA for their efforts in community relations, this intensity of indiscriminate sectarian abuse not only betrays a staggering level of ignorance amongst perpetrators. It also augurs very badly for any reappraisal of the Association by the Ulster Protestant/unionist/loyalist community that might challenge the conviction that the GAA is anything other than an organisation steeped in republicanism and anti-British hatred.

Irish Amateur Boxing Association (IABA)

The Irish Amateur Boxing Association organises and controls amateur boxing across Ireland, inclusive of both jurisdictions. Boxing clubs in Ireland are represented and supported at county, provincial and national level. Boxing clubs affiliate to the IABA and are then entitled to compete at each of these three levels.

The IABA has established four 'provincial councils' for Ulster, Leinster, Connacht and Munster, with special representation for Antrim, and Dublin. Although Antrim (Belfast) and Dublin are of course not among the four traditional provinces of Ireland, additional arrangements were put in place due to large volumes of working-class youth joining boxing clubs in these two areas. As with many other sports organised around an All-Ireland administration, the question of allegiance for boxers from the Ulster Protestant/unionist/loyalist community has always been a vexed one. This is perhaps further compounded by a strong tradition of boxing success historically emerging from, and supported by, Belfast patrons.

There are many notable examples of boxers from this community securing Olympic success for Team Ireland and preferring to align themselves with the established boxing fraternity on the island rather than declare for Great Britain. Wayne McCullough (Shankill Road) and Dave 'Boy' McCauley (Larne) perhaps are the most noteworthy.

Famously Ulsterman Barry McGuigan MBE (from County Monaghan) became WBA featherweight champion in 1985 whilst pointedly eschewing both Union Jack and Tricolour, preferring to fight under a flag of

Peace. Promising prospect Carl Frampton (from the loyalist Tiger's Bay area of Belfast) is the holder of the World Super Bantamweight title, has gained a silver medal representing Ireland in the EU Amateur Boxing Championship, and is managed by McGuigan. Unfortunately, what seemed to be a functioning non-sectarian model of sporting endeavour for both communities was undermined somewhat in 2012 when a club from loyalist Belfast's Sandy Row compiled a 57-page report outlining sectarian attacks on its members whilst competing in nationalist areas. This was contested by the IABA but the publicity around the matter has proved damaging to the sport's perceived neutrality.

Conclusion

In all of the sporting codes under consideration, a pertinent theme emerged in the context of cultural, political and religious division as represented by community sporting allegiance. It has been oft stated that Protestant/unionist/loyalist cultural expression (as represented through sports or elsewhere) defines itself in terms of separatism, exclusivity, exceptionalism, arrogance and perceived elitism. The implication being that collaboration and common purpose with shared expressions of 'Irishness' – through sporting endeavour (or cultural alignment) – are eschewed by this community.

However, when we review responses from the nationalist tradition within Northern Ireland and the Republic of Ireland toward sporting institutions and individuals from this community, we can clearly identify a partitionist mistrust (even antagonism) anchored within a deeper perception of 'difference'. Protestants/unionists/loyalists may indeed harbour solemn reservations regarding their Irishness. Crucially however, this is seriously compounded by nationalist opinion that seemingly rejects any expression or representation of 'Irishness' that does not subscribe to a de-Valerian idyll.

I have always viewed with interest – in a sporting context – how the trappings representing the British or Northern Irish states have been regarded or presented as somewhat unsavoury. How pride in this community's culture, traditions and sporting successes somehow equates with the rightly unpalatable manifestations of extremist groups like the National Front and British National Party. Yet in contrast, the unmitigated and uninhibited pride that Irish sports fans (and citizens) take in the celebration and promotion of their state, culture and traditions rarely if ever sees any admonishment for the blanket waving of the Irish Tricolour.[8]

Nationalism of any hue seems always to find a welcoming domicile for celebration, affirmation and pride within any sporting code. That popular sport also provides a fertile breeding ground for triumphalism, jingoism and sectarianism is a truism that still impedes the unfettered and joyous celebration of collective sporting achievement on this island. If the Orange segment of the Republic's national flag is truly to symbolise a recognition of another valid tradition within the state (and the island as a whole), then perhaps the most immediate and far-reaching developments to acknowledge this might take the form of real and pragmatic changes and reforms to sporting bodies. Whilst sport is often by definition adversarial, it should nevertheless be possible to create 'national' allegiances or forums where both traditions are meaningfully accommodated and respected in a common cause. Rugby Union has to some degree addressed this (whilst acknowledging the aforementioned limitations).

Similarly, Protestant/loyalist/unionist communities should be able to meaningfully reengage with those unique characteristics that previously identified them as different and distinctive within their shared British family; namely, their 'Irishness'. In order for them to do this, Irish cultural and sporting identity must be seen to denote more than simply the 'Catholic/nationalist/republican' monolithic tradition. From a policymaking perspective, we cannot underestimate the potency of partitionist/separatist opinion in ROI in this regard. And at the sharper end of things, from those northern nationalists who relentlessly seek cultural domination and the eradication of British culture from Northern Ireland.

Put simply, if Ulster Protestants did not already feel significantly different to their neighbours, then difference would most certainly be thrust upon them.

Notes

1. Derek Lawrenson, 'Team GB in Rio? Rory McIlroy Says He Owes a Lot to Irish Golf But Feels More British', *Daily Mail* [online], 9 September 2012.
2. The one notable exception to this is Higgins's now infamous threat to have loyalist paramilitaries shoot Dennis Taylor.
3. Edinburgh historically also featured clubs with sectarian origins, but both Hearts and Hibernian seem to a large degree to have transcended the problem.
4. Derry City in the north-west also, significantly, withdrew from the Irish league to play in the ROI's League of Ireland. As with other decisions of this nature, this move reinforced the drift toward an almost exclusively nationalist support base for a club that had previously been religiously 'mixed'. Interestingly,

sport once again reflected the changing socio-religious demographics of the city itself along sectarian lines.

5. Cliftonville Cricket Club – 'Our History' <http://www.cliftonvillecricketclub .co.uk/wordpress/ourhistory/> [accessed 1 August 2013].

6. The IRFU later explained that when Ireland played rugby in Northern Ireland it was deemed to be an away match, therefore only 'Ireland's Call' was played.

7. It might be noted that northern/Ulster county members predominantly voted against these changes.

8. Explanations citing associations between emblems of British identity and her colonialist past crimes seem a little dated in the twenty-first century. In fact, it could be argued that this would be akin to associations of the Irish Tricolour with IRA atrocities.

9

No One Likes Us, We Don't Care: What Is to Be (Un) Done about Ulster Protestant Identity?

Robbie McVeigh

> We are, we are, we are the Billy boys, we're up to our
> necks in Fenian blood, surrender or you die ...
>
> ('Billy Boys', Billy Fullerton)

> Could you find me? Would you kiss-a my eyes? To lay
> me down, in silence easy, to be born again, to be born
> again ...
>
> ('Astral Weeks', Van Morrison)

Introduction

My title begs the question of who 'we' are. This question is neatly framed by two perspectives: 'we' might be 'Billy Boys'[1] singing the 'famine song'; but 'we' might equally be Van Morrison singing 'Astral Weeks'.[2] We are a population defined – sometimes by ourselves and sometimes by others – as 'Ulster Protestant'. Broadly this population is defined by two relationships. First it is Irish – or at least defined in relation to its place in Ireland. Second, it is amorphous and ambiguous. It resists the tendency to neat categorisation. Thus the Northern Ireland census has at times been at pains to insist that people cannot be 'Protestant'. There was nothing new in this. As far back at 1861, the Irish census indicated, 'Members of Protestant Denominations are requested not to describe themselves by the vague term "Protestant", but to enter the name of the Particular Church, Denomination, or Body to which they belong'. Back in 1861 they also helpfully re-aggregated this disparate bunch as 'Total Protestants'. Then, as now, it was understood in this way by everybody interested in the sectarian zero sum game. At this point, its key meaning is 'not Catholic'.[3]

We need to begin by acknowledging that there is a veritable cornucopia of 'Total Protestants'. Indeed the tendency to schism and dislocation might be one of the defining elements of our identity. That said, there are two archetypes – one the loyalist, the other the committed applicant of the Westminster confession. This already implies a complex synergy between religion, politics and ethnicity. But any member of the 'uniformed organisations' of the Protestant churches, or the PWA might also be seen as definitive. Moreover, historically at least, the appellation included large numbers of people who were Irish and nationalist and republican. In other words, there is neither spatial nor temporal homogeneity with the term 'Protestant' as it is used in Ireland. Neither 'Kick the Pope' bands nor United Irishmen have a monopoly on Protestant identity.

It is also a given that this identity is currently (perhaps also perennially and definitively) 'in crisis'. While the appeal to 'No one likes us, we don't care' appears apposite to the contemporary self-identity of alienated Ulster Protestants, the reality is that most Protestants – especially those of the alienated variety – are more perturbed by the perception that no one cares. 'No one cares about us – and we don't like it' might be a more accurate characterisation of the present Protestant malaise. This inversion – like Marx with Hegel – moves us closer to the underlying reality.

On the one hand it seems trite to stand the old Millwall FC chant[4] on its head; however, it does touch on something real in Protestant angst. We think the world should care but nobody is really buying the reinvention of Orangefest as an inclusive cultural phenomenon; we think that the Scotch-Irish in the US should care but they won't even come and watch *On Eagle's Wing*; in Scotland they organise a worldwide 'homecoming' but don't even invite those most obsessive of expats, the Ulster Scots, to the party; most of all, we think the Brits should care – and all they can do is go on about how Irish it all is and insist they would never protest in that way about the Union Jack.

This sense of being disregarded echoes Henry McDonald's premise that this is 'the least fashionable community in Western Europe'. Here we begin to find the Protestant reflection of the Catholic MOPE syndrome (the 'Most Oppressed People Ever'). In contradistinction Ulster Protestants are perhaps suffering from the MUPE syndrome – 'Most Unfashionable People Ever' – at least in their own minds. Perhaps this is why the identification with Israel and Israelis is so widespread among northern Protestants. However the reality is that in post-GFA (Good Friday Agreement) Ireland, Ulster Protestants are not even significant enough to be 'unfashionable' – you don't have to look very hard to find far more unpopular groups – Roma or Albanians, for example – in European popular consciousness.

That nobody cares is the real issue.[5] The continuing concern with being misunderstood and disliked is relatively easy to unpack. On the one hand there is a metropole/colony tension, a sense of being the ones who make the sacrifice for Britishness at the frontiers while those in Whitehall regard us with metropolitan disdain – 'what do they know of England who only England know?' There may well be something in the notion that the British reaction to the flag protest is rooted in the fact that it represents the purest form of British nationalism – the logic of imperialist nationalism. In other words, British distaste for loyalism is a form of displacement that confirms the British self-image of tolerance and multiculturalism. This helps keep repressed all the nastier aspects of nationalism lurking behind, for example, the Olympic festivities. In this sense Orangefest isn't that far removed from London 2012 or the Last Night of the Proms. But this only compounds the Ulster Protestant sense of grievance. They have the party; we are the sacrifice.

Ulster might not be right

There is also a different perspective on this Ulster Protestant sense of grievance. This suggests that – if no one likes us or indeed cares – the fault often lies with us rather than them. It isn't – like everything else presented in post-GFA conflict resolution jargon – simply reducible to questions of perception. We aren't just misunderstood or bad at PR – many of the political and cultural forms with which we have been associated are inherently unlikeable, if not repugnant. This is a view I share. In other words, this reading starts from the point of view of Susan McKay's contentious *Northern Protestants: an Unsettled People* (2000). Anyone – Ulster Protestant or otherwise – reading that text will find it challenging. McKay doesn't offer much in the sense of an alternative but what she does offer is a brutal, unflinching account of what she feels is wrong with unionist and loyalist 'culture' and identity in the North. There has been a particular focus on racism in loyalist communities as if this were the only blot on the post-Good-Friday-Agreement union-ist copybook. But, there isn't any contradiction between sectarian and racist youth culture – so the struggle against fascism in the Second World War is much more distant to loyalist youth than songs about being 'up to our necks in Fenian blood' and burning Lundy (although not as distant as the Somme of course). From this perspective, popular

manifestations like the song 'The Pope's a Darkie' carry their own crude
logic rather than suggesting some tension between anti-Nazism and
contemporary racism and sectarianism. Once a community has inter-
nalised a methodology that accepts the logic of not having a Fenian
'other' about the place, it's very easy to turn to expelling anyone else
who is 'different'.

This idea that 'Ulster might not be right' has always been there
among Irish Protestants – northerners and others. There are a number
of key references in terms of the broader work and historical context.
Geoffrey Bell provided a critical but sympathetic overview in his *The
Protestants of Ulster* (1976). Flann Campbell's *Dissenting Voice* (1992) is
very good on that sense of a continuing tradition, recording the whole
tradition of Protestant radicalism and moving it beyond one or two
aberrant individuals. The *Further Afield* collection has a whole series of
contemporary contributions that all continue to insist on the possibility
of being Protestant and radical (Hyndman 1996).

My own chapter in *Further Afield* situates some of the personal biography (1996: 298–304). There's no simple, straightforward explanation for
what places us on a particular political trajectory. I have written elsewhere
about the importance of the punk movement in the north in generating
a different notion of what it was to be Protestant. Beyond this, however,
I still insist on the centrality of my Protestantness to my radicalism –
to reclaim the right to be Protestant and progressive, emancipatory,
revolutionary – to be a dissenter. I place myself squarely and positively
within the Irish dissenting tradition. I feel very much part of the Protestant
community and proud of it, though that does take a bit of effort at times.
More personally, I continue to insist on my own right to occupy some of
this space. Until I discovered Stiff Little Fingers and The Undertones and
Ruefrex, the coolest cultural icon I had was the pole-swinging band leader
at the front of a 'Kick the Pope' band. In this sense, I have always known
what it is to be a Protestant Boy as well as a Dissenter.

So there is a wealth of wider work around the progressive Irish
Protestant tradition – insisting that the progressive strain was and
is just as important – and just as Protestant – as the reactionary one.
This rightly reclaims people like the United Irishmen and the weaver
poets from people who wanted to claim them as forebears of unionist/
loyalist reaction. Thus if we choose to distance ourselves from our most
reactionary brethren, we don't necessarily have to identify with someone
else's history. Different forms of radicalism – nationalism, republicanism,
trade unionism, feminism – are all a part of Irish Protestant history – this
should make progressive politics much easier.

But not even the most sanguine of dissenters could claim that this has been the majority voice of Protestants in Ulster – at least since the defeat of the United Irish movement. And if we want to understand present discontents, we need to understand this dominant strain – and put it in context. To do this we need what might be characterised as a 'political economy of Ulster Protestantness'. This is a proper, grounded sense of the economic and social and political conditions that generated significance to the notion of the 'Ulster Protestant'. In contemporary discussions it sometimes feels like the only message young Protestants get is 'the Somme' and concomitant tales of Protestant victimhood. We are constantly urged to 'Remember 1690' or 'Remember 1641'. But Protestant history doesn't begin or end in 1603 with the plantation or 1641 with the Portadown massacre or 1690 with the Boyne or, indeed, 1914 with the Somme. Moreover, commemorating is very different from understanding. In Ireland, history repeats itself, the first time as tragedy, the second as farce, and the third as a 'community relations' project.

In other words, we northerners need a more grounded sense of our place within Irish and Irish Protestant identity. And we need to develop our capacity for self-criticism. It is common sense, not apostasy, to engage with the question of whether Ulster is – by definition – always right. And even if we accept the caricature of the inherent evilness of the Catholic Church and Sinn Féin – the notion that this then justifies our every action is a pretty hollow one. If they were all terrorists and institutional paedophiles – as many loyalist websites tend to suggest – wouldn't that be a horribly perverse other against which to set our moral compass? We need to begin by searching for what is best in ourselves rather than what is worst in others.

Uneasy silences: the political economy of Ulster Protestantness

At one level Irish Protestant history is explained by the political economy of settler colonialism – it all turns on the imagined and real relations with the colonised. Either they form a subordinated majority on whom the settler population is dependent and of whom they are eternally fearful;[6] or they attempt to build a society which is no longer in any relationship with the colonised. In this latter context the project becomes genocidal, at least by default.[7] For most of its history, most of the Protestant minority in Ireland defined its relationship with Catholics through one or other of these approaches. The colonial state model created a context in which Catholics were necessary but would 'know their place';[8] the Stormont approach attempted to ignore and exclude Catholics completely.

Thus we can employ a fairly simple model of ethnic interface here – where a dominant group needs to make sense of those it has subordinated. Either it tries to get rid of them altogether or it attempts to 'keep them in their place'. The first approach is neatly summed up by the invocation to 'Kill All Taigs' which adorns many gable walls in Protestant areas – it is explicitly genocidal. The notion of not having a Catholic about the place frames the same philosophy more politely – it insists that we want to live in a polity in which they no longer exist. The second approach is captured by the notion of 'housetraining' – the racist demotion of Catholics to the status of animals is no accident. Here the approach is about creating a polity in which Protestant privilege is safeguarded and maintained but which allows a place for Catholics.[9] These dual tendencies define the current crisis in Ulster Protestant identity.[10] Both of these methodologies have been adopted at different times and both continue to be offered as solutions to Protestant grievance.

It bears emphasis that most of this history was lived by us as Irish Protestants rather than 'Ulster Protestants'. This history was often stereotyped as 'Anglo-Irish' but this labelling fails to understand the cross-class identity of the Protestant bloc in Ireland. The quintessential Anglo-Irish person was 'Irish in England and English in Ireland and only truly at home on the Dublin-Holyhead ferry'. (The northern subsection was the 'fur coat brigade'.) Brendan Behan identified the Anglo-Irish more succinctly as 'a Protestant with a horse'. This essay is more concerned with Protestants without horses and without the capacity for seasonal migration. The last all-Ireland census in 1911 shows a breakdown of: 503,482 Church of Ireland, 424,359 Presbyterian, 60,114 Methodist, 7570 Baptist.

That is 'us' – a hundred years ago – all of them were primarily Irish.[11]

In other words, 'Ulster Protestant' identity didn't really exist until the twentieth century. While the roots of the partition of (nine-county) Ulster unionism from Irish unionism lie in the Ulster Defence Union formed to oppose the Second Home Rule Bill of 1893, there was no clearly distinct 'Ulster unionism' until 1905. Before that Protestants in Ireland – like their churches – were Irish. Unionists were Irish and loyalists and Orangemen were Irish – organising and belonging to all-Ireland institutions. Theirs was an Irish identity – profoundly sensitive to its two defining features – its privilege and its minority status. Of course, there were more Protestants in the north and fewer in the south. But majoritarianism wasn't really an option – Protestants had to stand their corner as a relatively privileged minority on the whole of the island or find some other identity to organise around.

Even the Ulster Unionist Party only traces its formal existence back to the foundation of the Ulster Unionist Council in 1905. Before this, unionists from the north had been part of a less formally organised Irish Unionist Alliance that emerged after the introduction of the first Home Rule Bill in 1886. The Irish Unionist Party was an alliance of Irish Conservatives and Liberal Unionists that split from the Liberal Party over the home rule issue. Though most unionist support was based in the Six Counties that ultimately formed Northern Ireland, there were unionist enclaves throughout southern Ireland, particularly Cork and Dublin. The initial leadership of the Ulster Unionist Party all came from outside what would later become Northern Ireland, with people such as Colonel Saunderson from Cavan and Edward Carson from Dublin – both members of the Irish Unionist Party.[12] However, after the Irish Convention failed to reach an understanding on home rule and with the partition of Ireland under the Government of Ireland Act 1920, Irish unionism was itself partitioned.[13]

But this was only possible by a further partition – the brutal repudiation of one third of the Ulster Unionist Council with the exclusion of Donegal, Cavan and Monaghan. Thus 35,393 men and women from Cavan, Donegal and Monaghan who had signed the Covenant and the Declaration were to be summarily excluded from the new unionist project. This was not without implications:

> If it is now open to one portion of the Province for its own safety to desert the rest, there was never any meaning in the Covenant at all. If we were not all 'to stand by one another' what was the object of the Covenant? The facts about the three Counties were as clear when the Covenant was signed as they are today, and they have not altered. The position of Ulster as a whole remains the same. Why were we asked to come in and sign if, when the emergency comes, we are to be thrown over?[14]

With some prescience these soon-to-be-excluded Covenanters argued:

> [The Six Counties] is too small for a Parliament, and it is bound to become parochial with its 52 Members as compared with 128 for the Southern area. Are not nine counties a small enough area for a Northern Parliament? Anyone looking at the map will see what

a ridiculous boundary six counties would present. Donegal cut off with its harbours and rivers and no access to it except the six counties. Cavan and Monaghan form a natural boundary to the South of Ulster, and Monaghan runs up to a point between Tyrone and Armagh into the very heart of the Province. ... An argument that has been used is that the three Counties contain a majority of Nationalist and Sinn Feiners. That is true. But so does Derry City, Fermanagh County, Tyrone County, South Armagh, South Down and the Falls Division of Belfast. Yet no one proposes to exclude them. The truth is that it is impossible to fix upon any exclusively Unionist area. There are more Unionists in the Southern area than there are Nationalists in the three counties and no provision whatever is made for them. ... We appeal to our fellow Unionists in the six counties not to desert us and not to violate their Covenant when they can take us in with perfect safety to themselves. We appeal to the Unionist Members of Parliament to see that the Province of Ulster is not partitioned. ...

Thus we find Irish/Ulster Protestant identity partitioned traumatically not once but twice over a relatively short period. But it is only really with the second partition – the partition of Ulster – that we find Protestants finally thinking about a polity without Catholics at all. This imagined community that underpinned the Stormont state's sense of self from first to last was, of course, still a class system. It had working-class and rural labourer Protestants firmly at the bottom and the 'fur coat brigade' squarely ensconced at the top. There is thus a desperate need to break with the notion of a continuity of Ulster Protestant identity from plantation to flag protests. Even after partition, there are at least two key phases defined by the state formation of Northern Ireland – Stormont (1920–72) and post-GFA (1997 onwards) with a key transition between these formations in the intervening 'Direct Rule' period. The essential point is that the 'Ulster Protestant' only really emerged with partition – before that, northerners were Irish Protestants with some sense of regional identity (albeit that of a nine-county 'Ulster'). Thus is bears emphasis that partition divided Ulster and Irish Protestants as much as it divided Ireland and Catholics. Being 'Ulster Protestant' only becomes definitive in consequence of the emergence of a consciously and profoundly sectarian Northern Ireland state – ironically at the point at which Ulster and Ulster Protestants are summarily divided. But the really pertinent question is what is being generated in the context of the new, more stable, less formally sectarian post-GFA state? And what space does it create for Protestants? It is from this sense of location – of historical and relational specificity – that we face the current crisis of Ulster Protestant identity.

The Good Friday Agreement and its discontents

It helps to make sense of the post-GFA state from this historical perspective. That said, the contemporary Northern Ireland state is not a fixed entity – it is still becoming. But we see an ongoing tension around the relation to Catholics (and increasingly 'others' with a growing minority ethnic population). So Catholics are about the place – but they are also supposed to have accepted the line in the sand – the state remains British (and the flag still flies). Flag protesting is a key manifestation of the outworking of these tensions. The two strands of ethnic domination – exclusion and subordination; the colonial model and the 'Stormont' model – continue to run through the contemporary crisis of Protestant identity. Although they continue to dominate Protestant political thinking, neither is going to get us out of the mess that we are in.

What does it mean to be Ulster Protestant in this context? There is clearly an emerging gulf between the Protestant 'winners' and 'losers' which is demarcated in terms of class as well as politics. It is both a middle-class/working-class divide and a divide between the working and the workless. We can begin to sketch two new ideal types of Ulster Protestant identity in this context. One is shaping a new social formation that can establish a relationship with Catholics whilst maintaining their subordination, both economically and culturally; the other continuing to dream of a state in which Catholics do not exist – in which they 'go home'.

It is probably a mistake to try and discern the politics of the flag protests from the statements of prominent figureheads such as Willie Frazer or Jamie Bryson.[15] They are simply too idiosyncratic to be representative. A more authentic voice is to be found amongst the largely young, urban Protestant working-class people who populate the protests. They are alienated, resentful and organised. They voice the lived experience of a community whose actual experience of disadvantage is aggravated by a misplaced sense that their Catholic peers are significantly better off than them. The resentment is a natural outcome of a polarised society in which one community, having monopolised power for a long period, is now required to make compromises, to 'share' a future.

It is important to begin by asking whether there is any progressive reading of the flag protests – or of broader Protestant alienation. It is necessary to accept that there is a politics – it isn't simply a local variant of the nihilistic consumerism of the English riots of 2011. There is a politics to it even if we don't like the politics. It is also generally true that people are better blocking roads than drinking Buckfast, even if it's about as reactionary a focus as you could get. The paradox of alienation is that it bonds the alienated together.

These young Protestants experience significant educational disadvantage compared to Protestant middle-class young people. They are far removed from the labour market and defined as anti-social within their own communities and seen as a threat by wider society. Young Protestants, often male, construct gangs, proudly proclaiming themselves 'hoods', owning and taking pride in a label that badges them as outlaws, as unwanted. Such gangs have employed social media to communicate and organise and this practice has been evident in the capacity of flag protesters to organise outside traditional structures. It has given them the opportunity to effectively bypass structures that previously would have exercised control. The more traditional print and television media has tended to portray the use of social media in its most negative guise, focusing on those who have attempted to use the supposed anonymity of Facebook as cover for sectarian abuse and threats. But, less publicly, Facebook and Twitter have been a vehicle for organisation and information-sharing.

Finally, whatever anyone thinks of them, the flag protests have put Northern Ireland back on the map – they made the world care a little about us again. Undermining the mood music of post-conflict, they insist that Ireland has not seen the end of history. But the content of the protest gives more cause for concern than hope. There is a profound irony in all of this – this is history repeating itself as farce – it is tempting to look for the satirist 'Hole in the Wall Gang' when the only buses running are in republican West Belfast.

Whilst young northern Protestants share many of the characteristics and worldview of alienated young people in developed societies across the world, their sense of resentment is local and specific. Beyond this there is a general perspective that Catholics are always the winners and Protestants, especially loyal, working-class Protestants, the losers. These are not good politics – for Protestants or anyone else. There's something of the Somme about this – great mobilisation and suffering directed at the wrong target – another section of the working class. Even if they choose to repudiate any notion of Irishness or republicanism, they still have to find some way to become a 'class for themselves' – flag protesting and Fenian-baiting just won't do it. While their Catholic peers are not better off in any tangible sense – in terms of employment or income or morbidity or mortality – they are seen to be 'winning'. Young

Protestants may well be worse off than their parents and grandparents. The Protestant class alliance that underpinned Stormont has gone. But this sense of loss is equally pronounced in terms of the politics of belonging. This new state – whatever it is – is not theirs: whatever the New Stormont is, it definitively is not a 'Protestant Parliament for a Protestant People'.

There isn't a huge amount of theory to accompany this angst and grievance. There is the odd interesting piece giving an Ulster Political Research Group outlook; and *Long Kesh Inside Out*[16] gives some UVF thinking. Often a few token points are made about Protestant culture and identity followed by an anti-SF rant. That said, however, the politics are all too real. As with the flag-protesting youth, we have to move away from the notion that these manifestations of Ulster Protestant politics are just some sort of atavistic relic. These people continue to represent one key construction and element in 'Ulster Protestantness' in the new post-GFA social formation – albeit one that sees itself as losing.

Alongside this alienation, however, we begin to see something akin to a 'New DUP' phenomenon. A generation of younger, able unionist politicians has appeared. They are slick and articulate and appear very different from their parents and grandparents although mysteriously one seems to have emerged from the other. Thus the 'drink the devil's buttermilk'/ 'save ulster from sodomy' activists – or at least their children – seem to be fairly relaxed at a wine reception for the equalities coalition. Perhaps most of the fundamentalist wing have retired/died or followed Jim Allister into the wilderness of North Antrim. This flipside of loyalist defeatism is peopled by Protestants who present themselves as 'winning'. They tend to be relatively liberal and politically confident – a bit like slick young US republicans. And they have 'won' in a way that the majority of the Protestant working class definitely have not.

It is no easy task to second-guess this new generation of unionist politicians – for every act of inclusion there's a volte-face on Long Kesh or parades. There are plenty of unreconstructed bigots still about so the new less sectarian elements have to be adept at accommodating sectarian attitudes. The DUP have recently launched a manifesto on education in Protestant working-class areas but they still attack Sinn Féin's 'ideological jihad' against grammar schools. Perhaps the DUP can be so bad on comprehensive education because they are mostly grammar-school boys – they just don't see the failure of the current education system for working-class Protestants. Or perhaps they simply see contemporary political advantage as trumping class loyalty. These politicians love their working-class roots almost as much as they love their middle-class advantages. This might be the trope for any post-GFA class analysis – certainly it is definitive of the Protestant 'winners'. We see a new political class emerging who are still 'doing alright' and have made their peace with having Catholics about the place (at least in private) and want to make the state work to their further advantage. In reality most are responding to the objective political conditions and the big change is the recognition that Protestants are not a comfortable majority anymore. So – tactically – the method to protect the Union is to act reasonably, some of the time anyway.

Despite this new loyalism, however, there is no ready political resolution to the political and cultural abyss young Protestants have been cast into. There is nothing approaching a broad, left-of-centre mobilisation. Indeed, since the United Irish movement, it might be argued that the 'Protestant problem' is that the political offer is only ever conservative, when push comes to shove. In other words the Irish Labour Party or the Northern Ireland Labour Party or the PUP always capitulated in the face of the 'loyalty test'. Protestants are politically trapped within unionism and loyalism and royalism. From this perspective Britishness continues to be a straitjacket that prevents any progressive political identity emerging.

In short we find contemporary Protestantness profoundly divided – primarily on class terms but also more loosely as 'winners' and 'losers' in the GFA/St Andrew's settlement. The 'losers' still clinging to the notion that it is possible to create a polity without any relationship with Catholics; the 'winners' tentatively edging towards a polity that can persuade Catholics of the benefits of unionism.

For all the froth around the GFA and the new 'good relations' state, it isn't a very attractive construction – and the flag protests are a symbol of this rather than a cause. The next census will in all likelihood indicate a Catholic majority in Northern Ireland – in other words the writing is on the interface wall. We should do what we should have done 100 years ago – embrace rather than fear our minority status. Finally, there is one further – if slightly more cynical and selfish – reason to be bold, to be positive and progressive. If northern Protestants are outvoted into a 32-county Ireland we will also be negatively affected by the accompanying resentment – there won't be any deal to be done.

All of us need some way out of the current impasse. In terms of my own framework, neither ethnic subordination nor exclusion is going to work – in the sense of producing a polity with enough process toward justice and equality to ensure stability. The colonial state model didn't work before 1921 and the Stormont model didn't work afterwards. The ongoing flag protests are a key indication that the GFA state isn't going to work either. Britishness, unionism and the Northern Ireland state create a series of straitjackets that prevent innovative thinking. The structures that have trapped us in counterproductive and self-destructive reaction have to be ditched – Britishness, 'Ulster', the Northern Ireland state. All of the reactionary baggage we load onto our youth should be consigned to the dustbin of history: loyalty, royalty, Orangeism, Fenian-baiting and Taig-hating – throw in the collarettes and the coronation mugs. We need to stop sacrificing ourselves on the whim of British imperial nationalism – that should be the main lesson we learn from the Somme.

Transcending alienation and resentment – what is to be (un) done?

So what is to be done and undone? I have suggested that much of our history needs to be repudiated rather than repackaged. But this recognition is a liberating one. Unionism is neither a birthright nor a cultural imperative but a political choice. So – at least in our unusually fortunate situation – is national identity. This pushes us remorselessly towards the question of the possibility of Protestant Irishness. Even for the most loyal of us, the repressed still returns. As David Ervine said, 'how the hell can you not be Irish when you are born and reared and all things affect you on the island of Ireland?'[17]

It hardly needs to be said that we all need to resist essentialist posturing for lots of reasons – we aren't just Protestants or 'Ulstermen' or Ulster Protestants – we have class and gender and sexuality identities and each of these should and sometimes does fracture the classic sectarian bifurcation. And we can't simply replace 'Irish' with 'British' on our EU passports and assume that our lives will be transformed. That said, northern Protestants have to come to some different and better sense of their relationship to the island and its peoples.

This approach allows us to draw again on a deep well of understanding. Of course, there are the obvious Protestant nationalist and republicans thinkers that people should read. The Tone of 'protestant, catholic and dissenter' and Yeats of 'no petty people'. But we also need a broader sense of what it means to be Protestant in Ireland. Thus the middle-class Shaw sets out his stall: 'I repeat that I am an Irish Protestant' (1926: xvi). He then proceeds to insist:

> Nothing can be more anomalous, and at bottom impossible, than a Conservative Protestant party standing for the established order

against a revolutionary Catholic party. The Protestant is theoretically an anarchist as far as anarchism is practicable in human society: that is, he is an individualist, a freethinker, a self-helper, a Whig, a Liberal, a mistruster and vilifier of the State, a rebel. (1926: xxiii–xxiv)

Shaw's prophetic counterfactual vision of what the role of Irish Protestant would be under Home Rule has pathos. But it continues to offer a template for progressive identity under reunification:

> When England finally abandons the [Protestant] garrison by yielding to the demand for Home Rule, the Protestants will not go under, nor will they waste much time in sulking over their betrayal, and comparing their fate with that of Gordon left by Gladstone to perish on the spears of heathen fanatics. They cannot afford to retire into an Irish Faubourg St Germain. They will take an energetic part in the national government, which will be sorely in need of parliamentary and official forces independent of Rome. They will get not only the Protestant votes, but the votes of Catholics in that spirit of toleration which is everywhere extended to heresies that happen to be politically serviceable to the orthodox. They will not relax their determination to hold every inch of the government of Ireland that they can grasp; but as that government will then be a national Irish government instead of as now an English government, their determination will make them the vanguard of Irish Nationalism and Democracy as against Romanism and Sacerdotalism, leaving English Unionists grieved and shocked at their discovery of the true value of an Irish Protestant's loyalty. (1926: xxiii–xxiv)[18]

But perhaps the best example of all of this to-be-rediscovered Irish Protestantness is that of Sean O'Casey.[19] His life story asks a huge amount of young northern Protestants – particularly of the flag protestors – why did he Gaelicise his name? Why did he join the Irish Republican Brotherhood and the Irish Citizen Army? Why did he play the uilleann pipes and play hurling? And what reference could this have for young working-class Protestants in contemporary Northern Ireland? Well, his autobiography should be compulsory reading for all of us. How was a young Irish Protestant to engage with both his poverty and his relative privilege? How was he to negotiate his relationship with his church and with the Orange Order? What kind of politics offer Irish Protestants a way forward? He confronts both Orangeism and Catholic reaction with equal vigour. Sometimes he wins and sometimes he loses but he maintains optimism of will until the end. It is all there in six volumes of O'Casey's autobiography – written in beautiful, modernist prose but speaking directly to disgruntled young Protestants in Ireland.

In other words, once our Irishness is engaged with, there are cultural resources available from which young Protestants could construct a more generous, outward-looking worldview – John Hewitt, Wolfe Tone, Anne McCracken, Yeats and Beckett, Stiff Little Fingers and Van Morrison.[20] How young Protestants might go about this should be a matter of their choosing but they desperately need a better offer than the current impoverished diet of Ulster Scots, a flag, and militaristic, sacrificial and imperial accounts of the First World War.

It bears emphasis that none of this should be read uncritically – it is part of the narrative of Irish Protestant identity. Mitchel's racism, Maud Gonne's anti-Semitism – and Yeats and George Bernard Shaw on fascism – like Carson's[21] imperialism or anti-socialism – or all the silences on gender – need to be acknowledged and understood. But these biographies are the stuff from which a new, more settled identity can be forged.

A recurring problem for alternative voices within the Protestant community is that the very act of constructing a positive and generous worldview creates a break with the community. Progressive politics is necessarily grounded in a concern for others. It involves a commitment to social change and a rejection of the urge to conserve. It also requires optimism and confidence. The Protestant community is short on optimism and generosity, but the resources do exist to construct a more positive worldview that can offer opportunity and hope to its young people.[22]

That 'no one likes us' because we often have unlikeable politics (and racism and sectarianism is only a part of this) may be an unpalatable truth for many Protestants. Ultimately, however, recognising that our politics are based on choice is profoundly liberating. Politics aren't hardwired culturally or genetically. The choices made since the United Irish movement have often been reactionary and self-destructive. And all this leads to the broad conclusion that only a reconnection with Irish and Irish Protestant identity offers a way out of the morass.

The existential choice between 'Ulster' and 'Irish' identity is the definitive political choice for northern Protestants. We can continue to cling to our majoritarian 'Ulster Protestant' status in the Six Counties hoping that the next census won't confirm the inevitable; or devising some other schemes for repartition; or entertaining even darker fantasies involving Catholics 'going home' that would rebalance the sectarian headcount. Or we can accept that we are an Irish Protestant minority – accept the inevitability of reunification and begin to embrace and celebrate the positive aspects of this prospect. At the heart of this perspective is the recognition that being a minority isn't such a terrible thing – it can be both progressive and liberating.

In so far as peace has created a space in which it is somewhat easier to explore identities, the contemporary situation is better. We see some opening up of a more liberal, progressive Protestant space and voice. In terms of prospects, things look pessimistic at the moment. But then so do the prospects for radical, transformative politics in most parts of the world. More specifically, the structural context for the hegemony of unionism is ever more fragile in the north of Ireland. And this is about more than the ticking time-bomb of demographic transition – everyone knows that when Catholics become a majority in the Northern Ireland, ethnically based unionism is finished. Other factors also threaten the status quo. For example, if Scotland becomes independent – unionism implodes. Most menacing of all for unionism is the capriciousness of the British. As Patrick Mayhew said, 'there can be no proper reason for excluding any political objective from discussion. Certainly not the objective of a united Ireland through broad agreement fairly and freely agreed'.[23] This uncertainty was compounded by the GFA – the conditional nature of Northern Ireland means that the state operates on the basis of uncertainty permanently.

In this context, for Irish Protestant identity to survive at all in the longer term, there has to be an alternative to unionism. The reality of this analysis is that unionism – particularly working-class unionism – is less likely to change proactively and positively than to have change thrust upon it. But the inevitability of that change is already fairly inescapable. And those of us who remain dissenters – who continue to insist on the possibility of a radical Ulster Protestant voice – achieve two things. First we present a small but important phase in the 'genealogy' of the 'dissenting voice'; younger activists who come to think as we do and did – even if it's in a generation – will be able to discern a continuity in progressive Protestant thought in Ireland. Second, it reminds everyone that politics is a choice – unionism is not a genetic or biological imperative – it is a choice of politics made by many Protestants in Ireland but also rejected by many others.

In the Protestant tradition of speaking truth to power, of testimony, of singing redemption songs, if we achieve nothing else, we continue to testify that Protestant reaction is not inevitable – politics is a choice, not an ethnic or cultural imperative. Here we can stand with the archetypal Ulster

Protestant – arch-contrarian and sometime racist – John Mitchel who said he could never give up his struggle against British imperialism, even when the cause looked hopeless, because this would render 'England's brute power', 'resistless, and therefore righteous' (Mitchel 1854: 70).

Wolfe Tone said, and we should continue to say; Protestants in Ireland – like everyone else – need to make choices – to be racist or anti-racist, to be sectarian or anti-sectarian – to be imperialist or anti-imperialist.

This moves us further towards the conclusion that what we need is a revising or rediscovery of Irish Protestantness, in all its complexity. It bears emphasis that there are two slightly different dimensions to this – first, we need to re-engage with what it means to be Protestant in Ireland – culturally, socially and religiously. The consequences of this aren't so terrible – who in their right minds wouldn't swap the reality of a day by the seaside in Rossnowlagh for a 'tour of the north' around north Belfast under a hail of abuse and Belfast confetti? This is where it will stop for many people – a more comfortable relationship with our Irishness and our island; with our Catholic neighbours and fellow citizens.

However, there is also a specific political dimension to this. As Protestants we are profoundly lucky that there was, of course, always a radical Irish option. This is the point at which – existentially and politically – we stop being settler colonialists and formulate a completely different type of relationship with the Catholic Irish. This, of course, happened heroically and in a remarkably advanced political form with the United Irish movement. But it has continued in different forms ever since. This is what Flann Campbell characterised as 'Protestant democracy'. It is arguably where Protestants should find themselves – supporting vigorous protections for minority rights, constitutional protections, etc. In other words, playing their full part in creating an Ireland that can manifest Tone's vision of a union of Catholic, Protestant and Dissenter and, in which they can, for the first time, genuinely and actively 'cherish the children of the nation equally'.

Conclusion

This essay has argued that we find a solution primarily in our Irishness – or, more specifically, our Irish Protestantness. Thus there are two interconnected processes that will take us out of the current crisis. First, northern Protestants have to come to terms with their Irishness. They need to reconnect with the idea of what Irish Protestantness means. Second, they have to make sense of what politics emerge from this reality. Some of us will hope that most Protestants – free of the shackles of Britishness and unionism and the Northern Ireland state – would choose a more progressive politics – democratic, inclusive, feminist, socialist. But this isn't a given – they might end up in the Blueshirts[24] like Ernest Blythe. Many may not want any formal politics at all. It bears emphasis that politics is a choice.

Of course, other aspects of identity remain crucial to how we identify and organise. But Irishness remains central to who we are and what we are going to do on this island. Part – but only part – of any reconciliation with Irishness might be a re-engagement with our Irish radical politics. Without being too chauvinistic, it is ours – Irish Protestants framed it and named it. We finally disarticulated Irish nationalism from royalism and Jacobinism and sectarianism. This wasn't all a product of principle – we also did this for pragmatic and self-interested reasons – we needed to create a pluralistic republic in which Protestants had an equal place. Nevertheless it was done.

Ultimately, however, the key point for Protestants is not that Irish identities or republican politics are naturally progressive – because often they are not. Irishness as much as any other nationalism or identity can be problematised and deconstructed. Moreover there is no guarantee in Ireland that progressive forces win. Rather the key issue is that the currently hegemonic British, imperial, colonial identity is naturally and inevitably reactionary. In other words, there is no hope of radicalising 'unionism' or 'colonialism' or 'imperialism' – whatever changes we want, we need to start by ditching these old, reactionary identities and politics. Of course, less sectarianism and racism and imperialism would be good for Catholics but the key issue here is that it would be good for Protestants.

My core argument is that the central choice for Protestants is about politics rather than ethnicity – it is a choice, and that it's bad politics rather than prejudice or misunderstood culture that have got us where we are today.

So, which song will we sing? 'The Billy Boys' or 'Astral Weeks'? 'Croppies Lie Down' or 'Brave Henry Joy'?

The future of the northern Protestant remains unwritten. If there's one essential thing about Protestants in Ireland it's that they resist the tendency to essentialise. How else could a people stereotyped by Calvinist taciturnity produce the lyrical genius of a Best or a Morrison? And if Ian Paisley and Van Morrison have one thing in common, it is the belief in the possibility of revolutionary transformation, the capacity for transcendence, the aspiration to be born again.

Notes

1. Billy Boys originated in the 1920s as the signature tune of the Brigton Boys, a Glasgow loyalist street gang led by Billy Fullerton. Fullerton was a member of the Union of British Fascists, started a Glasgow branch of the Ku Klux Klan and was awarded a medal for strike-breaking during the 1926 General Strike. Poet Edwin Morgan wrote after his funeral: 'Go from the grave. The shrill flutes are silent, the march dispersed. Deplore what is to be deplored, and then find out the rest.' The 'rest' included imprisonment for violence against his wife: Chris Watt, 'Billy Boys' Glasgow Godfather "Was a Thug Who Beat His Wife"', 17 October 2010, <http://www.heraldscotland.com/news/crime-courts/billy-boys-glasgow-godfather-was-a-thug-who-beat-his-wife-1.1061960>.

2. It was announced in 2013 that Van Morrison was to become a 'freeman' of Belfast. The emphasis was very much on where Van came from, 'Van the Man' as east Belfast boy made good. But the emphasis could equally have been on where Van travelled to and the influences he absorbed as a child from far beyond east Belfast – gospel music, jazz, Leadbelly, Jackie Wilson – that turned him into a world-class musician. In 2012 Van was the headliner of the first East Belfast Arts Festival. He also managed to sneak a sample of 'The Sash' into his *Irish Heartbeat* album with the Chieftains.

3. If you can ignore the fact that the largest denomination of 'Protestants' actually defines itself as 'reformed Catholic' that is probably as good as it gets – one of my relatives got round this uncomfortable reality by referring to Church of Ireland as 'Protestant Episcopalians'. Although, of course, this isn't the whole story either – in 1861 the sum total 'other' was the 393 Jews identified in the census alongside 'Total Protestants' and 'RC'; by 2011 the growing other '0.8% other religion' and '16.9% no religion or none stated' had become central to demographic debates as well as riffing on the old joke – were these Protestants or Catholics of 'no religion'?

4. The chant 'No one likes us, we don't care' was adopted by Millwall fans as part of a 'resistance identity' toward external critics such as the press and the government. Rangers supporters in Scotland adopted the song for similar reasons.

5. It also bears emphasis that Ulster has some very certain defenders – including both southern and northern Catholics who feel the pressing need to constantly articulate the case for Ulster Protestants. We mightn't like the people who like us and they mightn't be very likeable – but we can't pretend that they don't exist.

6. This was classically illustrated by the South African 'Swart Gevaar' or 'Black peril'.

7. Here the notion of 'balance of cruelty' becomes more important than any idea of creating a better society. Thus contemporary 'tit-for-tat' arguments about loyalist violence draw on a long history of claim and counterclaim about genocide in Ireland (McVeigh 2008).

8. From the Penal Laws through the establishment of the Church of Ireland to disenfranchisement, Catholic subordination would be symbolically and actually maintained.

9. 'Vote Deepens Unionist Rifts', *BBC News* [website], 28 May 2000 <http://news.bbc.co.uk/1/hi/northern_ireland/767782.stm> [accessed 1 May 2014].

10. Thus we have a First Minister who can still – in 2013 – endorse the notion that land should not be sold to Catholics.

11. There are also some 140,000 other 'non-RC' people in Ireland in 1911 – 'Church of England' (46,039), 'Church of Scotland' (2503), Independents (780), Plymouth Brethren (755), 'Information refused' (1171) and 'other' (88,232) who may or may not have regarded themselves as Irish Protestants.

12. We also see the Ulster Defence League and the British League for the Support of Ulster (Jackson 2011: 311).

13. By 1916 the Ulster Unionist Council accepts the principle of permanent partition, although the Irish Unionist Alliance protests against the proposed settlement. But this established the principle of partition and in 1918 a separate Southern Unionist Committee formed. In 1919 the Irish Unionist Alliance split and Lord Middleton formed the Irish Unionist Anti-Partition League.

14. 'Ulster and Home Rule. No Partition of Ulster'. Statement by the Delegates for Cavan, Donegal and Monaghan (Monaghan 1920: 2–8) (cited in Mitchell and Ó Snodaigh 1985).

15. But we should note a depressing circularity in the context of our title: *BBC News* [website], 'Loyalist Flag Protester Jamie Bryson Defends Alleged Singing of Sectarian "Billy Boys" Song', 13 September 2013 <http://www.belfasttelegraph.co.uk/news/local-national/northern-ireland/loyalist-flag-protester-jamie-bryson-defends-alleged-singing-of-sectarian-billy-boys-song-29577518.html> [accessed 1 May 2014].

16. *Long Kesh Inside Out: a Forum for Former UVF/RHC Political Prisoners!* [website]. <www.longkeshinsideout.co.uk> [accessed 1 May 2014].

17. Interviewed in William Crawley's BBC Radio 4 broadcast, 'Northern Ireland: Who Are We Now?', first broadcast 31 December 2012, <http://www.bbc.co.uk/programmes/b01phfn3>.

18. Ironically the nearest example to any Protestant assuming this role after partition in the Irish Free State was Ernest Blythe – the aggressive Irish language policy that was seen as so offensive by unionists was primarily driven by a Presbyterian from Lisburn who himself regarded this as a means of transcending sectarian difference in the new state.

19. Sean O'Casey (John Casey) 1880–1964, writer, socialist, pacifist, Irish Protestant, 'one of ourselves'. As Casey himself wrote: 'It had often been recorded in the Press ... that Sean was a slum dramatist, a gutter-snipe who could jingle a few words together out of what he had seen and heard. The terms were suitable and accurate, for he was both and, all his life, he would hold the wisdom and courage that these conditions had given him' (1963b: 231).

20. I grew up in the town that Alice Milligan was from and yet was taught nothing of her work or relevance or historical importance. She was excised from the memory of Protestant Omagh with all the precision of a Stalinist censor.

21. A. T. Q. Stewart quotes Tim Healy approvingly in his assessment that Carson, '[a]lthough a Unionist [...] was never un-Irish': 'It was no part of his intention to dismember Ireland, or to see Unionism survive in the form of a Home Rule parliament in Belfast – rather the contrary was true – but having used the resistance of the Ulster Loyalists as the trump card to defeat Home Rule, he became to some degree their prisoner. Paradoxically, the very success of the Ulster cause ensured the ruin of his own.' (1981: 134).

22. One relatively small, but significant step would be a better and fairer education system. There are few, if any, examples of Protestant secondary schools

serving Protestant working-class areas that can educate and inspire their young people. Orangefield Secondary School developed a reputation in the 1960s for being progressive and liberal, inspiring as diverse a range of pupils as Brian Keenan, David Ervine, Gerald Dawe and Ronnie Bunting. But it is doubtful if such a school would now be possible in the demoralised and under-resourced secondary sector with Boards of Governors fearful of being out of step with the dominant community voices.

23. Cited in Fraser (2000: 72). The Downing Street Declaration confirmed this reality.
24. Pro-Treaty army which emerged after the Irish Civil War to provide physical force protection to political groups such as Cumann na nGaedheal from anti-Treaty IRA elements.

Bibliography

Bell, G. (1976), *The Protestants of Ulster* (London: Pluto).

Campbell, F. (1992), *The Dissenting Voice: Protestant Democracy in Ulster from Plantation to Partition* (Belfast: Blackstaff Press).

Fraser, T. G. (2000), *Ireland in Conflict 1922–1998* (Abingdon: Taylor and Francis).

Hyndman, M. (ed.) (1996), *Further Afield: Journeys from a Protestant Past Belfast* (Belfast: Beyond the Pale).

Jackson, A. (2011), *The Two Unions: Ireland, Scotland and the Survival of the United Kingdom* (Oxford University Press).

McKay, S. (2000), *Northern Protestants: an Unsettled People* (Belfast: Blackstaff).

McVeigh, R. (2008), '"The Balance of Cruelty": Ireland, Britain and the Logic of Genocide', *Journal of Genocide Research* 10 (4).

Mitchel, John (1854), *Jail Journal: Five Years in British Prisons* (New York: Office of *The Citizen*).

Mitchell, A. and P. Ó Snodaigh (1985), *Irish Political Documents 1916–49* (Dublin: Irish Academic Press).

O'Casey, S. (1963a), *Autobiographies I: I Knock at the Door, Pictures in the Hallway, Drums Under the Windows* (London: Macmillan).

O'Casey, S. (1963b), *Autobiographies II: Inishfallen, Fare Thee Well; Rose and Crown; Sunset and Evening Star* (London: Macmillan).

Shaw, G. B. (1926), 'Preface for Politicians', in *The Plays of Bernard Shaw* (London: Constable).

Stewart, A. T. Q. (1981), *Edward Carson* (Dublin: Gill and Macmillan).

10

Celebration and Controversy in America: At Home with the Scots-Irish Diaspora

John Wilson and Alister McReynolds

Introduction

The chapters in this book explore various perspectives on Ulster Protestant identity and in this chapter we look at a unique subset of this group, specifically those who migrated to America in the eighteenth century. They left on ships from ports such as Coleraine and Londonderry as early as 1718, over a hundred years before the main Irish Famine migration of the 1840s. On arrival in America they were known by several names, but here we will generally refer to them in modern nomenclature as the 'Scots-Irish' (see discussion below). In looking at these Ulster settlers we will discover that many of the same issues facing Ulster Protestants also relate to this group. For example, while many scholars recognise the impact and achievements of the Ulster settlers on the formation of the United States, any statements highlighting the remarkable achievements of this group (for example, they gave the USA at least 11 Presidents, several Vice Presidents, State Governors etc.) is swiftly countered by damning mention of their role in the slave trade or their involvement with the Ku Klux Klan. Much as modern mockery is given to claims of an 'Ulster Protestant culture', there are many, and for similar reasons, who do not want to see the Scots-Irish raised up and praised, because, quite simply, for some this is seen as setting up a competition with 'the Irish' in America, and carrying forward a negative and confrontational distinction between Ulster Protestants and unionists and Irish nationalists and Catholics.

However, if we are ever to fully create a context of mutual trust and understanding within the conflict of identitites in Ulster we must first recognise there are distinctions between different identities, that each identity has its own strengths and weaknesses, and that each group should be free to express its identity, for good or ill, wherever it manifests itself on the world stage.

An identity by any other name?

The terms Scots-Irish and Scotch-Irish are both used to refer to inhabitants of North America descended from Ulster settlers. These settlers initially arrived in Ulster via Scotland where they had faced religious and political persecution, but they later discovered similar and other variants of such religious distress in Ulster itself, hence they set sail for America. But what do we call this group, given they have different names, and why should that matter?

The issue of which name to use is often presented as an 'essentialist' debate about the 'correct' term to use for this group. There are those who argue the correct term is 'Scotch-Irish' since this was the term first used to refer to the settlers, both by themselves and others, thus it has historical precedence. We accept there is historical precedent here, but not that such precedence must determine modern usage. Montgomery (2004/2013) argues that the correct name is 'Scotch-Irish' and supports this argument with several historical examples of its use in letters and newspapers, while Kerby Miller (2004) suggests that one of the very first groups of settlers from Ulster who arrived in New Hampshire in 1718 rarely if ever used the term 'Scotch-Irish' and often referred to themselves as 'Irish Protestants'. Miller argues that 'Scotch-Irish' was only used in legal or other disputes with the authorities over rights to land, for example. Both Montgomery and Miller offer evidence from a small number of letters, newspapers, or from the activities of a single settlement, and while these are instructive they could hardly be considered definitive. As H. Tyler Blethen (2002) notes of the Ulster settler: 'In North America they usually called themselves "Irish," while outsiders customarily referred to them as "Irish Presbyterians" or "Protestant Irish." The Oxford English Dictionary dates the first American appearance of "Scotch-Irish" to 1744.'[1]

Historically, then, one could argue that there are several names one might appropriately use. It is also the case, however, that one of the oldest societies established to represent Ulster settlers in America is called 'The Scotch-Irish Society of the United States of America', and, until recently, the American census recognised an identity category named 'Scotch-Irish'. Countering this is the fact that there are other groups in the USA who also claim to represent the Ulster settler heritage and they call themselves such things as the 'Ulster Scots Society of America', or the 'Maine Ulster Scots Project'.

Perhaps one of the most important points made in this debate is that we should respect the term which actual members of the settler group use to refer to themselves (Montgomery 2004/2013). But we are not aware of any major survey which would confirm which name this group prefer. So once again the evidence seems equivocal here. We have already noted that there exist both 'Ulster Scots Societies' and 'Scotch-Irish Societies', whose members, one assumes, are happy to call themselves 'Ulster Scots' and 'Scotch-Irish' respectively. Indeed, in 2012 the United States decided to remove the census option to designate one's identity as 'Scotch-Irish', and while this raised protests from members of the Northern Ireland Assembly, there was no concerted counter-reaction against this decision in the United States. The argument for removing the designation 'Scotch-Irish' was that members of this category could locate themselves under other available options such as Irish or Scottish, or they could be designated simply as other.

It is interesting to note when the *Belfast Telegraph* (Symington 2012) reported that MLA Gregory Campbell had written to the United States Ambassador to complain about the census change, both the *Belfast Telegraph* and Mr Campbell used the term Scots-Irish, not Scotch-Irish, a term which had been used in the the census. The online newsletter *IrishCentral* (Malone 2012) does use the term Scotch-Irish and quotes a US government spokesperson as saying that 'While the ancestry tables will all look the same, the interpretation of the "Scotch-Irish" and "Other groups" estimates will change. ... Individuals reporting Irish-Scotch are no longer tabulated as "Scotch-Irish" but rather are included in the "Other groups" category.' Note here how the term 'Irish Scotch' is mentioned as one that may be used by some individuals completing the census – yet a further option, it seems.

One of the best-known and most recent books on the Ulster settlers in America is called *Born Fighting: How the Scots-Irish Shaped America* (Webb 2004: see also Leyburn 1962). This book was written by ex-US Senator James Webb. Webb makes clear in the book that he is descended from Ulster stock, as are the people he talks about in his book, and they are, for Webb, 'Scots-Irish' (the term is also used in most reviews of the book, and by the famous American author Tom Wolfe). Similarly, recent academic texts have adopted the same position; Patrick Griffin (2001) covers a number of bases with his title *The People with No Name: Ireland's Ulster Scots and America's Scots-Irish*. And for those seeking their Ulster heritage and its links with the United States, William Roulston (2005) gives us *Researching Scots-Irish Ancestors: the Essential Genealogical Guide to Early Modern Ulster, 1600–1800*.

So what are we to make of all this? The term 'Scotch-Irish' may have some claims to historical precedence but this does not mean we must use this term, particularly if there has been a modern shift towards 'Scots-Irish'. Further, it seems to be the case that many people in the USA who are of Ulster heritage make use of both Scots-Irish and Scotch-Irish, and indeed also Ulster Scots.

As stated, we recognise there may an argument for historical precedent in using the term 'Scotch-Irish', and it can be argued that it was the term most commonly used in America from the 1880s or earlier. Nevertheless, as Blethen (2002) notes: '"Scots-Irish" has recently been coined by academics, out of deference to present-day Scottish sensitivities. A cursory Internet search elicited 30,800 hits for "Scotch-Irish" vs. 12,200 for "Scots-Irish," but a search of Amazon's book titles found only forty-six "Scotch-Irish" versus eighty-two "Scots-Irish." Popular usage has apparently not kept up with scholarly fashion.'

But there may be other issues lurking behind which name is appropriate. Perhaps we should ask why, since the Ulster settlers used various names, as did others to refer to them, did they decide on the term Scotch-Irish? One argument is that they did so to distinguish themselves from the later arrival of the 'Famine Irish' who came from across the whole island of Ireland, and who were mainly Catholic. This seems reasonable, if it simply helps provide a relevant distinction between two immigrant groups. However, this neutral description is given a different twist in other hands. A number of Irish scholars have argued that as the poor bedraggled Famine Irish arrived on the streets of America and became even more hated than 'the blacks', the Ulster settlers strove not only to descriptively distinguish themselves from these other Irish immigrants but to deny any link or relationship to the Famine Irish. While there may be some truth to this, a number of researchers have also pointed out that the Scotch-Irish Society in states such as Georgia actually went out of their way to raise funds for the Famine Irish and to support them where they could as part of their broader diaspora (David Gleeson, personal communication, see also 2001).

This notwithstanding, the modern incarnation of the Scotch-Irish Society of America makes it very clear that the Scotch-Irish are not 'Irish'. On their 'History and Origins' page, they say of the Ulster setters that:

They had sailed from ports in Ulster, the northern province of Ireland, but their language and customs were manifestly not Irish: one could still recognize the signs of their migration from

Scotland earlier in the seventeenth century: the name Scotch-Irish was coined for these people, and is borne with pride. ('History and Origins' 2014)

Given the argument that a distinction between the Famine Irish and the Scotch-Irish originally emerged for negative reasons, that is to disassociate the Scotch-Irish from the Famine Irish, this may partly explain why some writers are reluctant to have the term Scotch-Irish modernised into Scots-Irish, since this may leave unchallanged the negative associations imposed on the term 'Scotch-Irish'; specifically, that they denied recognition of the poor Famine Irish because they did not want to be associated with their poverty and status. This would also explain why an argument for the use of Scotch-Irish is projected well beyond the arrival of the Famine Irish. If the term Scotch-Irish can be shown to have been in use before the arrival of the Famine Irish then it can hardly have been coined to distance the Scotch-Irish from the Famine Irish. But in this case we end up with the original terms 'Scotch' and 'Scotch-Irish' being historically projected back between 300 to 800 years, with the term Scotch-Irish being seen by some as a translation of 'Scotus Hibernus'. Yet if this were so why did the term 'Ulster Scots' later emerge, when there already existed a perfectly useable term in Scotch-Irish? Indeed the Ulster Scots Agency of Northern Ireland refers to itself in translation as 'Ulster Scotch'.

To make matters even more complicated consider a further claim by the Scotch-Irish Society of the USA:

> The Scotch-Irish Society of the USA is truly American. We believe that we can broaden, deepen, and enlarge the principles from which our nation has drawn the sustaining power for its development by recalling past achievements, remembrances, and associations ('History and Origins' 2014)

We see here that the Scotch-Irish are not simply the Ulster-Scots in America. As one representative of the Scotch-Irish Society made clear to the first author, 'the Scotch-Irish are not Ulster Scots but Americans'. Logically, of course, if one follows the immigrant trail then the Scotch-Irish would first have to have been Ulster Scots, who in turn would have to have been Scots. But is this any different from the position of Italian Americans or Polish Americans, or indeed Irish Americans? Well, yes, because unlike many of these other immigrant groups the Ulster settlers did not really have a recognised homeland, hence they viewed themselves, in many ways, as the first modern Americans. It seems many Ulster settlers suffered a kind of cultural amnesia as they morphed into Americans, as John Shelton Reed, co-founder of The Center for the Study of the American South put it:

> You ask people what their ethnicity is and a lot of Scotch-Irish people either don't know or if they know it they just (don't) acknowledge it. It's not something they really identify with. They're just plain old Americans, plain vanilla. (Shelton Reed, quoted in Ewart 2012)

But if the Scotch-Irish are Americans, what does that make the Ulster Scots? And where does that leave the relationship between Scotch-Irish and Ulster Scots? How do the Scotch/Scots-Irish view the Ulster Scots and Ulster itself? Consider the following aim from the Scotch-Irish Society of the USA:

> The Scotch-Irish Society of the United States of America was founded to promote and preserve Scotch-Irish history and culture of America's Scotch-Irish heritage and to keep alive the esprit de corps of the Scotch-Irish people. ('Home' 2014)

Does this include consideration of where the Scotch-Irish came from and who they were originally? If so there is no avoiding the Ulster Scots, and, indeed, some would argue the Scots. It is here some Irish nationalist commentators see an opportunity to suggest a simple solution to all of this, arguing that since everyone came from the same island to America, i.e. Ireland, everyone is Irish. Consider the following quote from the Spring 2012 edition of the *Newsletter of the Scotch-Irish Society of America*. Kevin Myers, the renowned Irish columnist, recently wrote that 'There's no end to this nonsense of subdividing society, defining and redefining "identity", or even worse, "culture", like a coke-dealer fine-cutting a stash on a mirror. The outcome is a multiply divided community, sects in the city, with almost everyone having their own mini-culture. Healthy societies don't dwell on identity' (Myers, quoted in 'Letter from the President' 2012) Most societies, healthy or otherwise, do, of course, reflect on identity in many forms, from family affiliation through county affiliation, to state affiliation and finally to country affiliation. Identity is always multifaceted and complex, so this is not really the problem; the problem is exclusion and denial of identity, even within the same subculture. So who then are the Scots-Irish and how do they view themselves and the place and people they had left behind?

In the remainder of this chapter we want to consider this issue by offering a brief overview of why so many left and went to the USA in the first place, and we argue that the very religious and personality traits claimed by the Ulster Scots and the Scots-Irish suggest that since Ulster settlers were not leaving an ancient homeland – that is, somewhere they could look back to as a place of first origin – America became home, and hence this is why many of them consider themselves simply Americans. Further, we speculate that across generations the nuances between Scots-Irish and Irish may have become weakened in America, and hence this may explain why the census figures for Irish have remained high, while those for (Scotch) Scots-Irish have diminished until finally being removed as an option by the United States government.

The Scots-Irish and the view from America

One of the main reasons for the Ulster Protestant migration to the United States in the eighteenth century was the establishment's efforts not only to keep Catholics out of power but also their efforts to control and subdue Protestant Dissenters. Many of the very same people, in particular Presbyterians, who had fought to defeat the Catholic King James II now found themselves discriminated against as 'The Ascendancy' sought to control the potentially significant political force represented by Ulster Protestants. Official recognition of Dissenter marriages was denied, and failure to attend Anglican services or to accept Anglican Episcopal authority became prosecutable offences. In 1704, the Test Act stated that all public office holders had to take sacraments in the (Anglican) Church of Ireland. Such constraints led many to seek religious freedom in the new world, a kind of religious exodus. The *Encyclopedia of the Irish in America* refers to Rev. James McGregor who led his flock to New England as 'the Moses of the Scotch-Irish in America' (Glazier 1999)

On top of these religious issues many Protestants also had to contend with protectionist economic policies that impacted upon Dissenter-led industries in linen and wool. This created economic hardship as well as religious discrimination. Many Dissenters refused to accept such a culture of control and opted, for economic as well as religious reasons, to emigrate, with some 250,000 taking this road during the eighteenth century. But it should be noted that there were also positive economic reasons for such a move, one being the availability of plentiful cheap land which was a great inducement, especially since so many farms set up under the Plantation of Ulster were disappointingly small. Thus we can understand the attraction for Hugh McLellan to come from Ballymoney in the 1730s and to purchase 200 acres for £15. Albeit the land could accurately have been described as hostile wilderness and jungle (see McReynolds 2013).

A number of related elements flowed from this Ulster migration which create a difficulty, and perhaps a paradox, in assessing the interconnectedness of the Ulster Protestant and the Scots-Irish in America (see Gleeson 2001). First is the fact that the Scots-Irish played a major role in the American Revolutionary War. Having already gained a fearsome reputation for their frontier fighting ability against the native Indians, the Scots-Irish stamped their mark in the fight against the British; so much so that George Washington is famously said to have remarked that he would make his last stand with his Scots-Irish troops. What is interesting here is that it was those who fought with the British, not against them, who would have been seen as 'loyalists'. Those fighting the British were essentially 'Republican'. Indeed, it has been argued that many Scots-Irish who wished to remain loyal to the Crown moved north to Canada rather than fight against the Crown. From this viewpoint, Ulster loyalists looking to America for their connection with the Scots-Irish must contend with this paradox; that those who left Ulster for America fought against the Crown as Republicans, while those who stayed remained loyal to the Crown.

We should also note that while the violent nature of the Scots-Irish was a positive characteristic in time of war, critics of the Scots-Irish have cited their tendency to use violence as a ready means of solving a problem as a negative attribute. To some extent, that is inescapable when we consider the words of James Logan's self-confessed motivation for organising the main eighteenth-century exodus from Ulster.

> At the time we were apprehensive from the Northern Indians. ... I therefore thought it might be prudent to plant a settlement of such men who formerly had so bravely defended Londonderry and Inniskillen [*sic*] as a frontier in case of any disturbance ... These people if kindly used will be orderly as they have been hitherto and easily dealt with.

However, the latter experience was not the truth for everyone and another Quaker, John Woolman, who was at the forefront of the abolitionist movement in eighteenth-century America, was to witness instances of ruthless Scots-Irish violence as he traversed America. This experience was shared by fellow pacifists such as the Moravian Church, who had converted whole tribes of Native Americans to Christian pacifism and yet suffered the violent outrages of gangs such as the predominantly Scots-Irish Paxton Boys. Woolman's biographer Edwin H. Cady (1966) put it succinctly:

> They established decisively the frontier axiom: 'The only good Indian is a dead Indian'. In frontier minds – many of them affected by Scotch-Irish Calvinism – arose a myth, as a pseudotheological rationalization of that hatred, which varied the familiar myth that Americans were led in the wilderness like the children of Israel to the Promised Land. This myth said that Indians were cursed Canaanites, and it had become the sacred duty of God's people to stamp them out. (Cady 1966)

Notwithstanding this, it has to be said of Scots-Irish violence that too much has been generalised from isolated incidents. A recent study into the Scots-Irish and the question of violence has counteracted some of the notion of the 'referral' of Scots-Irish violence as a cultural phenomenon in today's society. This particular research was carried out by three academics at Louisiana State University and examined the extent to which higher rates of violence in 'the south' were a remnant of the unique culture of the Scots-Irish in those southern states.

The research was particularly focused on determining whether the high rate of female homicide in the region could be connected to, 'the lasting effects of the Scots-Irish on the southern culture of violence among females'. The initial standpoint included a belief that the Scots-Irish culture of violence would have exerted a uniform effect on both men and women. Contrary to that, however, the findings were that the gender-specific roles within Scots-Irish southern culture meant that the 'business' of violence and crime was seen as 'man's work'. In fact the study showed that the Disadvantage Index was a more accurate tool as a correlation indicator and that, 'areas with higher percentage of Southern born Scots-Irish women will be more likely to show lowered rates of female homicide' (see Berthelot, Blanchard and Brown 2008).

That fighting ability which James Logan had discerned and attempted to deploy became invaluable at the time of the American Revolution. Consider the brilliant move by Colonel Henry Knox, despatching 2000 troops to fetch 60 tons of abandoned (formerly British) ordnance using 400 oxen and move it 300 miles from Fort Ticonderoga to Boston across snowy wastes in the middle of winter. And to then place it on

Dorchester Heights above Boston Harbor. There, the British General Howe initially tried to strike back, but couldn't get the angle of elevation and was forced to withdraw from Boston Harbor.

Withdrawal meant leaving behind an abandoned town and 250 pieces of large-calibre artillery. Thus was struck the first blow of the American Revolution against General Howe and the cream of the British forces. The American patriot expedition was led by a 25-year-old officer and former bookseller, whose father had sailed from Londonderry with Rev. John Morehead in 1729. Thereafter we are told that that officer, Henry Knox, was regarded by Americans as 'an object of admiration and regard' (Callahan 1958).

But it would be wrong to consider Scots-Irish violence, cruel or courageous, in isolation from another core characteristic associated with the Scots-Irish and their Ulster and Scottish heritage; namely their healthy respect for education and learning. As the ideological implications of the American Revolutionary War spread across Europe, core Enlightenment values originally developed by such Ulster Protestants as Francis Hutcheson began to take hold in many Irish Catholic and Protestant minds. Francis Hutcheson was born in the townland of Drumalig just outside Saintfield in Co. Down. As Professor of Moral Philosophy at Glasgow University (where one of his most famous pupils was Adam Smith), he was described as the 'father of the Scottish Enlightenment'. He was nonetheless Scots-Irish (he registered as a pupil of Glasgow University as ethnicity 'Scotus Hibernus'; see Simpson Ross (2010)).

The Enlightenment, the American War of Independence and the French Revolution all bear traces of Scots-Irish thought. Hence, one might argue that an intellectual legacy of Scots-Irish/Ulster Scots thought, enlivened by an original independence and strong fighting ability in the United States Revolutionary War, can be traced in the formation in 1791 of the Society of United Irishmen, whose aim was to unite Catholic, Protestant and Dissenter in Ireland's cause against England.

Finally, and completing the circle, the failure of the United Irish rebellion led many of its leaders and followers to flee to America where their ideological views fitted well with the core elements of Republican politics in the United States and where, claims Gleeson (2001), they could actively work on the removal of the British from Ireland '… without seeming un-American'. Here is a core problem for modern Ulster Protestants – or more specifically the Ulster Protestant loyalists – as they look in vain to their brethren in the United States. Those from Ulster who left its shores seem to have ended up less concerned about loyalty to the British Crown than those who remained behind. Hence, attempts to bind with the Scots-Irish politically may prove more difficult than binding with them on the core and more neutral level of ancestry, or perhaps a love of the intellectual and the promotion of education.

Yet on the level of ancestry, as we have seen, there is also a problem in that many Americans of Ulster descent do not look to Ulster, nor even think of themselves as Scots-Irish; they are simply Americans.

This creates another potential paradox.

As the modern Ulster Protestant and Ulster Scot looks to their cousins in America they behave as an inverse or reverse form of diaspora. They seek to acknowledge their heritage and links with the Ulster settlers in the United States, while many of these settlers cannot or do not reciprocate, as they view their heritage as exclusively American.

Indeed, we would go so far as to suggest that if one finds an American who is unaware of or uninterested in anything but their American roots you have probably, paradoxically, found a Scots-Irish person.

The problem is that one of the main motivations of the eighteenth-century migration was religious freedom, which for many was a reason for leaving Scotland for Ulster in the first place. Hence, on arriving in the United States, and eventually finding religious freedom, the United States became home.

Unlike the Famine Irish, or the rebels of 1798, the Scots-Irish actively sought exile in order to find somewhere they were free to profess their religion, and they found this in America. This may be why some say that the Scots-Irish are the first modern Americans.

But what then of the modern Scots-Irish in America and their relationship – or lack of it – with the region of their forefathers?

If the claim above is correct we should not be surprised that there was little outcry when the term 'Scotch-Irish' was removed from the United States census, since many of the descendants of Ulster settlers do not understand or do not care about identity issues on the island of Ireland.

As each generation has moved on, all that is left of the social and cultural memory of Ulster for many is that they have heritage links to somewhere in Ireland and hence they are ostensibly 'Irish'. As one young student put it, her granny told her she was from Antrim and that her family came to America in the eighteenth century. So when the student looks up Antrim they discover that it is in Ireland, hence they conclude they are Irish.

An interesting thing seems to have taken place over the centuries.

While there was always a hard core who knew and remembered they were Scots-Irish, the actual number expressing this in the United States census has always been small compared to the number expressing Irish identity; around 5 million Scots-Irish, against 39 or 40 million Irish.

Many commentators have always been suspicious of this and it is often claimed that many of those who designate themselves as Irish are actually Scots-Irish. Given the numbers of Ulster settlers that migrated to the United States across the centuries, and given standard birth rates, there may be some truth to this, but it is very hard to prove. One piece of interesting anecdotal evidence however may be gleaned if one compares census figures with figures for religious affiliation. Here one finds that the numbers of Irish in some American states tend to be higher than the number of Catholics; in some cases there are more than twice as many people with Irish identity as there are Catholics. An informal review of these figures suggests that this mathematical difference is most prevalent in southern states such as Georgia, South and North Carolina, Kentucky and Tennessee. But it can also be seen to a lesser extent in other states such as Oklahoma and even Alaska. Given the strong relationship between Irish identity and Catholicism it is unlikely that the figures suggest a significant conversion of Irish Catholics to Protestantism. More likely is that once removed from Ulster the political nuances (of partition, nationalist and loyalist affiliations, Northern Ireland and southern Ireland designations, etc.) become less relevant, hence many Americans who know their ancestors came from Ulster may simply align with the European identity 'Irish'. Hence, by accident and ignorance the identity of the Scots-Irish becomes ever further eroded and ever more distant and inaccessible for the descendants of the original American settlers from Ulster.

Conversely, this also means that it becomes ever more difficult for Ulster Protestants and Ulster Scots to reach out and find the descendants of the original Ulster settlers.

References

Blethen, H. Tyler (2002), 'Review: *The People with No Name: Ireland's Ulster Scots, America's Scots Irish, and the Creation of a British Atlantic World, 1689–1764* by Patrick Griffin (Princeton, NJ: Princeton University Press, 2001)', *William and Mary Quarterly Reviews of Books* 49 (4).

Berthelot, E., T. C. Blanchard and T. Brown (2008), 'Scotch-Irish Women and the Southern Culture of Violence', *Southern Rural Sociology* 23 (2): 157–70.

Cady, E. H. (1966), *John Woolman the Mind of a Quaker Saint* (Washington Square Press).

Callahan, N. (1958), *Henry Knox, General Washington's General* (New York: Rinehart).

Ewart, R. (2012), 'Every Revolution Begins with a Spark, Ethnic Americans, Assimilation & Dependency!', *The Federal Observer* [website], 17 June <http://www.federalobserver.com/?s=shelton>, [accessed 8 August 2014].

Glazier, M. (ed.) (1999), *The Encyclopedia of the Irish in America* (University of Notre Dame Press).

Gleeson, D. (2001), *The Irish in the South* (Chapel Hill: University of North Carolina Press).

Griffin, P. (2001), *The People With No Name: Ireland's Ulster Scots, America's Scots Irish, and the Creation of a British Atlantic World, 1689–1764* (Princeton, NJ: Princeton University Press).

'History and Origins' (2014), *The Scotch-Irish Society of the United States of America* [website], <http://www.scotch-irishsocietyusa.org> [accessed 14 August 2014].

'Home' (2014), *The Scotch-Irish Society of the United States of America* [website], <http://www.scotch-irishsocietyusa.org/index.html> [accessed 12 September 2014].

'Letter from the President' (2012), Newsletter (Spring 2012), *The Scotch-Irish Society of the United States of America* [website], <http://www.scotch-irishsociety usa.org/SISNewslSpring12.pdf>, 1 [accessed 12 September 2014].

Leyburn, J. G. (1962), *The Scotch-Irish: a Social History* (Chapel Hill: University of North Carolina Press).

Malone, Bernie (2012), 'Scotch-Irish Will No Longer Be Included in Official US Census Figures – POLL', *IrishCentral*, 6 January <http://www.irishcentral.com/news/scots-irish-will-no-longer-be-included-in-official-us-census-figures-136800793-237426421.html> [accessed August 2014].

Miller, Kerby (2004), 'The New England and Federalist Origins of "Scotch-Irish" Identity', in William Kelly and John R. Young (eds), *Ulster and Scotland, 1600–2000: History, Language and Identity* (Dublin: Four Courts Press).

Montgomery, M. (2004/2013), 'Scotch-Irish or Scots-Irish: What's in a Name?', *The Ulster-Scots Language Society* [website], <http://www.ulsterscotslanguage.com/en/texts/scotch-irish/scotch-irish-or-scots-irish/> [accessed 14 August 2014]. Originally published in: *Tennessee Ancestors* 20 (2004): 143–50.

McReynolds, A. (2013), *Kith and Kin: the Continuing Legacy of the Scotch-Irish in America* (Ballymoney: Colourpoint Press).

Roulston, W. (2005), *Researching Scots-Irish Ancestors: the Essential Genealogical Guide to Early Modern Ulster, 1600–1800* (Belfast: Ulster Historical Foundation).

Simpson Ross, I. (2010), *The Life of Adam Smith* (Oxford: Oxford University Press).

Symington, Matthew (2012), 'Unionist MP's Anger as US Drops "Scots-Irish" Term from Census List', *Belfast Telegraph*, 16 January <http://www.belfasttelegraph.co.uk/news/local-national/northern-ireland/unionist-mps-anger-as-us-drops-scotsirish-term-from-census-list-28703425.html>.

Webb, James (2004), *Born Fighting. How the Scots-Irish Shaped America* (New York: Broadway Books).

11
Convergence

Graham Reid

Jack Watson was serving in the Royal Artillery. He and a colleague were ordered to report to a barracks in Tipperary. Their journey from Belfast proved something of a nightmare. They eventually arrived at the barracks in the early hours of the morning, but could find no one awake. Waking up in a large hall, that might have been a gymnasium, Jack found that he could not move. Terrified, he called to his colleague ... but he was in a similar situation. Had they been struck by some mysterious illness? After initial panic and frantic struggling they realised the truth ... in their exhausted state, without realising it, they had lain down on a newly painted floor and were stuck fast in their Army greatcoats! This was a couple of years before the First World War ... and before it would end they would be in many other 'sticky' situations.

Before leaving for the front Jack met up with his brother-in-law, Company Sergeant Major William John Graham of the Royal Irish Rifles, at Borden Camp in Surrey. Sergeant Major Graham was also a professional soldier before the outbreak of the war. He was an only son and Jack was married to his only sister, Agnes. The two men were never to meet again. Jack was wounded in Belgium and spent time recovering in an *estaminet*, being tended by the landlord's daughter. He recovered, rejoined his unit and eventually, like many thousands of other Ulstermen, fetched up on the Somme, in 1916.

William Graham also made it to the Somme. Both men survived that awful battle. William, by now a Second Lieutenant, pushed on towards the Battle of Cambrai. On the way his unit pushed the Germans out of the little village of Mouvres. William received a wound to his hand, but continued to lead his men. The Germans counter-attacked ... pushing the Rifles back, out of the village. William John Graham was killed by a sniper's bullet during their retreat. His colleagues had to abandon his body. A couple of days later, when they in their turn retook the village, his body couldn't be found. He was presumably buried by the Germans. His name is listed amongst the missing on the Cambrai Memorial. He was 26 years old.

William Reid, born on the Shankill Road, was a foreman painter in the Belfast shipyard of Harland and Wolff. He had worked on the *Titanic*. For very many years Belfast people didn't talk about the *Titanic*. There was a great sense of communal shame about the ship sinking on her maiden voyage. It was said that grown men wept at the news of her sinking. This was an era when men took fierce pride in their work, especially so the men who worked on that ship. It was to be many years later before Belfast people had the confidence to quip: 'Well it was all right when it left here'. Given the fact that the shipyard workforce was predominantly Protestant, sectarian rumours were soon flying around. It was said that Catholic workers had been sealed up in the hull of the ship and that was why it sank. Another accusation was that the Protestant riveters cursed the Pope with every rivet they 'shot' and that's why it sank. Another, non-sectarian theory, was that it was a challenge to God. Men claimed the ship was unsinkable, so God decided to prove them wrong. Today we have 'Titanic mania'… a 'Titanic Quarter' and a £100 million museum, which would have been unthinkable to the men who built *Titanic*.

William Reid was also a member of the original UVF, founded by Sir Edward Carson and Sir James Craig to resist the imposition of Home Rule in Ulster. William also signed the Covenant in 1912. Many apparently signed it in their own blood. His family history does not record if William did such a thing. Despite being the father of four children when Sir Edward Carson pledged the UVF to the war effort in 1914, William marched away. These men, who formed the bulk of the Thirty-Sixth Ulster Division, also fetched up on the Somme. Whether William Reid ever encountered William Graham or Jack Watson during the war is not recorded.

Back in Ulster in 1919, living at No. 3 Coolderry Street, Jack Watson fathered his fourth child, a girl, Norah. Years later Norah would marry William Reid's youngest child, Joseph. Perhaps the two old soldiers eventually met at the wedding. Whatever, Joe and Norah Reid were my parents. Norah's mother, Agnes, had died in 1928. Shortly after this Jack Watson moved out of the family home to live with his mistress at Ballyaughlis, near Drumbo. Norah at nine years old became the 'little mother' to her five siblings. As a baby she had lost an eye when her sister, Alice, knocked a hatpin into her cot.

My mother's grandparents, the Grahams, who lived at 67 Coolderry Street, had lost both of their children. When I was born my mother decided to keep the family name alive, so I was called Graham. The name still lives in the family through my own son and my youngest grandson. I am fiercely proud of the name and of those three men and the Ulster Protestant tradition they represented.

Growing up I saw little of Jack Watson, he and my mother being estranged, but I did come to know him a little bit when he was an old man who served thick, strong tea in pint mugs and offered two-inch-thick slices of bread. He and my mother were reconciled before he died. The only stories he ever told me about the war were of the paint-struck overcoat and the *estaminet* landlord's daughter. He didn't elaborate on whether there was a romantic element to the latter story. Perhaps it was implied by his emphasis on the fact that it was the daughter of the house who ministered to his needs. I never did ask him outright. Nor did I ask how he could cross a freshly painted floor and not be aware of it. He wasn't really the sort of man you questioned. He'd been a hard man ... one of five brothers. According to my mother they cleared many a public house in their day. He was an Orangeman, but not a fanatical one to my knowledge. I did ask him if he'd signed the Ulster Covenant. He said he hadn't, although he agreed with its sentiments. As an 'oath bound' soldier, as he put it, he felt it would have been wrong to do so. During the sectarian troubles of the '20s he was a carter. There was a wooden partition down the middle of York Street, to keep the warring factions apart. Snipers operated on both sides. One day as Jack drove his horse and cart along the street, his 16-year-old helper was shot dead on the cart beside him. According to Jack he just calmly trotted along, waiting for his own bullet ... but it never came. To my ears it sounded like a recklessly brave thing to do, but then here was a man who had come through the entire First World War. Survived many battles, including the Battle of the Somme. Which side shot his helper he never knew and it's unlikely the killer knew his victim. Also during that troubled period he used his horse and cart to 'flit' a Catholic neighbour, ignoring dire threats of what would happen if he did so.

William Reid died when I was still quite young, so I never had any conversations with him about his wartime experiences. The dearth of stories coming down through the family would seem to attest to the fact that, like so many, it was something he just didn't talk about. (Unlike his son, my Uncle Willie. He'd been a territorial before the outbreak of the Second World War. With the start of hostilities he was mobilised and sent to fight in Burma. He seldom talked about anything else.

According to my mother he talked as if he'd won the entire war on his own!) Once when my father couldn't take me to a promised football match at the Oval, my grandfather stepped into the breach, to prevent my being disappointed. Later I recall being annoyed at being asked to drop back and walk with him on our way to the Salvation Army ... he walked very slowly by then. My grandmother didn't approve of the cinema ... a house of sin she called it. Grandfather on the other hand would often slip in to watch war films.

Despite the family having been burnt out of Ardoyne in the 1930s, there was never any sectarian talk in the house. Although my aunt did say that as the removal van left the street my father played 'The Sash' on a wind-up gramophone. The Reids then moved to the Ballygomartin Road. William Reid was not an Orangeman. Later on I found it hard to reconcile the idea of this little Christian gentleman having fought on the Somme, or of his having been a member of the UVF. My father certainly was never an Orangeman. To my knowledge he never voted unionist in his life. He was a socialist who only ever voted Labour. He was a labourer in the shipyard. He and my mother separated when I was two years old. They never divorced, but never lived together again either. I remained close to both of them. When Joseph Stalin died my father stood and cried in our house. He took his own life shortly after the deaths of his parents ... who died within months of each other.

I was brought up by my mother in 67 Coolderry Street, the house her grandparents had rented since its construction. Both were dead by the time I was born in the front bedroom. My Uncle Bobbie, my mother's youngest brother, took over the house when they died. My parents moved in with him. When Uncle Bobbie moved to Canada in the late '50s my mother stayed on. She was there until she herself died in 1981. The house has since been demolished, but I have two bricks from it in my study in London. After the marriage break-up my father returned to live with his parents on the Ballygomartin Road.

As a boy I remember going for a walk with my mother one Sunday afternoon. Her favourite walk was up to the City Cemetery, the main Protestant burial ground then, at the corner of the Falls and Whiterock Roads. Her mother was buried up there and later her father would be too, before it became a virtual no-go area for Protestants. At the top of the Donegall Road I envied some boys who were playing football. We weren't allowed to play games outside on Sunday. When I questioned why they were, I was told that they were Catholics and that their Sunday ended at twelve o'clock. So my early consciousness of the religious difference was that Protestants were deprived ... not allowed to play outside on Sunday. When I was growing up Sundays were strictly observed by Protestants. 'Good clothes' were worn. From quite an early age until I was 15 and had left school I wasn't allowed outside on a Sunday, because I didn't have a good suit, or rather I did, but my mother had to pawn it. She never had the money to redeem it, so it was lost. Privileged position my eye!

June was the start of our collecting material for the 11th July bonfires. People had to be wary. Any decent piece of wood or even furniture left unattended could be commandeered and added to the pyre. When the schools broke up for the summer holidays at the end of June, we went into overdrive. We would head for the Lagan towpath, hatchets down belts, ready to chop down the trees … well, saplings and branches. Getting there from where we lived entailed cutting through some middle-class areas. We would often raid orchards on our way … convincing ourselves that the rock-hard, bitter little crab apples were worth the risk. There was always the danger of being stopped by the police and having our names taken. Having our names taken! This happened quite a lot for one reason or another. Our names were taken for playing football in the street; trespassing on the railway; lighting fires in the back entries; or just standing at the street corner. Back to the bonfires. We always strived to have the biggest bonfire in the district. We mounted raids on other streets' material and fiercely defended our own. It was common practice to build a hut in the middle of our pile, so that we could mount guard overnight. The police were very down on this, because of the risk of fire … either arson by a rival gang, or an accident. The allocated 'leader of the bonfire' had his name taken … entered in an RUC notebook.

I was very proud when the day came that I was the allocated leader. I couldn't wait to get my name put in the RUC notebook. The RUC must have had a huge budget for notebooks! They took all these names but it was only on a very rare occasion that they took things further. I was never taken to court, but one or two were, usually for the crime of playing football in the street. A fine of 10 or 15 shillings was usually imposed. To us in the '50s and '60s, 10 or 15 shillings was quite a large sum.

To my recollection Catholics were never mentioned during this bonfire period. Or rarely, perhaps in an abusive song. Our rivals were fellow Protestants trying to steal our wood, or set our fire alight prematurely on the day. We always held off as long as possible before erecting the pyre. Yes, once or twice rather inept effigies of the Pope were put on the top of the pyre and a cheer would go up when the flames reached it ... but it only happened rarely. We always tried to delay lighting our fire until all the others in the district were blazing. Quite often interfering adults would cause it to be lit early so that the 'wee ones' could see it. That happened the year I was 'leader of the bonfire'. I was furious. The RUC took me seriously enough to put my name in a notebook, the neighbours ignored my status. Another tricky issue was when the Eleventh fell on a Saturday or a Sunday. If it fell on the former the fire would be lit mid-evening ... so that it wasn't burning fiercely into Sunday. If it fell on a Sunday, then the match couldn't be struck until after midnight ... such was the respect for the Sabbath.

After the Eleventh ... the Twelfth. I can't recall ever being up early enough to see the Orangemen marching to the Field when I was a boy. I could make it at around 5 p.m. for their return. One ambition was to carry the string of the banner, but I wasn't a member of the Junior Orange Order, nor did I have any really close relative in the Order who didn't have a child of his own. Of course it would have entailed rising very early and walking a long way. I wasn't Protestant enough for that.

On the Twelfth day some of the adults would retire to the front first-floor lounge of Moses Hunter's pub. This was situated on the corner of Donegall Road, Shaftesbury Square, Bradbury Place. I was in it once ... when my Uncle Bobbie was home from Canada ... although I was too young to drink, in fact too young to be in a pub at all but for the day that was in it. When we were too young to know better we wondered if Moses Hunter was a Catholic, working on the theory that no self-respecting Protestant would work on the Twelfth day. The first-floor lounge offered a fine view of the Orangemen on their way to and from the Field at Finaghy. Pallets of strawberries were a great favourite on the day ... again the speculation was that the sellers must be Catholics ... they didn't support the Twelfth, but they took advantage of it. If they were Catholics they were allowed to carry on their business unmolested. Some years later I was a bus conductor on the Shankill Road on the Twelfth. I was accused of being a 'Fenian' because I was working on 'the day'. This came just as the bus passed the top of the street where I actually lived. As was to be proved during the later Troubles, establishing facts was never a priority in Belfast. If Moses Hunter was a Catholic, it was Protestants who were buying his drink. If the Catholic vendors were selling strawberries, it was Protestants who were buying them. It was Protestants who were happily riding the bus up the Shankill Road. There was never any logic in sectarianism.

There was an IRA 'border campaign' in the '50s. During an outing with friends near Maghera (quite a way from the border!) we had to make a long detour because a bridge had been blown up. Protestants generally didn't worry about the campaign. They were convinced the RUC, especially supported by the 'B' Specials, could deal with it. For us lads in the city the 'B' Specials were no heroes. They were a menace. They kept moving us on from the corner. They threatened to take our names ... again ... when we pointed out that it was the corner of our own street. We'd sullenly move away and gather at the other end of the street. An hour or so later they would appear there too ... and move us on again.

Growing up

Money was not plentiful. We gathered at the corner almost every night ... and surrounded by a semi-circle of spit, took the reputation of every young female who passed up or down the road. Apart from going to the cinema, chasing girls was the main preoccupation of our lives. I had a lot of jobs as a young man ... and in every place I worked the workforce was mixed, Catholics and Protestants. There was one girl in a certain factory and I thought she was absolutely beautiful, I desired her like no other. It became known that she fancied another fella ... from Sandy Row. He refused to talk to her, because she was a Catholic. I found such conduct absolutely unbelievable. For me and my mates they really only had to be females ... to hell with religion ... get your priorities right!

A cousin and myself had a brief flirtation with republicanism. We read an article on Michael Collins in a *Reader's Digest*. It was a highly romanticised account of his fight for Irish freedom ... and we decided he deserved our help. One night we set out to walk to Dublin and join up. The railway ran to Dublin ... so off we went, full of enthusiasm ... that got us as far as Dunmurry. We decided we'd go home and save up the train fare. Then we discovered to our horror that Michael Collins was dead ... and had been for some time ... so died our flirtation.

My mother always urged us to treat people as we found them. Never to judge them on grounds of colour or creed. It was a lesson I absorbed. It was how she lived her life. I was brought up with some people who believed that every bad day in their lives was the fault of the 'other side'. That was never the case in my immediate family. When I was 15 I joined up ... the Junior Leaders Battalion, RAC. I was sent to Bovington Camp in Dorset. It was a great melting pot of colours and creeds and my mother's advice was very useful. One day on field craft exercise on the top of a hill the Sergeant pointed out T. E. Lawrence's cottage ... it meant nothing to me then ... nor the fact that he died in the Military

Hospital at Bovington, at that time still standing. The fact that Thomas Hardy had lived just down the road left me cold too. We were taken to Dorchester Museum one day, where there was a reconstruction of Hardy's study ... but I wasn't to read any Hardy until many years later. *Jude the Obscure* was one of the books I studied for 'O' Level and has since become a favourite novel of mine. Also there have been many return trips to Dorset and visits to Lawrence of Arabia and Hardy sites. Most Sundays I would walk the couple of miles from Bovington Camp to Moreton village where T. E. Lawrence is buried, but then it was to see a girl, not to pay homage. Then chasing girls was still the priority. That particular girl is still a friend over 50 years later. When Thomas Hardy died his heart was removed and was buried in Poet's Corner in Westminster Abbey. His body is buried in Stinsford churchyard. A few graves away lies his great admirer, Cecil Day-Lewis.

My first leave from Bovington was at Christmas, 1960. The night before I was due to return to camp a policeman knocked on our door. My father had taken his own life. The policeman was wearing a Glentoran scarf and I chatted to him about football. Although we lived close to Windsor Park, home of Linfield, I supported Glentoran, as did ... suddenly now past tense, 'had' ... my Father. I was granted a compassionate extension to my leave. My father was buried from a funeral parlour on the Crumlin Road, not from his home. There was still a stigma about suicide. At the time attempted suicide was still a crime, but ...

I attended the funeral in uniform and greatcoat. It didn't appear to excite or irritate anyone. Standing by his grave in the City Cemetery didn't elicit any hostile reaction either. Not something that would have been advisable after 1969.

Returning to camp proved something of an ordeal. Army greatcoats and difficult journeys becoming something of a family tradition. First the long night crossing to Heysham. I watched the lights of Belfast falling away behind us ... a Belfast without my father. He hadn't left any note. We had no way of knowing why he did it. Yes, he'd just recently lost his parents ... but didn't he have me? Wasn't I reason enough for him to want to live? There were also my three siblings. Guilt, hurt, confusion, a sense of having failed him in some way. A million confused memories as we crossed the dark water. I needed the comfort of my family, not to be journeying back to England on my own.

Off the boat in the cold early morning, tired, hurting. On to the train and the long journey to London. Wearing an Army uniform, making me play a role I didn't in the least feel up to. Ate the sandwiches my mother had made for me. The train arrived at Euston Station. My train to Wool, in Dorset, left from Waterloo. The journey across London. All my sandwiches long gone. Feeling tired, hungry and frustrated. Asking my father questions in my head. Why? Why? Why? Receiving no satisfactory answers.

London mainline stations were the haunt of predatory homosexual men in those days and it appeared young soldiers were their favourite prey. They would try to grab your case, by the way they were going to help you. They took some shaking off, what with their aggressive, threatening behaviour. These looked like men of my father's age. At Waterloo I discovered my train was considerably delayed. The seedy men circling. In the end you tried to tag on to groups of ordinary-looking men and women. Tried to look like you were part of a group. The hunger was growing. I had one last half-crown in my pocket.

Paddy and the pies

I was very partial to Lyons' individual fruit pies in those days. Were they one shilling then? Half a crown. Two pies and a cup of tea. Selected my two at a station buffet and proffered my coin. The woman refused to take it. I was devastated. 'Sorry Paddy, it's Irish, I can't take it.' It might have been Irish, I bloody well wasn't – standing there in a British Army uniform. She couldn't be persuaded. I told her it was all I had, that I was hungry, that I was returning from leave and my train was delayed. 'Sorry Paddy' and she turned her attention to her next customer.

A long hungry haul to Dorset. Late leaving London, very late arriving at Wool. There was no transport waiting. Trucks used to meet the trains up until a certain time. It was well past that certain time. It was a four- or five-mile walk to camp. I had to carry my suitcase, not a modern affair then, no handle and wheels. It was dark. It was darker than dark. Once I left the lighted area around the station I was plunged into a pitch black Dorset night. It was difficult even to see the border between the grass verge and the road. It was a long trudge, the suitcase growing heavier all the time, switching hands becoming more frequent. There wasn't even an isolated telephone kiosk from which I could maybe call the camp guard-room. Even if there had been, an Irish half-crown wouldn't fit the slot, Paddy! Everyone was asleep when I finally arrived. I had to waken the hut NCO. Thankfully he was friendly and sympathetic, not attributes he'd ever shown before. I cried myself to sleep that night and for many nights afterwards, quietly in the darkness. It was unsoldierly conduct. C. S. Lewis was right – grief is like a physical pain. Life in the Army was never the same for me again. A transfer to the Infantry at Oswestry only delayed my final departure from the Army.

Restless

Toing and froing to England for a number of years ... Huddersfield, Manchester, Hayes in Middlesex. For a spell working on a boat plying between Belfast and Liverpool. I was interviewed for a job on a Head Line boat, Belfast to Philadelphia. I got the job and was given a date to sail. Stormy seas seriously delayed our return from Liverpool to Belfast. As we limped slowly up the Belfast Lough, the ship I was due to sail to Philadelphia on sailed slowly down and passed us on its voyage out. So instead of 'Philadelphia here I come', it was Manchester. I couldn't think of a worse reason for turning someone down for a job, or denying them a house than because of their religion. That wasn't the way my mother brought us up. So I joined the Campaign for Social Justice in Northern Ireland. They sent packages of their leaflets, which I used to distribute around Manchester ... in pubs, cafes, hospital outpatients' departments and libraries. There was a great irony here. As I tramped the streets there were signs in windows: 'Flat to let. No blacks or Irish need apply.' Try convincing an English landlady in the 1960s that you were British, not Irish. 'Sorry Paddy, it's just been taken.'

As a teenager I was not a great reader. When I did read a book what I enjoyed most were the dialogue sections. One wet day I dropped into the West Didsbury branch of the library, distributed my leaflets; but lingered to shelter from the rain. It was rain ... it was Manchester. To pass the time I browsed and made a wonderful discovery ... whole shelves of books that were all dialogue ... playscripts! Delighted with this discovery I joined the library and read all the scripts they possessed. Shaw and O'Casey pleased me most, especially the former – still my favourite playwright.

Many jobs and girls later, 1965, I met my wife. I'd returned home to replenish and return to England. Met a girl who was different. Delayed my departure. Fell in love, got engaged and on 10 September, 1966 got married in St. Thomas' Church on the Lisburn Road. We went to live on the Shankill Road. To my mind 1966 marks the beginning of the Troubles. The murders of Peter Ward and John Patrick Scullion, attacks on the police. A hand grenade was thrown at policemen in McDonnell Street. Tensions were building up. There was talk of a 1916-like rebellion, only this time in Belfast on the fiftieth anniversary of the original rebellion. There'd been the sectarian antics of Ian Paisley ... an attack on the Governor of Northern Ireland. The reckless parade through Cromac Square that preceded it. The Divis Street riots, orchestrated by Paisley. I was working on the night shift in Mackies Engineering works. As we made our way up the Springfield Road we could 'hear' the rioting.

August 1969 saw the attack on the Apprentice Boys in Londonderry and then the Battle of the Bogside.

Gerry Fitt made a reckless and irresponsible intervention. He called people onto the streets of Belfast, to take the pressure off the Bogside, and then we were all in it! Who did what to whom, why and when, etc. It was argued about at the time ... it is still argued about. I had one child and was terrified that our home might be attacked and she'd be hurt, or worse. With other local men I became a vigilante. We tramped around the streets in the early hours of the morning. I can't speak for everyone but my only weapon was a stick. We never encountered any Catholic attackers, but we were charged with stopping fellow Protestants stealing coal from back-yards and breaking into houses and robbing the meters. A lot of people had gone to stay with relatives in safer areas. Eventually I moved my own family up to the Ballygomartin to stay with my aunt. To stay in the house where my father had killed himself. He never met his granddaughter ... he never met any of his grandchildren. I attended a founding meeting of the UDA on the Shankill Road. We were assured there was an organisation and that the leaders were in place ... just sign on the dotted line. Anyone who didn't want to join was asked to leave. Myself and another neighbour did. Many decent, well-intentioned men did join ... and many of them lived to bitterly regret it. We eventually left the Shankill Road and went to live in Donaghadee, with our three children. My first three plays, *The Death of Humpty Dumpty*, *The Closed Door* and *Dorothy* came from that period on the Shankill Road. *The Hidden Curriculum* owed something to that and something to my experiences as a schoolteacher in Bangor.

Politics

I tend to vote in every election nowadays, more to make the system work than with any great conviction. During my years in Northern Ireland I voted three times, once for Terence O'Neill and twice for the 'converted' Brian Faulkner. For a lot of people in Northern Ireland it's a matter of voting against someone rather than voting for someone. If anyone calls me Paddy now, with or without fruit pies, I contradict them. I'm British and very proud of it. At a reception hosted by Charles Haughey in the Mansion House in Dublin I wrote 'British' in the nationality section of the visitors' book. I was roundly attacked by the then Artistic Director of the Abbey Theatre, but that's what I am. Not Northern Irish/British ... just British. I love Northern Ireland because it's British. Having said that I have very warm feelings for the Republic of Ireland ... despite that letter of condolence to the German people on the death of Hitler ... my early work was staged in Dublin. I have many friends there and respect them as Irish, so therefore expect them to respect me as British.

Seamus Mallon rightly described the Good Friday Agreement as 'Sunningdale for slow learners'. I supported the Sunningdale Agreement. It wasn't perfect, but to borrow from Michael Collins ... it could have been a stepping stone to a 'perfect' agreement ... in so far as any political agreement can be perfect. It should have been given time to bed in and be seen to work in the interests of both sides in Northern Ireland. Again the primitive roar of Ian Paisley came thundering down the years to wreck it. It's salutary to look through the publication *Lost Lives* and just reflect how many were lost since the Sunningdale Agreement was wrecked in 1974.[1] We are where we are, and as I don't live in Northern Ireland now some might say it's none of my business, but we do have memories and I have many friends and loved ones who do live there. We shouldn't be where we are. We should be somewhere better, with better people in charge of things. The people who are in charge should be 'on a charge' for all manner of appalling crimes and for incitement to all manner of appalling crimes. Ian Paisley shook my hand as I left his church one Sunday morning. He asked me where I was from and I said 'London'. 'Oh, a terrible place, terrible place', he said. It reminded me of a young music teacher I met when I gave a talk at a Catholic school in Country Antrim. She also said London was a terrible place. 'At least they don't shoot you because of your religion', I said. 'No', she replied, 'they don't need an excuse.'

***

I have visited the Western Front many times. I found my 'Uncle Bill's' name on the Cambrai Memorial to the missing: Second Lieutenant William John Graham, Royal Irish Rifles, 1917. In Mouvres Cemetery Extension there are a number of British war graves. One is dedicated to an unknown Second Lieutenant of the Royal Irish Rifles, who died in 1917. I wonder? I mentioned him in a play once, *Lengthening Shadows*. Described him from letters his colleagues sent. Described how he met his death.

An aunt, on my mother's side, said the *Titanic* sank because my stupid Granda forgot to put the waterproof paint on it. They're all dead now – aunts, uncles, grandfathers, grandmothers, mother, even an ex-wife. I know why they all died ... but my father ... I don't know why my father died.

Note

1. D. McKittrick, Brian Feeney and Seamus Kelters (1999), *Lost Lives: the Stories of the Men, Women and Children Who Died as a Result of the Northern Ireland Troubles* (Edinburgh: Mainstream).

12

Labour Aristocracies, Triumphalism and Melancholy: Misconceptions of the Protestant Working-Class and Loyalist Community

Gareth Mulvenna

Introduction

Although all working-class Protestants are not per se loyalists, it is loyalist constituencies which are ostensibly inhabited by working-class Protestants; those who have borne witness to the proliferation of a number of socio-economic problems over the past three decades in particular. In 2004 a Northern Ireland Department for Social Development Task Force survey entitled 'Renewing Communities' drew attention to the problems affecting Protestant working-class areas of inner-city Belfast such as Sandy Row, Shankill and the Village.[1] Philip Orr has highlighted how the report diagnosed 'low educational attainment, low aspirations, physical and mental problems and apparent acceptance of economic inactivity', drawing attention to 'fragmentation within the community' and 'an absence of strong, benign and effective local leadership'.[2]

This chapter seeks to explore how this situation has come to be by exploring two key themes which are often associated with Northern Ireland's Protestant working class, with particular reference to the loyalist component of that community. The first theme surrounds popular discourses in relation to the concept of 'labour aristocracies' – notably the manner in which the use of this term has obscured the realities of the Protestant working-class experience. It is argued that descriptions of the Protestant working class as historically 'privileged' has created a distorting effect on commentaries about the current malaise in the Protestant working class and loyalist community. The second theme explored is the perceived notion of Protestant 'triumphalism' and the extent to which this ultra-nationalistic phenomenon has shaped expressions and external perceptions of Protestant working-class identity socially, culturally and politically.

By combining analyses of these two themes it is intended that this chapter shall demonstrate that a more nuanced understanding of the Protestant working-class experience can lead to a better understanding of its hopes, fears and aspirations as an integral part of the overall British working-class community.

The chapter ultimately illuminates the key factors behind the Belfast Protestant working class's journey from being a proud British working community to being perceived as a 'lumpenproletariat' and concludes that by recapturing something of the civic life that existed before the Troubles, things might slowly be turned back in their favour, re-empowering a community which for so long has been bereft of strong leadership and kinship networks.

Loyalism and the Protestant working class: #flegs and 'poor white trash'

On Monday 3 December 2012 an amendment motion was passed by Belfast City Council which meant that the Union flag which had flown over the dome of Belfast's City Hall for 365 days a year for many decades would be retired for all but 17 designated days. Sinn Féin and the SDLP had originally demanded that the flag be drawn down completely but it was only the intervention of the Alliance Party, who tabled the amendment, that saved the disappearance of the Union flag from Belfast's civic centrepiece altogether.[3] For something which amounted to a symbolic neutering of unionist and loyalist identity in Northern Ireland's capital city the months which led up to the vote saw surprisingly little coverage of the upcoming motion. In mid-November however a leaflet accusing the Alliance Party of 'un-unionist activities' in relation to the upcoming motion was distributed by DUP and UUP councillors in Belfast. When the motion was passed loyalists, enraged by what they viewed as the continuing erosion of their cultural identity, took to the streets in protest.[4] One of the most important mediums for following the progress of the flag protests was through the social networking sites Twitter and Facebook. While loyalists used Facebook to set up discussion groups informing their followers of where flag protests would be staged, many people uninvolved in the protests used Twitter to vent their frustrations at how the protests were affecting their daily lives.

One of the trends which emerged on Twitter throughout the first week or so of the flag protests was the use of the 'hash-tag' entitled 'flegs', i.e. #flegs. This play on the perceived pronunciation of the word 'flag' by working-class loyalists[5] became an integral part of the discourse used by many people on Twitter. Indeed 'flegs' entered the wider lexicon and was used by journalists and others. The use of a colloquialism such as 'flegs' and the continuing reference to the protestors' attire of sports and leisure clothing demonstrated an obvious contempt for the loyalists' socio-economic background. The journalist Eamonn McCann tackled this issue in the *Belfast Telegraph* in the second week of January, stating:

> Flags is the word – not 'flegs', much as a number of commentators seem to relish the chance to sneer at a section of the less well-off without fear of being labelled offensive.
>
> If they derided Dubliners' accents in the same way, they'd be told to button their lips if they can't keep a civil tongue in their heads.[6]

McCann's assertion probed, or at least should have probed, searching questions of those involved in the peace process and the so-called 'silent majority' who used the term 'fleg' liberally in their online discourse. Henry McDonald once played to this constituency in *The Observer* when he commented that working-class loyalists comprised the 'least fashionable community in Western Europe'.[7] This sort of comment seemed positively endearing when considered against the denigration of people who came onto the streets based on their accents and clothing. Depressingly some of the main protagonists of this abuse were working-class Catholics – a community that should know better than most the damage and frustration that can be caused when a community is pushed to the fringes of society.

The flag protests and the manner in which they were debated – in crass social class terms – around Christmas 2012 and the months after brought to bear, more than ever before, the vast chasm that had emerged in post-ceasefire Belfast. While the stoppages, and to a certain extent the climate of fear which the protests caused, did no favours for the economy in Belfast many of the people decrying the loyalists on the street and the effect that their actions were having on retail and hospitality in the city seemed unable to comprehend an important factor. The protesting loyalists did not see the 'new' city centre as a place in which they were welcome anyway. While the city council congratulated itself on the commercial rebranding of Belfast as 'Our time, our place' it relegated in people's minds the long-simmering disconnect between the city centre economy and the reality of the socio-economic backgrounds of a large number of the young loyalists who emerged on the streets before and after Christmas.

When the protesting loyalists marched from Protestant working-class areas such as the Shankill, Newtownards Road and Tiger's Bay to the City Hall on various occasions in the run-up to Christmas, the city became a contested space and a cleavage emerged between those who felt fulfilled by the Cathedral Quarter and Victoria Square and those who felt socially and economically marginalised – a process which had been crystallised in the removal of the flag. In 1997, long before the 'new' city had emerged Shirlow had observed that '... while sectarian animosity is still visible among all social classes, a growing body of evidence supports the thesis that the middle classes, irrespective of their religious affiliations, increasingly share similar lifestyles and socio-economic pursuits, which are mutually agreeable and inherently less antagonistic'.[8] With the realignment of the retail and hospitality industries into Victoria Square and the Cathedral Quarter by the mid-point of the last decade (circa 2006 onwards) a new middle ground was created which accelerated the 'mutually agreeable' and 'less antagonistic' lifestyles and socio-economic pursuits Shirlow had observed a decade previously. During the flags controversy it was these very people that complained about the effect that the protests were having on the city centre economy. Crucially this middle ground had failed to comprehend that the economy which had blurred any previous sectarian lines among the middle classes in Belfast had actually alienated further those who felt they had no stake in the city centre economy or the peace process. Indeed, another campaign was launched in January 2013 in which people were encouraged to 'Take Back the City' by which they would be 'Backin' Belfast'.[9]

As well as the latter campaign's function as a thinly veiled gimmick to prop up the bars and restaurants of Belfast city centre during the traditionally quiet post-Christmas period, the 'riots' of January 2013, confined to a small enclave in East Belfast as they were, were no challenge to May 1974 by way of comparison; when the Ulster Workers' Council strike demonstrated the Protestant working class's ability to bring Northern Ireland grinding to a halt. This was a slightly easier battle for the new urban middle class to win. A toxic mixture of economic instability and constitutional uncertainty fed into the events of December 2012 and January 2013, and elements within the Protestant working class projected a confused and ambiguous message which didn't chime with those who had enjoyed the apparently cosmopolitan city centre of Belfast.

In the two decades before the flags controversy there had been a lot of soul-searching carried out by working-class Protestants in relation to their socio-economic identity, particularly in the period immediately after the Belfast Agreement. In an article written for *The Blanket* in 2002 the late Billy Mitchell, with typically admirable candour, drew comparisons between the 'poor white trash' of the American Deep South and the Protestant working class of Northern Ireland.[10] Mitchell was a former UVF leader who had been a follower of Ian Paisley for a time during the 1960s.[11] Having grown up in abject poverty in Glengormley, a then semi-rural suburb just outside north Belfast, Mitchell eventually served 14 years in jail for his part in the killing of two Ulster Defence Association members on 7 April 1975 during a loyalist paramilitary feud.[12] Mitchell's observation about the Protestant working class in 2002 was formed on the basis of lived experience. As well as coming from that community himself his work in the LINC Resource Centre on Belfast's York Road in the years before his death brought him into close contact with the Protestant non-working and underclasses in areas such as Tiger's Bay and Rathcoole in the city as well as south-east Antrim towns like Larne. Responding to some of the themes in Mitchell's article Brian Kelly, also writing in *The Blanket*, agreed with the analogy between the 'poor white trash' in the USA and the Protestant working class in Belfast:

> ... in many ways it is an analogy that fits: callously abandoned in social and economic terms by the rulers of a society to which they have so enthusiastically proclaimed their loyalty over many, many years; sneered at, manipulated by, and regarded with a mixture of pity and contempt by 'respectable' elements in their 'own community'; and diverted from pursuing joint struggle alongside their fellow workers from the Falls or the Short Strand by their entanglement in a deep-rooted, reactionary historical tradition, like the Southern white working class during the civil rights era they are too easily held up as 'the culprits' in the recent upsurge of sectarian barbarism.[13]

Although Kelly's pejorative criticism of Protestant working-class social and political culture would have rankled with most grassroots loyalists such as Mitchell, his bemoaning of the lack of opportunity for consistent working-class solidarity in Northern Ireland would have had a sympathetic ear in many quarters of Belfast's Protestant working class with its once-proud Labourist traditions. Events in the ten years after the Belfast Agreement would have caused much consternation to those within that constituency as they tried to wrest control from the unwieldy criminal elements in their midst. Less than a year before Billy

Mitchell passed away, in September 2005, working-class loyalist areas of Belfast exploded in what at the time was regarded as an apocalyptic bout of rioting and anti-social behaviour. Various theories abounded about the violence, with some considering that it was the modern loyalist paramilitaries reminding society of their potential muscle in the wake of interference in their 'crime empires', while others suggested with an apparently unironic sense of mist-clearing polemic that a new loyalist 'underclass' had emerged in the wake of the Belfast Agreement. Some journalists used the riots as a means by which to attack the loyalist working class and the historical dominance of Protestants in the Northern Irish labour market. Briege Gadd suggested that Protestant workers had been knocked off their 'top dog podium' by having the 'certainties' of traditional employment terminated.[14] In his cultural and religious criticisms of the Protestant community more widely, but with particular reference to the working class, Max Hastings was unambiguous about the situation as he saw it: 'When unification comes, Northern Ireland's Protestants may be amazed by the wealth and happiness which accrue to their children, once they shed the baggage of Cromwell as icon, the Orange Order, mafia rule and institutionalised bigotry.'[15] Gadd and Hastings both used condemnatory language and were seemingly unable to conceal their delight at the collapse of the grand narratives of civic, cultural and political unionism and Britishness which had held the Protestant/unionist/loyalist community together in perceived dominance of their Catholic neighbours for so much of recent history. These analyses were unhelpful and did not get to the crux of the underlying problems which have stunted social and economic progress in Protestant working-class communities across Belfast.

Labour aristocracies, civil rights quandaries and community fragmentation

Much of the present in Northern Ireland is so often anchored in its turbulent past. In this respect there has been no better demonstration of the seemingly constant repetition of history than when the flag protests emerged. Gadd, for example, is confident in her analysis that the Protestant working class were the 'top dogs' who constituted a labour aristocracy in Northern Ireland. The truth is that ordinary working-class Protestants had never felt anything but anxiety about their position within the Northern Ireland state or its economy, and thus the UK as a whole. Whereas the overwhelming majority of studies about Northern Ireland's turbulent contemporary political history have portrayed the late 1960s as a period when the country was at war with itself due to the competing forces of Civil Rights campaigners protesting against forty-odd years of unionist misrule, while the Protestant/unionist/loyalist community and the Royal Ulster Constabulary and 'B' Specials beat down the 'traitors' within the Catholic community for daring to criticise their cherished Stormont Parliament. This narrative fits in with the long-held perception of 'Protestant Exceptionalism'; a concept and false consciousness which appeared to be drip-fed from 'Big House' unionists whose main uses for the Protestant working class were industrial labour, votes and later – in the 1960s – street agitation.

It came as a surprise to many when during the flag protests of the winter of 2012–13 the loyalist working class began to talk about their 'civil rights'. In terms of the familiar lexicons of Northern Irish social and political discourse this was a new development. Protestants have however never felt anything but anxiety about their position within the Northern Ireland state and thus the United Kingdom as a whole. The flag protests in 2012–13 were a stark demonstration of this; but were things that different at the dawn of what became known as the 'Troubles'?

In February 1969, during heightened tensions between the Civil Rights campaigners and the government, Raidió Teilifís Éireann (RTÉ) filmed and broadcast a 'news special' which attempted to capture the mood music on the Falls and Shankill Roads. On the Shankill reporters followed Alex Scott, who came across as just a typical working-class Protestant living in an extremely loyalist area which has been described as the 'heart of the Empire'.[16] Far from being the hot-blooded and impassive *Herrenvolk* that many viewers in the Republic of Ireland would have expected, Scott seemed quite overwhelmed by everything that was going on around him in his little world. Interviewed in his front room, Scott's main concerns lay with his young family. The narrator reminded the viewer that the Scott family's attitude to the social and political malaise is informed not by the recent history of Ireland, or of the world, but 'the history of the small community within these narrow streets …'.[17] Scott and his family referred to the better relations which exist between the young people. They described youths meeting up at dancehalls in Belfast City centre and bemoaned the fact that it is the older generation, who remember the previous Troubles of the 1920s, who are bitterer at the state of Northern Ireland in 1969.[18]

When the talk turned to Prime Minister Captain Terence O'Neill the mood in the film changed and Scott's friend, who had remained silent up to this point, sitting beside him on the family sofa, interjected angrily – 'He'll (O'Neill) be out next ... sure he's sacking all our Ministers. He's selling us out. He's letting these Civil Rights marchers march, and when we wanna march we can't march.'[19] Scott and his friend are symbolic of the forces, not always mutually exclusive, which have always been at the heart of Northern Ireland's Protestant working class, in particular since the formation of the state in 1921. Scott represents the ordinary Protestant working man who is loyal first and foremost to his family, then to his immediate community and then to his country. Scott's friend on the other hand sees the denial of his cultural right to march as paramount and his dismay at Catholics apparently being given preferential treatment by the state in this respect is indicative of the solicitude surrounding potential 'sell-out' and 'surrender'.

Due to the inexorable rise of Paisleyism and the undermining of O'Neill's tenure as Prime Minister in the latter half of the 1960s, the Protestant working class found itself in a state of flux. While a number of young men joined the recently formed UVF at this time to assist in agitation and the undermining of O'Neill's credibility[20] there was also a tangible sense of frustration at the perceived partisan stance which the Northern Ireland Civil Rights Association had adopted – indeed some Protestants saw the campaign for Civil Rights as exclusionary. It wasn't just that some were convinced that NICRA was a Trojan horse for an emergent Irish republican conspiracy in the wake of the fiftieth anniversary of the 1916 Easter Rising; ordinary working-class Protestants simply could not comprehend how they were any better off than Catholics. Although Billy Mitchell was a biblical and political follower of Paisley at this time, he explained that class unity should have been the defining feature of the Civil Rights campaign. He was one of many working-class Protestants at the time who viewed the movement as being constitutionally driven rather than representing a true appeal for working-class solidarity in opposition to the Stormont regime:

> The 1960s wasn't just about being seduced by Paisley. I think the Civil Rights movement had a role to play in it too: 'One man, one vote for Catholics', 'Civil rights for Catholics'. The whole thing was sectarian – Hutchy's father was right;[21] I got a slum quicker than a Catholic, but it's still a slum. If it had been about uniting the working class – and I think that's something that the likes of Cathal Goulding would have wanted – but it came to us as working class Prods that this is simply about civil rights for Catholics: 'One man, one vote'; I didn't have a vote. Unless you were a property owner you didn't have a vote.[22]

The perception of inequality in housing was particularly vexing for residents of working-class Protestant areas such as the Shankill. Mitchell recalled how conditions in the Falls and Shankill were similar and also underlined the manner in which bosses in the large industrial work-places used the threat of the Catholic working class replacing Protestant workers if they considered dissenting:

> We needed better housing too ... I remember the old Shankill – there was absolutely no difference in the housing in the Lower Shankill and the Lower Falls. In the early days when Ballymurphy was built for instance it was nearly all Prods that lived there so there's no difference in a house in Ballymurphy and New Barnsley or the old houses on the Shankill and the Falls. There might have been a difference in jobs but Mackie's philosophy was 'if you don't like it there's a hundred Taigs'll take your job tomorrow' – that was exploitation.[23]

While deindustrialisation occurred in other parts of the UK after the 1960s, and the shipyards of the Clydeside, Tyneside and Merseyside suffered, these working-class communities did not have the added stresses of political violence to contend with. If one considers the shipyard as the main employer of working-class Protestants then it is perhaps neces-sary to further put into perspective their experience as workers there. A shipyard worker who had been interviewed by Sam Hanna Bell during the first half of the century highlighted the degrading effect of lining up to be chosen for work (cited by Megahey in 2009):

> You always left your pride and dignity at home when you went down to the Cattle Market. Everybody was pushin' so as the foreman would get a good view of you when he came out. It was damnable to hear your mates squabbling among themselves about who was standing in front of who. It was humiliation all right.[24]

Between 1960 and 1985 manufacturing declined by 45 per cent and by 1985 Harland and Wolff (with a large government subsidy) employed only 4000 in comparison with 26,000 in 1945.[25] During this period of economic freefall the violent atmosphere of the early 1970s in Northern Ireland brought a sense of deep anguish to both sides of the community. Catholics suffered indiscriminately at the hands of roam-ing loyalist murder gangs, while both Catholics and Protestants had to endure the IRA's bombing campaigns which were intended to destroy the commercial vitality and viability of Belfast city centre in an effort to force the British to retreat on economic grounds.

This combination of violence and deindustrialisation affected the Protestant working class in a unique manner which is perhaps best understood by referring at least in part to Paul Willis' classic 1977 study *Learning to Labour*. In Willis' study he noted that the 'lads' (a group terminology used by Willis to describe his working-class research subjects) had formed an 'oppositional culture' to education, conditioned by social and economic circumstances to believe that they were predestined to an unskilled job in the industrial workplace.[26] There has been a general consensus, perhaps too easily unquestioned in every instance,[27] that the Protestant working-class attitude in Belfast to education was similar to that of the lads in Willis' study. Due to the process of deindustrialisation, however, the jobs that would have been available to the forebears of Willis' lads and young Protestant working-class males in Northern Ireland from the 1970s onwards had become redundant. While working-class Protestants may have had easier access to employment, though no more privilege in their working conditions than their fellow workers across the water, their housing conditions were very often every bit as squalid as those of their Catholic neighbours. One need only look at Bill Kirk's 'Sandy Row 1974' photographic exhibition to witness the poor living conditions of working-class Protestants in the 1970s.

The need for slum clearances in the post-war era brought to bear another important process – redevelopment. Slum clearances began in the Shankill area during the late 1960s and early 1970s. The resultant redevelopment gave rise to the Belfast Urban Motorway project. Modernisation, however, did not account for the effect on community and kinship during a period in which people were already experiencing drastic upheaval due to the onset of the 'Troubles'. As Ron Wiener demonstrated in his seminal work *The Rape and Plunder of the Shankill*, the strong sense of community which had been present in the Shankill prior to the conflict was decimated and redevelopment pushed working-class people further out into the suburbs, thereby breaking up solid community and family networks.[28] The Shankill, with an ageing population, has never truly recovered from this. Divorced from the violent context of Northern Ireland at the time what happened to the Shankill is similar to what had happened to another proud working-class community – London's East End – during the late 1950s. As Phil Cohen has noted, plans to '"modernize" the pattern of East End life' were a disaster and did not allow for 'any effective participation by a local working-class community in the decision-making process at any stage or level of planning'.[29]

While housing in districts such as Dagenham and Greenleigh were substantially better than the slums that people had previously inhabited, there was no way in which planners could conjure the sense of community that had existed for generations. The strong kinship network which had sustained community morale was destroyed. If one views the Protestant working class with a similar perspective, albeit in tandem with the violence of the early 1970s and the resultant population movements across Belfast, and in some cases further afield, it is more possible to envisage a disorientated component part of British working-class life struggling to adapt to what had ostensibly become 'a place apart'.

Without community, without identity?

In tandem with the deindustrialisation and poorly planned redevelopment experienced by the Protestant working class in Belfast, the early 1970s also bore witness to a breakdown in previously solid social and civic structures due to the high levels of violence. A casualty of this was an already dying sense of 'Empire Britishness' which had, cosmetically at least, emboldened the worldview of the poorest Protestant workers.[30] More importantly the displacement of organisations such as the Boys' Brigade and the Scouts by the youth and senior wings of loyalist paramilitaries in many instances led to the dwindling of a finer sense of purpose which would have perhaps buffered the degrading effects of unemployment. The emergence of paramilitaries in Northern Ireland during the late 1960s and early 1970s contributed to a hypermasculine environment and allowed for a short-term means of community identification among young Protestant males in lieu of industry.

Nelson has described how the social breakdown experienced in the early 1970s affected Protestant working-class communities in particular, stating that 'Traditional bodies like the Orange Order were already alarmed that their control of the social order was slipping and were very concerned about the rise in teenage violence, under-age drinking, Sunday drinking in clubs, etc. They blamed paramilitary groups particularly for encouraging these trends. But the sort of people who looked with distaste on the Orange Order also objected to dealing with gunmen whom they saw as lawless and sectarian.'[31] The early years of the Troubles inevitably brought challenges to the traditional social order of society within Protestant working-class areas which were by now hollowed-out imitations of previously strong communities. Schisms became increasingly apparent with the prominent emergence of the UDA. While many ordinary Protestants would have lamented the negative impact that the UDA's existence was having on working-class areas, there were also many who, in the words of Nelson, regarded the paramilitaries 'like the curate's egg – good in parts'.[32] A microcosm of the increasingly quiet admiration that many Protestants perhaps felt for the loyalist paramilitaries at this time is somewhat accurately described by Bell, who has written of Gusty Spence's transition from perceived villainous sectarian murderer in the mid-1960s to loyalist folk hero by the early 1970s, when graffiti began to appear on gable walls in working-class Protestant areas which confidently declared that 'Gusty was right'.[33]

While the British economy was nosediving and the shipyards that had provided employment for many Protestants went into decline, there was scant opportunity for people to form new working identities. In loyalist areas the questioning of authority only really began in earnest when members of the UDA and particularly the UVF and Red Hand Commando were imprisoned during the 1970s. Up until then the narrative had appeared straightforward and in many ways reflected the rest of the British working class. For young men, particularly in working-class Protestant communities, the fledgling paramilitaries often provided them with an over-inflated sense of prestige just as jobs were beginning to disappear. When the conflict eventually petered out in the wake of Thatcherism these same young men and in many cases, their sons, found themselves faced with an increasingly feminised labour market in which they were obliged to take jobs that their fathers and grandfathers would have baulked at. In this respect the Protestant working class once again saw their experiences reflected in the industrial classes in the UK with McDowell noting 'In the UK, today still a predominantly white country, male manual workers are, of course, the group currently most threatened by deindustrialisation, economic change and the growing dominance of the service sector. Rates of unemployment are consistently higher for men in old manufacturing districts ...'[34]

The 'decade of centenaries' – triumphalism or melancholia in loyalist commemoration?

The decade and a half since the signing of the Belfast Agreement in 1998 have brought into sharp focus the contentious issue of parading and commemoration in Northern Ireland. The years 2012 to 2022 have been termed the 'decade of centenaries' and much interest has understandably fallen on the 100-year anniversaries of historical events such as the Ulster Covenant (1912), formation of the UVF (1913) and the Battle of the Somme (1916). There are many ways in which the commemorations of the Somme sacrifice in 1916 and, further back, the Battle of the Boyne in 1690 by loyalists are symbolic of a continuing need among working-class Protestants in particular to reaffirm a sense of civic and cultural community and belonging, rather than being designed solely to denigrate their Catholic neighbours. In his searing polemic on British multiculturalism and post-imperialism[35] Paul Gilroy, writing about Britain's continued citation of the anti-Nazi war, condemns that culture of remembrance as neurotic. He states that

> Making it a privileged point of entry into national identity and self-understanding reveals a desire to find a way back to the point where the national culture – operating on a more manageable scale of community and social life – was, irrespective of the suffering involved in the conflict, both comprehensible and habitable. That memory of the country at war against foes who are simply, tidily, and uncomplicatedly evil has recently acquired the status of an ethnic myth. It explains not only how a nation remade itself through war and victory but can also be understood as a rejection or deferral of its present problems. That process is driven by the need to get back to the place or moment before the country lost its moral and cultural bearings.[36]

It is perhaps safe to assume that if given the opportunity Gilroy would extend his vision of postcolonial melancholia to the Protestant community's commemoration of the Battle of the Boyne in 1690 and the Somme sacrifice. In fact if anything remembrance of these events may be, according to Edna Longley, '*exempla* or history-lessons: a heritage-pack as survival-kit'.[37] By blending something of Gilroy and Longley's observations on remembrance and commemoration it is possible to envisage why a large number of people in Northern Ireland and the rest of the UK remained perplexed and vexed by the Protestant working-class sense of social and cultural identity. In the context of the loyalist community's current sense of displacement and alienation from the peace process it is crucial to comprehend the reasons why such events are commemorated in the first place. In many respects the remembrance of these past events and the manner in which the Twelfth of July in particular is celebrated are representative of Protestant working-class attempts to form a sense of autonomy in a society from which they feel increasingly cut adrift. The narrative following the flags controversy is that Sinn Féin is involved in a 'cultural war' on Protestants and that their intent is to 'de-Britify' Belfast. While this perception is tangible it is clear that the loyalist community will fail to move forward by ring-fencing itself. Despite the very obvious socio-economic problems which exist in these communities, self-isolation and the 'No Surrender' ethos have led to an outsider image of loyalist triumphalism and lack of compromise.

In the summer of 2013 a Civil Rights camp was set up at Twaddell Avenue in North Belfast by loyalists who were angry at the Parades Commission decision to ban an Orange Lodge from completing its walk back to the hall in Ligoniel. Those who were involved in setting up and supporting the camp are aware of how it has been perceived but are adamant that it is a new, non-violent, reaction to injustices against loyalist culture; and representative of a bigger picture. Winston Irvine, PUP media spokesperson stated that 'whilst there is a very crude manifestation of it [loyalist fears] around parading, there is a much deeper malaise institutionally that isn't always being recognised or understood or acknowledged ... that has to be given some expression to; and we would certainly hope that a deeper, more critical analysis, would speak to the deep-rooted fears and concerns about the withdrawal and the impingement of civil rights'.[38] It is only by repoliticising the Protestant working class (the deeper analysis alluded to by Irvine) that any progress might hope to be achieved. This process may prove arduous due to political apathy among the Protestant working class in light of constant broken promises by the Ulster Unionists and the DUP, yet by engaging with and understanding Protestant working-class attitudes to the Somme episode in particular, much more than supposedly mawkish sentimentality and 'triumphalism' can be usefully extrapolated.

The Somme commemorations work on two levels. On the one hand loyalists can articulate through the 1 July parades the important role that their forefathers played in securing the freedoms and liberties that they associate with being British. On the other, the Somme marks an essentially parochial remembering of the contribution to the war effort. In both instances a clearer understanding of the Protestant working-class psyche can be seen to emerge – a confident and strident British working-class community; and more insularly a loyalist identity which has been used as a means of protection from perceived British government betrayals on many occasions over the past forty or so years. As Walker and Officer have stated,

Ulster Protestant responses to the Battle of the Somme were suggestive of a cathartic self-realisation: what they had said, and been told, about themselves was seen to be vindicated. Yet this brought no real sense of security in terms of 'national' belonging, as opposed to the strong sense of ethnic self-preservation and survival which was perceived as having been forged through fire.[39]

These discourses have been replicated throughout the Troubles period as a means of self-sufficiency and defensiveness; and have to a degree stifled progress in terms of British identity, thereby causing a melancholy which has shrouded and occluded real social and economic progress. Like many regional communities within the UK, loyalists and the Protestant working class have made their own unique and important contributions to the maintenance of the Union but years of conflict have perhaps distracted this component community from the ongoing refashioning of British identity and multiculturalism which has occurred. Loyalist and Protestant identity in Northern Ireland was copper-fastened by the solemn pledges of figures such as Lord Carson a century ago. It is unlikely that this culture will fall away overnight, but loyalists must be best advised how to adapt and integrate more comfortably into a rapidly changing UK.

Conclusions

The problems currently facing the Protestant working class in Northern Ireland and in Belfast in particular must be considered in a proper historical context. While the experience of deindustrialisation historically has been compounded by global economic instability since the Belfast Agreement it is crucial to understand the Protestant working-class plight in terms of what it has lost as a community since the start of the Northern Ireland conflict. When violence erupted on the streets in the late 1960s and early 1970s working-class Protestants found that they were being blamed for the discriminatory practices which had been designed by the captains of industry and unionist politicians. To those opposed to the Stormont regime Protestant workers were regarded as the 'labour aristocracy'. In reality they were no better off than their socio-economic counterparts in cities such as Liverpool, Glasgow, Nottingham or Manchester; indeed in many cases they were treated more poorly in terms of pay and working conditions. Undoubtedly the Protestant working class did enjoy an upper hand in terms of access to jobs but to condemn them as being better off is to forget that they saw themselves as part of a wider UK industrial working community. Important oral testimonies have often been submerged or obscured by grander narratives about Northern Ireland's economic history. Interviewees of Sarah Nelson in 1984 highlighted the manner in which constant references to discrimination in the traditional industries have obscured the discriminatory practices in private employment; a group of Shankill housewives recalling, 'We knew we couldn't get a job in X [a Catholic-owned] bakery but we didn't complain, we just accepted it. Then they suddenly started complaining about "discrimination"!'[40]

This sense of frustration was further exacerbated when the civic pride in Protestant working-class areas of Belfast was hollowed out in the early 1970s. When violence and intimidation occurred in certain interface areas with the encroachment of militant republicans many church congregations dwindled to zero.[41] Others that did manage to maintain parishioners bore witness to the withdrawal of church leaders and their families to safer neighbourhoods. The link between the church and the community was in very many cases broken. Trade unionists who would once have provided reasonable voices and strong leadership qualities in their streets were cast aside with the emergence of more militant groupings such as the Loyalist Association of Workers in the early 1970s. In tandem with republican violence, there was and continues to be the stranglehold with which loyalist paramilitaries hold the urban Protestant working-class communities from which they evolved. The civic-mindedness that was lost in the early years of the Troubles has thus never been allowed to recover. The devastating effects of the changes experienced during this period are vividly recalled by the playwright Graham Reid who came from the Donegall Road area and lived on the Shankill Road in the 1970s. He has explained how normal life was ruined by the violence on both sides:

> When, as a bus conductor, I was the last bus into Short Strand Depot, I'd walk home … Up through the Markets, along Donegall Pass and up the Donegall Road. After I was married we lived on the Shankill Road. I'd leave my Mother's house in Coolderry Street … cut down Roden Street, cross the Grosvenor Road, into McDonnell Street … Up Albert Street, across Divis Street … Up Northumberland Street towards the Shankill … at all hours of the day and night … Then the big black shadow came.[42]

The Protestant working class in particular have long inhabited this 'big black shadow', finding that the effect that the early years of the conflict has had on it has been hard to extricate itself from. Things are moving forward slowly. Constant references to labour aristocracies and privilege by commentators in order to point-score will not aid that process. Loyalists must also play their part by recognising the manner in which they are perceived by outsiders. There is no need to surrender tradition, but if it gets to the stage that the rest of the UK is saying they don't like you ... you should care.

Notes

1. Northern Ireland Department for Social Development (2004), 'Renewing Communities' Task Force Survey (Belfast: DSDNI).
2. P. Orr (2008), *New Loyalties: Christian Faith and the Protestant Working Class* (Belfast: Centre for Contemporary Christianity in Ireland).
3. Despite this the Alliance Party and its members were subjected to continual protests and intimidation outside their constituency offices.
4. G. Mulvenna (2012), 'Belfast's Union Flag Debate Kicks Loyalist Communities While They're Down', *The Guardian*, 5 December.
5. 'Pride and Prejudice in Ulster', *Media Studies is Shit* [blog], 29 January 2013, <http://mediastudiesisshit.wordpress.com/2013/01/29/pride-and-prejudice-in-ulster> [accessed 17 September 2013].
6. E. McCann (2013), 'No Unilateral Fix to Hardship which Spawned Loyalist Rage', *Belfast Telegraph*, 11 January.
7. H. McDonald (2005), 'Return of the Angry Young Prods', *The Observer*, 2 October.
8. P. Shirlow (1997), 'Class, Materialism and the Fracturing of Traditional Alignments' in B. Graham (ed.), *In Search of Ireland: a Cultural Geography* (London: Routledge), 99.
9. V. O'Hara (2013), 'So, Who Helped Take Back the City?', *The Belfast Telegraph*, 21 January.
10. B. Mitchell (2002), 'Sectarianism: a Response to Hazel Croft', *The Blanket*, 8 August.
11. P. Taylor (1999), *Loyalists* (London: Bloomsbury), 146-7.
12. D. McKittrick et al. (2000), *Lost Lives* (Edinburgh: Mainstream), 532-33.
13. B. Kelly (2002), 'Belfast's "Poor White Trash" and the Dead Dogmas of the Past', *The Blanket*, 19 September.
14. B. Gadd (2005), 'Unionist Argument is Hard One to Sustain', *Irish News*, 11 October.
15. M. Hastings (2005), 'The Last Writhings of a Society Left Beached by History', *The Guardian*, 15 September.
16. R. Garland (2001), *Gusty Spence* (Belfast: Blackstaff Press).
17. Raidió Teilifís Éireann (1969), *RTÉ News Special*, 19 May.
18. Despite this it is interesting to note that Sarah Nelson observed during her time on the Shankill in the 1970s that it was actually the older generation, through lunch clubs etc., who maintained good relationships with their Catholic neighbours. Sarah Nelson (1994), 'Belfast: Walking the Shankill', in Ian S. Wood (ed.), *Scotland and Ulster* (Edinburgh: Mercat Press).
19. Raidió Teilifís Éireann (1969) – *RTÉ News Special*, 19 May.
20. D. Boulton (1973), *The UVF: an Anatomy of Loyalist Rebellion* (Dublin: Torc).

21. Reference to an anecdote told by Progressive Unionist Party leader and former UVF life-sentence prisoner Billy Hutchinson about his father, who was said to have stated that the only difference between the working classes in Belfast was that Protestants could get a slum quicker than a Catholic, but that ultimately housing conditions were equally as poor.
22. Author interview with Billy Mitchell. LINC Resource Centre Belfast, 12 June 2006.
23. Ibid.
24. M. Megahey (2009), *'The Reality of his Fictions' – The Dramatic Achievement of Sam Thompson* (Belfast: Lagan Press).
25. J. Stevenson (1996), *'We Wrecked the Place': Contemplating an End to the Northern Irish Troubles* (New York: The Free Press).
26. P. E. Willis (1977), *Learning to Labour: How Working Class Kids Get Working Class Jobs* (Columbia University Press).
27. G. Mulvenna (2012), 'The Protestant Working Class in Belfast: Education and Civic Erosion – an Alternative Analysis', *Irish Studies Review* 20 (4): 427–46.
28. R. Wiener (1975), *The Rape and Plunder of the Shankill* (Belfast: Notaems Press).
29. P. Cohen (1997), 'Subcultural Conflict and Working-Class Community', in P. Cohen, *Rethinking the Youth Question – Education, Labour and Cultural Studies* (Basingstoke: Macmillan).
30. See Billy Hutchinson's reference in another chapter of this book to two men on the Shankill arguing over whether they owned Australia (p. 194).
31. S. Nelson (1984), *Ulster's Uncertain Defenders* (Belfast: Appletree), 146–7.
32. Ibid.
33. S. Bruce (2007), 'Book Review: Crimes of Loyalty', *Scottish Affairs* 60: 145.
34. L. McDowell (2003), *Redundant Masculinities: Employment Change and White Working Class Youth* (Oxford: Wiley).
35. P. Gilroy (2004), *After Empire – Melancholia or Convivial Culture?* (Abingdon: Routledge).
36. Ibid., 97.
37. E. Longley (1994), 'The Rising, the Somme and Irish Memory', in E. Longley, *The Living Stream – Literature and Revisionism in Ireland* (Newcastle upon Tyne: Bloodaxe Books), 75.
38. Author interview with Winston Irvine, PUP Media Spokesperson. Civil Rights Camp, Twaddell Avenue Belfast, 25 September 2013.
39. G. Walker and D. Officer (2000), 'Protestant Ulster: Ethno-history, Memory and Contemporary Prospects', *National Identities* 2 (3).
40. S. Nelson, *Ulster's Uncertain Defenders*, 70–1.
41. One church building in particular, Macrory Memorial, underlines this phenomenon. It has lain derelict for over forty years on the New Lodge/Tiger's Bay interface of North Belfast since subscribers to the church's weekly offerings dwindled to zero in 1973.
42. G. Reid, 'Author's Note', *Love, Billy* (programme), April 2013.

13
To the Beat of a Different Drum: Loyalist Youth and the Culture of Marching Bands

Sam McCready and Neil Symington

A city built upon mud;
A culture built upon profit;
Free speech nipped in the bud,
The minority always guilty.
Why should I want to go back
To you, Ireland, my Ireland?
...
Her mountains are still blue, her rivers flow
Bubbling over the boulders.
She is both a bore and a bitch;
Better close the horizon,
Send her no more fantasy, no more longings which
Are under a fatal tariff.
For common sense is the vogue
And she gives her children neither sense nor money
Who slouch around the world with a gesture and a brogue
And a faggot of useless memories.

(Louis MacNeice – *Autumn Journal* 1939)[1]

MacNeice's long poem *Autumn Journal,* written in 1938, describes daily personal, social and political life during the lead-up to the Second World War. The poem is a significant illustration of how intertwined political, cultural and personal life are, whilst he also said that the most important events were still being made up of silly little ('foolish') things.

His *Ireland*, at that time, was still a 'bore and a bitch' where 'a single purpose can be founded on a jumble of opposites',[2] with children receiving 'neither sense nor money' and trapped by 'a faggot of useless memories'. These lines grip and challenge the reader and should cause us to pause for reflection, as they are perhaps as pertinent now as then. Whilst MacNeice wrote this autobiographical poem at a time of pending international crisis (and admitted that many parts dealing with Ireland may have been overstated), nonetheless it does offer us a prism through which to explore the views and voices of young people who have chosen to be part of loyalist marching bands.

The research[3] which this chapter draws upon set out to listen to this particular grouping.

Through their voices we hear their search into their past as a way of understanding, and thus expressing, their identity and feelings of where they belong. But, as Hewitt reminds us, any ancestral search is '... not just of the blood, but of the emotions'.[4] Their words in this study are not words of cultural self-pity or of cultural void but a story of pride in their history, their music and traditions. Their story of life in a band can be one of a complex interplay of the way in which parading flirts and floats between being a deadly serious business and being festive fun. This intermingling, on the occasions of parades and marches, is part of the challenge in understanding their culture and expression. A marching band is not just a band per se; it is a community institution with social and religious significance. It is the vehicle through which these young people explore and express their heritage, their identity, their art and their politics. This interface between culture and politics is of crucial importance when attempting to understand the wider Ulster Protestant experience.

As Declan McGonigle stated in 1991, 'Politics in the culture of Ireland can be understood as a cultural manifestation of allegiance and power – in this sense culture is more important than politics and operates on a more personal level'.[5]

The wider context

Young people and protest are not the exclusive preserve of Ireland, North or South. Over the last five years we have seen movements, involving young people, taking to the streets in Egypt, Bahrain, Greece, Spain, Syria and Turkey to show their protest and opposition to government decisions and policies with which they disagree. In the summer of 2013 people took to the streets of Brazil, again with young people to the fore; in protest against the huge government spend in the hosting of the 2014 World Cup, amidst growing poverty and cuts to health and education for ordinary people in Brazil. During World Youth Day (July

2013), hosted in Brazil, the Pope, when asked about his view on the young protestors, said:

> A young man is essentially a nonconformist, and that is a very beauti-ful thing. You need to listen to young people, giving them outlets to express themselves and ensure they don't get manipulated.[6]

The linking of *non-conformity* and *beauty* frees us to look at young people in a non-judgemental way in all they say and do. His emphasis on the necessity to listen and the importance of creating places and spaces for their self-expression resonates strongly with opinions and attitudes arising from our research and fits exactly into the purpose of the project from which we are drawing the material for this piece. But, before engaging with the voices of young loyalist bandspeople, there is a local context that is current and that has an impact and relevance. In Northern Ireland MacNeice's 'free speech nipped in the bud' and 'the fatal tariff'[7] loom and echo menacingly as the 'flegs'[8] are either hoisted or lowered.

A Belfast City Council decision to remove the Union flag from Belfast City Hall resulted in large-scale protests across Northern Ireland over a number of months, with young people (and some bands) at the front of those protests. What it highlighted was a growing frustration and unease with how the Protestant, unionist and loyalist culture was being treated or, as some would describe it; 'being under attack' and engaged in a 'cultural war'. In one respect the fact that young people were out organising, taking action and trying to show their opposition to the flag decision was proactive, but it was not always described or interpreted by others in language associated with being *non-conformist and beautiful*. The protests drew attention to the issue of culture and its expression. For some this was a welcome focus of attention in order to open up the debate around equality, identity and cultural affiliation. For others it was seen as just another example of loyalist's intransigence at play. One interpretation of the protest was that the young loyalist was, once again, becoming defensive, intolerant and uncritically loyal to a tradition and cause. They were expressing it in a loud and emotional manner that came from a place where perception was more important than the reality of events. On the other hand this could be looked at as a re-visioning of loyalism's own political approach and an attempt to make unified unionism a *'notion once again'*. Either way, as Rodgers said in 1955, of his upbringing in Belfast, 'It had two sides to it. Everything in Belfast had two sides to it'.[9]

In the same spirit in which Pope Francis I spoke about the protestors in Brazil (and the need for places and opportunities for self-expression) we ask you to suspend any preconceived notions you may have of loyalism, loyalist culture, bands, triumphalism, et al. and just *'listen to the band'*.

The research background and methodology

The Northern Ireland Youth Forum in their 2013 report *Sons of Ulster*[10] estimate there are about 30,000 members of around 640 bands in Northern Ireland; the genesis of this research idea originated in June 2012 following the year-long engagement between one of the authors of this piece and young people in a Loyalist Flute Band from the Randalstown area of South Antrim. The youth project itself was based around peace and reconciliation, leadership and community action through the Northern Ireland Youth Forum (NIYF). The ongoing contact between worker and young people was negotiated around the band getting their tunes perfected, taking part in competitions and parades and their work for the local bonfire scheduled for 11 July 2012.

This experience and exposure to band life drew admiration and intrigue from the worker as young people spoke about their life in the band, how they became involved and what it all meant to them. This included observing the skill and artistry of a 23-year-old Band Master as he led the band, with all the ability, enthusiasm and clarity of purpose that would impress in any aspect of business or sport.

The fieldwork with the band culminated on 12 July when 50 flute bands, flanking Orangemen and thousands of supporters paraded through their local village on the way to their field of celebration. Running in parallel with this project was a similar engagement with a young nationalist group from the Crumlin area of South Antrim. These young people were less than enthused about the idea of this parade and they described the marching and the bands as anti-Catholic, triumphalist and sectarian.

This view is neither new nor surprising, but given the author's newly acquired insight and relationship with the band and these young people in particular, these views and assumptions were challenged.

It was in this moment that the fundamental importance of telling the story of young people's relationship with Loyalist flute bands was realised.

To gain a holistic understanding of young people one must acknowledge where the leisure and cultural lives of young people intersect within their wider structural biographies ... neither the life of the individual nor the history of a society can be understood without understanding both.[11]

The NI Youth Forum identified (through conversations with their membership, examination of media stories, academic and practitioner research) that there was a sense that young people from the Protestant community were becoming increasingly frustrated with the debate around how they were expressing their culture and identity. More specifically, there was a sense from young people that their identity was being diluted by a perceived nationalist and republican agenda within the devolved institutions at Stormont. By examining then how this constituency construct and shape their lives and their leisure landscape, it was hoped to build awareness toward informing a contemporary and historical debate about culture and cultural expression within the loyalist community with particular reference to young people.

As the orchestra noise around the 'flegs' dispute increased from unionist and loyalist politicians, this noise turned to anger and frustration and the parade became the vehicle and means by which to challenge what the Orange Order and unionist politicians labelled as *cultural apartheid* and the *war on our culture*. Campaigns in Protestant communities often take root and play into the fears of the past and this seemed to be following this tried and tested formula. The influence of history was once again providing explanation and meaning for the bands.

In October 2012 the NIYF were awarded a research grant from the Northern Ireland Youth Council's 'Young Roots Programme' to explore the attitudes and experiences of young band members from the Protestant, unionist and loyalist community. The central aim of the action research was to allow young people a space to explore, debate and articulate their views and opinions around how they express their culture and commemorate their heritage, and determine how these behaviours are interpreted across society. Furthermore, the project aimed to bring together young people from different flute bands to discuss methods of expressing culture and identity and produce a written report, which captured young people's views, opinions and understanding about 'life in the band'. In summary, through this project, NI Youth Forum worked to develop an understanding of loyalist culture and how it manifests itself; and to explore how culture, heritage and identity are expressed through bands, the community, music and other associations.

The NIYF steering group (consisting of representatives of the bands) identified themes that the study would focus on and agreed to carry out the study through focus groups and one-on-one interviews, also inviting band members to offer their own written stories. Young band members were at the heart of the development, delivery and evaluation of the study. All in all 100 young people aged between 13 and 21 engaged with the research through focus groups, individual interviews and personal testimonies.

This was a constructivist research design whereby the questions asked were influenced by the participants. One of the aims of the research was to display the complexities of the world in which these young people live and gain an understanding and meaning behind their stories. The focus of the discussions was around meaning, values and experience.

Above all else, the young people involved wanted others throughout Northern Irish society to understand the cultural dynamic of marching 'Bands' and to appreciate their culture.

The findings

The study highlighted a number of important factors regarding young people's participation within flute bands. In the first instance it shed a light on young people's motivations and reasoning for joining the band initially.

For the vast majority this was an entirely personal decision. They wanted to be 'part of something', to 'learn an instrument', have 'a sense of belonging' or to 'learn about and celebrate their culture'. One young man also described it as 'the only opportunity we had to keep our culture alive'. Given the political climate some would say this opinion was not surprising, but it did underline the vital role the band played in the expression of their culture at this time. Given the position of the peace process and the overwhelming objection to violence by the general public, the band serves as a vehicle to protect the Protestant, loyalist and unionist culture and place it within the new N. Ireland dispensation. For many young Protestants it is one of very few ways to express their Ulster Protestant culture and tradition. This is well described by MacDonald as he writes, in 2008: 'young Loyalists have a military discipline of parades written into their genetic code and given the major shifts that have occurred since the Good Friday agreement, it is in the marching ranks of uniformed bands where young protestant males have found their place and that the bands are the most vibrant aspect of Ulster Protestant Culture in the 21st Century'.[12]

Examination of the Protestant culture and community has often led to them being dismissed as the 'voice of unreason',[13] as the 'servitor imperialists',[14] the 'Gasconaders' (boasters – Henry Joy McCracken)[15] and even as the 'mad variable'.[16] Such sentiments lead to many believing that, in most working-class Protestant communities, there are cultural voids and a disabling cultural self-pity that comes from the siege mentality that produces and induces an imaginative exclusiveness.

This is not borne out by our research. These young bandspeople asserted a range of positive reasons for their participation. These reasons connected to culture, friendship, family and fun. It was a natural part of what you did in their communities and MacDonald is accurate when he talks of this being the 'most vibrant aspect of Ulster Protestant culture'.[17] There was no talk of joining the band to fight for a cause or defeat an enemy, but the talk was about their pride and joy of being part of something that provided a place where they felt wanted, were trusted, felt secure and where they had responsibility. Their participation was based on a familial collective security, mutual trust and a sense of belonging. As one respondent explained:

> Putting on the uniform I felt a sense of pride and excitement … meeting the rest of the band and faces were lit up with excitement … when we started to march it was the proudest day of my life.

Here was honour, heritage, identity, art and politics merged. Here was cultural engagement operating at a very personal level.

When the benefits of belonging to a band were explored, what unfolded was further evidence of their pride and the development of skills and self-confidence from being part of this collective:

> We hope more people will learn about our culture.

> In the band you have a deeper understanding of our culture and identity and you can be proud of it. In this way no other culture is a threat.

One young man, aged 16, described his immense sense of pride on being part of the Ulster Covenant Parade (September 2012):

> I woke up two hours before I was due and I was pure thriving with excitement … Thousands of people standing watching us was class and marching past the statue of Sir Edward Carson just made me so proud to be a part of a once in a lifetime parade and knowing that I am a 'Son of Ulster' and just to have been there was truly unreal.

The sense of unity, pride and togetherness was enriching and palpable. Many young people spoke about marching for the first time, or marching in their hometown or village and, most importantly, waking up on 12 July and taking part in everything that cultural event had to offer.

The band meant more than playing music and parading in villages and towns throughout Northern Ireland. The young people talked about how being in the band gave them more self-confidence and allowed them to develop stronger communication skills. The band became a vehicle through which they could explore and learn about their own personal and community history, culture and sense of identity. The band allowed them to be proud to come from a Protestant, unionist and loyalist background and express that sense of pride in a safe environment.

As stated in the *Sons of Ulster* (Northern Ireland Youth Forum 2013) report, 'Loyalist flute bands instil pride of place and identity, as well as confidence and skills in the estimated 30,000 young people in their ranks. They are fundamentally important to the communities they represent, articulating the story of the past in the present, while providing hope for the future. Yet most of all, these bands are about cultural heritage.'[18]

When it came to asking young people about the way they celebrated their culture and identity we can see the clear connections to politics, religion and difference.

Tom Paulin, in 1984, referred to the Protestant culture as an 'unusually fragmented culture with a snarl of superficial or negative attitudes'.[19] When we asked young people to talk of how they celebrated their culture and identity through the marching band there was no such fragmentation or negativity. There was nothing about hatred, political idealism or revenge and there was no sight of MacNeice's 'nomad who has lost his tent'. It was a story of young people who had a purpose, who were developing musical skills and who had a sense of camaraderie. Young people who had a commitment and connection to the positives in their culture. There was a yearning in what they said of wanting others to learn more about what they did and for these others to feel less threatened by it. The language, when talking about their celebrations, was aspirational and affirmative. Perhaps there was more romance than reality in their comments, but the aspiration is of value and is a welcome break from a tradition that has seen an association with a Protestant culture that has often defined itself in terms of what it is against rather than what it is for. Whilst the certainties of 1690 and 1921 are still the ones they cling to, it is through these that the individual finds explanation and meaning. But Ulster politics by its very nature is conflictual, meaning that there is a divergence and a battle between two politico-religious systems that ends up being played out in expressions of cultural identity. By being in a band this will inevitably connect the members to that conflict.

Young people mentioned their key points in history e.g. the Battle of the Boyne (1690), the Somme (1916), the Ulster Covenant (1912) and other historic dates where people lost lives in the name of Unionism/ Britishness. Once again the search for ancestry went beyond blood and became more about emotions, sacrifice and allegiance. There were a lot of references to history and people who had lost their lives within their narratives. In the conversations they challenged any attempt to limit or remove their expressions of this aspect of their culture and identity. Any criticism was viewed as a direct attack on this strong sense of heritage:

I am keeping the tradition of my forefathers alive.

It is about the 12th July and what that date stands for.

My great grandfather signed the document (Covenant), but like many others, he had signed it in his own blood ... that blood would be the blood he would sacrifice for his country at the Somme in 1916.

Lives were lost, blood was shed, mothers lost sons and wives lost husbands. The culture goes back over 300 years in which it has faced pain and heartache.

My culture is honoured to remember our past.

It is here we see the clear connection between blood sacrifice, ancestry and emotions and here you have the spectre of MacNeice's 'useless memories'. An outworking of these emotions is often a *bonding* which has long been a part of a Protestant strategy, since the Plantation. Within this bonding, differences in class and gender are temporarily suspended until any period of threat is lifted. In this you have the blurring of diversity in Protestant communities and any dissent is treated as potentially disloyal. The rhythm of the drums beat out a connection to a national anthem that is aligned to being British, an allegiance to a national flag, to royalty, and the drums beat a clear message of belonging within the Protestant faith. The Ulster Protestant heritage becomes an amalgamation of these many diverse strands of religious affiliation, Britishness and an ethnic sense of being part of a group that belongs to Ulster ... and yet within this there is difference. A difference that can express itself in protest against anyone or anything that threatens to take any of this away. Any rubbishing of the culture or removal of its symbols provokes this 'backward pull of custom and forward pluck of morality'.[21] It is the chain of the past that must not be forgotten and draws upon the more austere doctrines of Calvinism and the refusal to yield. From here the Protestant community derives its legitimacy and inner coherence, and history is that important value that provides a source of reference. Any perceived threat to the Union has a way of uniting any potential diverse strands of unionism, even if seemingly they are unravelling in different directions. This is the power of the past. But as Hewitt reminds us:

> ... he must know where he comes from and where he is: otherwise how can he tell where he wishes to go?[22]

Furthermore, it is Faulkner in 1950 who tells us 'the past is never dead. It's not even the past'.[23]

This Faulkner–Hewitt stance reflects a mix of the importance of knowing what has gone before in order to know a way forward, whilst at the same time acknowledging that this *past* is always with us.

The next phase of the exploration with the band members was their relationship between the band, its community and religion, and this drew out further the religious-political relationship.

> We only participate in events and parades if there is a religious service or element involved.

> Being in the band teaches you right from wrong, alongside discipline, respect and history ... it lays a foundation.

When ideology interfaces with religion it becomes increasingly an important component of power and may be the pillar that provides this community with both excusatory legitimacy and which also – just like those historical resonances – acts as an inner coherence. It offers the pragmatist an apparently dignified way of legitimising what is going on around them. As these bands are traditionally drawn from working-class Protestant communities, it is here where evangelical religious institutions and the Orange Order combine to channel the mood and help regulate relations between their own communities and others. In particular they impact upon the relations between Catholic and Protestant communities.

Even if religious practice does not figure much in people's lives 'the domain of religion provides the symbols which help provide the sense of self'.[24]

Protestantism, by its very nature, tolerates a wide degree of scepticism. For example, you don't need to go to church to believe in God's commandments. But it is, as Wright suggests, 'scepticism within a context'[25] because everything refers back to the 'Book'. An essential aspect of Protestant freedom is having access to the Bible and ensuring children have read it. Working-class Protestants are often Bible-lovers even if they are not Bible-readers. It is a short hop from here to ortho-dox politics (i.e., party politics) and this is where parades, celebrations of culture and marches become fused and play a role in influencing the relationships between the two communities. When there is a threat to marching a 'traditional route', this can ignite a powder keg of fears that result in sectarian attacks. The Orange Order and the church become the defenders of the 'Christian faith, reformed and Protestant'[26] and the marches are the occasions for the shows of determination to resist any erosion of identity. In times of perceived threat there is little regulation in these communities over what is said about the other side and any traditional agreements and accommodations that may have existed are broken.

When the subject of the relationship between the band and national-ist communities came up many felt that, on the whole, 'Nationalists' did not understand anything about their bands, and viewed them as sectarian and a threat. This was well illustrated by a senior band member:

> Marching bands are very misunderstood. People think we go out solely to antagonise Catholics and other creeds but that is nowhere near the truth. We do it for the love of our tradition and our culture and the love of music.

This theme was picked up by others:

> They see us as bigots, bastards and huns ... this is wrong. They don't take the time to read or research what bands do. Bands do more than parade.

> They view the bands as bigots and sectarian thugs who trample over people's rights, because this is implied by sections of the media.

This then can easily lead to a belief that the other side – who have this lack of understanding of what the band stands for and what it does – has subversive intentions. The positive view of self may then regress to the old siege mentality, leading this community into a warped cultural cul-de-sac.

This theme of being *misunderstood* is not one to easily dismiss. In Smithey's book, *Unionists, Loyalists and Conflict Transformation in Northern*

Ireland (2011), we have an insight from a local Protestant minister on the way parades tap deeply into a shared experience and the emotions of the community observing it:

> I think the whole parades thing is so important to working class loyalism to a degree that most people don't understand ... it's not just about marching. It's about family. There's a nostalgia that my father and my great grandfather did this. It's hitting people at so many different levels. People just say, 'Oh it's a sectarian parade', but to many people actually it's not. There's a family link, there's an emotional [aspect], there's a physical [aspect], there's a spiritual [aspect], there's a mental [aspect]. It's hitting all those different buttons within people's lives. I guess unless you work in these areas [it's difficult to] understand it.[27]

Bands, parades, marches can evoke feelings of sharing and continuity. They provide that common bond that holds all participants and onlooking bystanders together.

In the early parts of this chapter we highlighted the positive aspects of joining the band and the benefits that accrued. Significantly, when we broadened the discussion and asked for perceptions of the other community toward the band, the mood shifts toward what Redpath refers to as 'Protestantism that shows its strength as a veto body more than an achieving body'.[28] The early tone and comments lean positively towards all that the band stands for but then comments flit nervously to defining the group in terms of what they are against. A collective view, rather than an individual one emerges regarding the nationalist community and the threat to culture is cited as the significant factor. But as the discussions and interviews progress, this flirtation with negativity and fear is left behind and comments and conversations reassert the positives:

> My culture and band has made me who I am. It has taught me the dangers with drugs and alcohol. It has taught me respect and discipline.

> Political parties try to make us out to be bigots and sectarian but we are not any of these. We are proud Loyalists.

The revolutionary and defiant aspects of Protestantism emerge to overwhelm the negative and backward-looking mentality. Reason and enlightenment come through to connect with folk-art and romance, offering a much more positive avenue for exploration.

However, the archaic and restrictive institutions – in the form of the church, Orange Order and parts of the state – are still there. The critics remain ready and armed with the usual responses, directing accusatory rhetoric towards this culture. They are still seen as being trapped in a history they do not understand. And many of the liberating, non-judgemental expressions of loyalist working-class culture remain camouflaged effectively from the wider world. However, the study did identify causes for optimism, and tentative pathways out of stereotypical straitjacketing.

In conclusion, we have attempted through this piece to provide insight into the lives of young people who are band members from the Protestant, unionist and loyalist tradition. The overriding message emerging is that 'The Band' transcends simple categorisation. It is not just 'a band'; rather, it is a community institution with social and religious significance. It is one hugely important vehicle for these young people to explore and express their heritage, their identity, their art and their politics. It is here the interface between culture and politics has crucial importance. Their story is one of family that offers collective security and a mutual trust and a sense of belonging. It is a story of young people with a sense of purpose. Somewhere where they can develop musical skills and hone moral and ethical values. It is a place where young people commit and connect to the positives in their culture.

Perhaps Kavanagh, in his poem 'The 12th July', has it right – '… from them we have much to learn … And young men out of Ulster who will dare … To drive a wedge in Dublin's lounge-bar panzers.'[29]

Notes

1. L. MacNeice, *Autumn Journal* (London: Faber & Faber, 1939).
2. Ibid.
3. Northern Ireland Youth Forum Report, *Sons of Ulster: Exploring Loyalist Band Members' Attitudes towards Culture, Identity and Heritage* (Northern Ireland Youth Forum: Belfast, 2013).
4. J. Hewitt, 'The Bitter Gourd' (Belfast: Lagan, 1945).
5. J. Redpath, Seminar Report 'Community Development in Protestant Areas' (Lisnaskea: McGonigle Community Relations Commission, 1992).
6. Pope Francis I, speaking at World Youth Day, Brazil, in 2013. Source: 'Postcard from Rio 8: Absorbing the Whirlwind that was Francis in Brazil', *Catholic Voices Comment* [website], <http://cvcomment.org/2013/08/01/postcard-from-rio-8-absorbing-the-whirlwind-that-was-francis-in-brazil/>.
7. L. MacNeice, *Autumn Journal*.
8. 'Flegs': this is a reference to a Belfast pronunciation of the word *flags*. It is used to represent a working-class perception of the issue.

9. W. Rodgers, extract from *The Return Room*, broadcast by the BBC in December 1955.

10. Northern Ireland Youth Forum, *Sons of Ulster*.

11. C. W. Mills, *The Sociological Imagination* (New York: OU Press, 1959).

12. D. MacDonald, *Blood and Thunder – Inside an Ulster Protestant Band* (Cork: The Mercier Press, 2008).

13. G. Bell, *The Protestants of Ulster* (London: Pluto Press, 1976).

14. M. Hechter, *Internal Colonialism – The Celtic Fringe in British National Development* (London: Routledge & Kegan Paul, 1975).

15. H. J. McCracken, letter from Kilmainham jail to his sister (January 1797), in Edna Fitzhenry, *Henry Joy McCracken* (Dublin: Talbot Press, 1936), n.p.

16. T. Nairn, 'The Break-up of Britain. Crisis and Neonationalism', *New Left Review* (105) 1977.

17. MacDonald, *Blood and Thunder*.

18. Northern Ireland Youth Forum Report, *Sons of Ulster*.

19. T. Paulin, *Ireland and the English Crisis* (Newcastle upon Tyne: Bloodaxe Books, 1984).

20. L. MacNeice, *The Strings are False. An Unfinished Autobiography* (first published 1941; London: Faber & Faber, 1965).

21. W. Rodgers, 'Conversation Piece: an Ulster Protestant', *The Bell* 4 (5) (August 1942).

22. Hewitt, 'The Bitter Gourd'.

23. W. Faulkner, *Requiem for a Nun* (New York: Random House, 1950).

24. F. Wright, 'Protestant Ideology and Politics in Ulster', *European Journal of Sociology* 14 (2) (1973).

25. Ibid.

26. Ibid.

27. L. A. Smithey, *Unionists, Loyalists and Conflict Transformation in Northern Ireland* (Oxford University Press, 2011).

28. J. Redpath, 'Community Development in Protestant Areas'.

29. P. Kavanagh, 'The 12th July' (1943; PKTrust@tcd.ie).

14
Blood Sacrifice for Queen and Country: Paramilitarism and Political Manoeuvrings

Billy Hutchinson

A British working-class life

I was born in 1955 on the Shankill Road. I lived in the end house on Matchett Street, just off Tennent Street.[1] The house on Matchett Street was next to waste ground which was apparently created by the Blitz. There was some sort of shop there and it was blown up. In 1972 I moved to Jersey Street. When I was a young boy I remember playing football on the street corner and playing cricket in the summer, we painted the stumps on the wall and you bowled and all that sort of stuff but you could never knock the stumps off because it was painted on! I clearly remember that you were never allowed to call anybody's parents by their first name – you always had to call them Mr and Mrs.

Matchett Street and the Shankill Road in general was a very working-class community and if you ask anyone from similar communities in the rest of the United Kingdom they'll probably have the same memories of the normal camaraderie that exists in an area where everyone knows everyone else and people look out for each other. We were told to respect the police. When we were playing football in the street, which you weren't allowed to do, you would have picked up your ball and ran when the policeman came. I remember one particular policeman who we dubbed the Durango Kid[2] because he was on a motorcycle and he'd chase us up and down the entries to get our names for playing football on the street. From a young age I was a Linfield fanatic.[3] Isaac Andrews, who played for Linfield at that time, went up and down the street every day and to me and my friends as young boys he was a big star. To put it in simple terms I remember fondly just playing in the streets and feeling safe – it was just a normal working-class life.

Soldiers, commemoration and the UVF: blood sacrifice

One of the interesting things looking back is that a lot of soldiers lived in the area. There was a family called the McQuittys who I was very friendly with and their father had been in the army – I think it was the Signals; and because of this they had travelled all round the world with him so they had around seven children who were born in different countries such as Singapore and Malta (so anywhere the British Army were stationed, it seemed to be this family had a child!). You heard all the stories about these exotic places from the family and being a child from a close-knit neighbourhood such as the Shankill it seemed like there was such a massive world out there. I heard all about campaigns in far-flung places from Aden to Korea. For me as a young boy these stories were fascinating. From an early age then it was all entwined with the ethos and ideology of Britishness, loyalism and unionism. That's how people told their stories – they'd been off serving Queen and Country. There was nothing abnormal about it. Interestingly despite these magnificent stories of service in fascinating foreign countries that you heard, you also heard people complaining about how they didn't get whatever they were due. On returning to Belfast and the Shankill in particular the men often said that they weren't getting the quality of housing they should have been getting after having fought in the various campaigns.

I was ten when the shootings at Malvern Street happened in June 1966.[4] My grandmother only lived round the corner from where the murders happened and I would pass the site often. Everybody in Northern Ireland was shocked at these shootings and although I was young at that time the notion of the fiftieth anniversary commemorations of the Easter Rising and the subsequent Malvern Street shootings brought a lot of talk about the IRA and the danger it posed to Protestants. At that stage the UVF was just a distant memory from the beginning of the century and the only time you'd hear about them was when the old hands were talking about the Home Rule Crisis, Carson and the sacrifice at the Somme. The discussions I heard adults having during that period in my upbringing; listening and learning, it was drummed into me that the IRA was wrong … that the IRA was a group of people who rose up against the British … that the IRA was an illegal army.

In the Shankill, the blood sacrifice at the Somme was obviously viewed differently to the blood sacrifice that Padraic Pearse and the others involved in the Easter Rising of 1916 saw themselves as being part of. Although the Ulster Volunteer Force was a militia that was set up by Edward Carson to fight Home Rule, the organisation ended up becoming a British Regiment (36th Ulster Division) and going off to fight in a World War which was basically a war over territory – over land that people were trying to claim. It was about a fight for freedom for people in a world context. I think that the IRA's notion of blood sacrifice is a narrower concern and is about reinforcing the idea of victimhood and suffering under 'imperial rule'. For the 36th Ulster Division their blood sacrifice was about protecting the well-being of the people in the communities from which they came, and many ordinary young working-class men died endeavouring to do just that. It is important to consider for a moment that the Ulster Volunteers started off by opposing the British government over the Home Rule crisis but ultimately saw the bigger picture at the time.

They were prepared to temporarily put to one side their opposition to Home Rule and work to safeguard the rights of all British citizens. It is obvious that the generals in the British Army sent young working-class men to their deaths, used them as cannon fodder and basically sent them into combat often ill-equipped. It is apparent that it was really the generals who were leading people into a slaughter and massacre. Donkeys leading lions. To me and other loyalists of my generation that blood sacrifice is quite humbling. Young men said, 'We have to go over the top' and very many of them died in doing so. In terms of the rest of the history of Ireland and Northern Ireland that sense of sacrifice remained a key ideology, particularly for loyalists involved in the modern conflict who knew that if they were caught they would be convicted under British law, even though they knew that the British law was wrong in terms of such things as Diplock Courts. They still did it. The IRA and Republican notion of sacrifice from 1916 onwards was constructed around being a victim and suffering under imperial rule. It seemed to be about reiterating that the British were the oppressors and that they've been oppressing the Irish for hundreds of years.

People from the Shankill were very often included in this perceived group of oppressors. My experience doesn't tally up with what republicans are still so often keen to tell me. One thing that I always remember from my early childhood is the deep levels of poverty on the Shankill and this was often highlighted when I visited my granny in the Hammer district of the lower Shankill.[5] She died in 1966 but I remember just a year before she died when I was eight or nine going with her to this gateway in Downing Street on the Shankill where she used to bring round big heavy bags of straw or hay from her house. In return she got clean bags of straw and hay, then took it back and put it into the mattress in her house and sewed it up with a big darning needle. Of course at the time I didn't know this was poverty – as far as I was concerned everybody did it. It was just normal life so I've got nothing to compare it to because everybody around me was doing the same thing. I can also recall this really old woman on Matchett Street who wore a shawl. She would have asked you every now and again to go and get her stuff out of the shop and you'd have went and got it for her and brought it back; and I always remember clearly the gas mantles being in her house. There wasn't even electric in her house, and this was the 1960s. A lot of people on the Shankill talked about the British Empire as if it were this wonderful thing, and I suppose some people did feel a sense of being better off because of it, but I can always recall Gusty Spence telling a story which underlies the futility of that false sense of superiority. Gusty had gone into a bookies on the Shankill shortly after leaving the army where he had served in Cyprus. There were two fellas standing in the bookies and they were arguing over who owned Australia, so one of them turned to Gusty and said 'Gusty, you're an educated man – you've been round the world ... tell him, don't we own Australia?' to which Gusty replied 'Of course you own Australia, but you haven't the arse in your trousers!' When the Empire declined, our sense of 'Empire Britishness' all but disappeared with it. The lasting monument of the war effort after 1945 was the National Health Service. This was our payback – health and education. With that our focus started to shift and the Northern Ireland Labour Party for example was at the forefront of challenging people's thinking at that time.

Growing up at the start of the Troubles

When I was a young teenager in the late 1960s I was doing all the normal stuff that any British teenager would be doing – listening to music, playing football. I also remember the great sense of community that came around during the start of July when my friends and I and other groups of young people on the Shankill would have had competitions to see who could build the biggest bonfire in anticipation of the Eleventh Night. At that stage the hit parade was being dominated by bands like the Beatles and the Rolling Stones but Northern Ireland, which had always been a socially conservative society, was beginning to adopt a different outlook. From 1966 on there was obviously a definite mood change in Northern Ireland. In the Protestant community there was the emergence of Ian Paisley whose voice was loud and clear. We might not have necessarily understood what he was saying but we understood that Catholics were different. The rise of the Civil Rights movement reinforced in many Protestant minds all the rabble-rousing that Paisley had been coming out with since the mid-'60s; it seemed to live out his premonition. The 'blood and thunder' and religious rhetoric of Paisley created a completely different atmosphere. Protestants were frustrated because while the Northern Ireland Civil Rights and People's Democracy were complaining about lack of housing and voting rights we working-class Protestants faced the same problems. Then, in the middle of all of this, rioting began to occur and at Easter 1969 the Junior Orangemen were attacked on their way back from Bangor by the residents of Unity Flats just before their return to the Shankill. That was the whole talk on the road and people went down and got involved in the riots.

Things began to change from then on – rumours began, people were glued to their radios and some people were even tuned into police radios to hear what was going on. Alongside this there was the global context – the student riots in France, Civil Rights in the United States and the Vietnam War on your black-and-white television in the corner when you were sitting down to your dinner. In Vietnam particularly you were constantly seeing death. It was in black and white, but you knew it was blood you were looking at. Civil Rights, unrest, death. All of these things were brought into your home through the television while at the same time the streets outside your house were beginning to descend into the same turmoil. It was an interesting time to grow up, but it was also an intensely confusing time because it was hard to work out what was really going on. Whereas a few years previously I'd been reading the paper from back to front to get the football news first, I was now becoming more concerned with what was on the front pages. As a young working-class lad from the Shankill there was no critiquing the media. You didn't question things – black and white was right. Whether you read it in a newspaper or saw it on the television it was right.

Approached by the UVF

My granddad and my uncle ran the Hammer Blues Club, which was a Linfield supporters club. I was brought up in the Linfield tradition, and I can even remember my mother singing songs to me about Joe Bambrick – 'Head, heel or toe, slip it to Joe'. I started going to Linfield games in the 1959–60 season and can recall going to away games on the bus. I remember seeing older boys on the bus playing cards and that type of thing and being fascinated by them. Around about 1968–9 I was going to home and away matches with my mates rather than my aunt and uncle. We always walked together from the Shankill over to Linfield's ground Windsor Park in south Belfast and then back again. After 1969 the police would have followed the large crowds of Linfield fans walking across town in order to ensure that no trouble broke out. You would always have got some sort of aggravation coming from Unity Flats and the police knew that, so when the police would try and push us up the Shankill and we were getting abuse from Unity Flats we would hold our ground and sing 'God Save the Queen'.

By the time the 1971–2 Irish League season came around I was later told that some of the older men on the Shankill who were involved with the UVF recognised that I had strong leadership skills and control over my peers, something which I feel they grossly overestimated. Around the end of 1971 these men came to me and said 'We don't want any hassle from the Bluemen coming past Unity Flats. We don't want them stopping and singing the Queen' so I asked why they were telling me, only to be told that there was going to be an incident (which never materialised) at Unity Flats and that there couldn't be any trouble from myself and the other young fellas returning from Windsor Park. They wanted me to ensure that there would be no trouble and asked me whether I could ensure that, to which I replied that I could. When I asked these men who they were, one of them said 'Well, who do you want us to be?' so I of course said that I'd like them to be the UVF and they told me that they were. I told them that the UVF was just writing on the wall and that they were beaten dockets who had run away.

When the day came that we were to go past Unity Flats without causing any bother I had come to realise that this was just a test by the UVF in order to vet my credentials. I had a friend who I'd go to the matches with whom I knew was prone to gossiping so when we reached North Street[6] I told him that the UVF had planned something and that we couldn't cause any trouble as there might be shooting or a bomb or whatever at Unity Flats, knowing full well that this guy would spread the word around the crowd very quickly. All the guys were stopping me and asking 'Hutchy, what's going on here? Can we not stop at Unity Flats and sing the Queen?' and I told them to hurry up to Townsend Street where we had been told to go. When we got to where the black taxis are in Millfield I said 'Do the Hula, and don't stop till we get to Brown Square Barricks!'[7] Once we got to Townsend Street there was a stillness and everybody was wondering what was happening. Then these two men who I mentioned earlier appeared from a side street and called me over and one of them said 'Right, that's it – you've done the business. We'll be back to see you.' That was the first stage of my proper induction into paramilitarism and I was 15 at the time.

Reforming the Young Citizen Volunteers

Around this time the Young Citizen Volunteers[8] were reformed to act as a junior battalion of the UVF. The whole UVF was restructured in 1972 and the YCV was part of that restructuring process – they were making a conscious decision to follow that lineage right back to 1913–16. There were important connections between the modern era and our forebears; they had come from the same streets and had the same surnames. These were young men who had died at the start of the twentieth century and who had come from the same backgrounds and had the same social class as people like myself. At this stage we had already toyed with the idea of forming a group because of the violence that was occurring around us so the approach from the UVF made sense. We had a reputation as young men who were prepared to go that extra mile. Quite a few of the YCV members at this time were young teenagers like myself and many of them would eventually be imprisoned for various activities carried out in the name of the organisation. Most YCV members would have aimed to move into the UVF by the time they were in their twenties. We all grew up together, had the same likes and dislikes, socialised together and got to trust each other.

A lot of prominent people started off in the YCV. My co-accused[9] Tom Winstone was a member of the YCV at the time; Eddie Kinner and Martin Snodden[10] were two important members who came along a bit later. There were around 28 of us initially and the UVF had to vet everybody that joined.

The leaders of the YCV at that early stage used to have to travel around Northern Ireland and in particular the greater Belfast area where membership was high. This was so that they could deliver lectures to young lads, many of whom would have been older than me, about what the YCV was and to gauge what we were prepared to do. These weren't grand lectures, they were just talks used to teach potential recruits about unarmed combat and training with weapons – stripping guns and putting them back together. Many of these sessions would have been held in church halls and other civic meeting places under the guise of karate lessons or other activities. In terms of the social and political context there were a number of factors that suggested to me at this time that we needed to use violence and one of them was the IRA, which was engaged in a blatantly sectarian campaign. The two cases I always cite, and I don't refer to them to justify anything I did as a paramilitary, are the bombings in September and December 1971 respectively of the Four Step Inn[11] and the Balmoral Furniture Showrooms.[12] The bombing of the Balmoral killed two babies.

The Four Step Inn bombing had a particularly bad effect on me because the two men who were killed in that explosion were people I knew and had grown up knowing. Ernie Bates and 'Joker' Andrews were two characters on the Shankill Road and 'Joker' had two sons, one of whom was also known as 'Joker', and his brother, 'Bear'. They were all known as Belfast hard-men in the vein of Buck Alec and Silver McKee and were well liked up and down the road. My feelings after the Four Step bombing were that we couldn't let this type of atrocity against the Protestant people continue – that we needed to begin to fight fire with fire because the British government weren't going to give us the protection that we deserved. There was a real fear after these bombings in particular that the IRA could come into our communities at any time and just shoot up all around them.

Loyalists versus the Crown Forces

People might ask of me – why did you not join the police or the army at this stage? To be honest the thought never occurred to me because I and my friends got involved in paramilitarism at a very young age. I was in the Sea Cadets[13] when I was even younger, but circumstances just dictated that the YCV was the grouping for me. I think for a lot of my comrades at the time it was a peer thing. Also, there was a strong feeling in an area such as the Shankill that the Stormont and British governments had not done enough to counter the IRA threat. That perception led to illegal forces springing up to do the job that it was felt the police and army just weren't up to. Remember, the RUC had been disarmed for a time between 1969 and 1971 and the 'B' Specials had been disbanded completely in 1969.[14] In October 1969 the first police officer to be killed during the conflict, Constable Victor Arbuckle, was shot dead on the Shankill during rioting in the aftermath of the recommendations outlined in the Hunt Report. On the same evening two men from the area, George Dickie and Herbert Hawe, were killed by the British Army. There was no irony in fighting the army – if we go back to the notion of the Home Rule crisis unionists then were prepared to do anything possible to resist it; the same was true in 1969 and thereafter.

Another example of this occurred in 1970. The King's Own Royal Border Regiment was stationed in the Milanda Bakery[15] in the Shankill area just off Snugville Street. At the end of September 1970 there had been a period of sustained rioting on the road due to something the army had done and during this loads of young loyalists attacked the Regiment's base. They knocked the big gateway of the bakery down with a hijacked bus and blocked the soldiers off so they couldn't get at them. Then one of the loyalists climbed up on top of the sanger and took their colours: 'captured the flag'. That was them in disgrace. At this particular time we had the King's Own on the run and after this, if I remember correctly, they brought in the 7th Horse Artillery[16] for reinforcements on the road. They came from the Crumlin down onto the Shankill and it was like the cowboy films I used to watch as a child – the cavalry always came when the Indians were nearly away anyway! The paras came in and restored order but the young fellas on the road weren't stupid. They knew that after three days of rioting they would soon be up against British soldiers who were well rested and refreshed, so they decided to give that a miss!

I suppose people might think it strange that loyalists were attacking the Crown Forces but it isn't a contradiction that particularly worried many of us who were getting involved in paramilitarism at the time. People on the Shankill suffered harassment and as I outlined earlier, death at the hands of British soldiers at that time as well. In fact, the attitude of those older men at the time who had served in Aden and Cyprus and such places was that what was happening – Protestants being shot by the British Army – was nothing short of a bloody disgrace; I heard them say this. When I later became involved in paramilitarism I saw the YCV and the UVF as being at the coalface in terms of bringing the war to the IRA. I certainly didn't see the army as an enemy per se, but neither did I see them as being on our side.

Shortly before becoming involved with the YCV I had become known to the police and army. One memory that stands out from around this time is travelling home from school on the bus one afternoon and they were both waiting for me at the bus stop. So I stayed on the bus and got off further down the road where I caught myself thinking 'What am I doing here? I'm a kid!' These adults were waiting for me and then all the other kids on the bus were saying 'No Hutchy, don't get off the bus – the army and police are waiting on you!' It was around then that I fully realised that I was doing something that other people my age weren't doing. What I had been doing with other people and what I had learnt were well above my years in terms of maturity and life experience. In a two-year period I had been forced to grow up very, very quickly. The police and the army had probably created an image of a person that didn't really exist. I existed, but not in the form or description that they had given me. Sometimes people are put into positions and they have no other choice. Sometimes things are bestowed on people and they have to take up the mantle. A lot of that happened to me. I never regarded myself as a leader, I never saw myself as brave, I never saw myself as hard – none of those things, but by the time the police and the army had finished with me everybody believed that I was all of those things. I was a kid, struggling with this overwhelming change in my life, and at the same time being interested in the normal stuff teenagers like such as music and football. My concentration was taken away from what I really wanted to do which was to get an education. Circumstances in Northern Ireland at the time and the culture in which I had become involved forced me to put that to the side.

Gusty 'on the run' and being sworn in

My memory of being sworn into the organisation is crystal clear. Gusty Spence swore me in while he was on the run in 1972. I don't mean this to sound disrespectful to anyone else who carried out swearing-in ceremonies, but when Gusty did them he did them right. I got a certain feeling – a buzz or a high – from being sworn in by a famous loyalist folk-hero from the area in which I lived. Gusty was being mentioned on the news every night at that time and I suppose for young men like myself he was the closest thing to royalty in that sense. This was a man who had had songs written about him. I spent a lot of time with Gusty when he was on the outside from mid-July until November 1972 until he was eventually rearrested on the fourth of that month. I would have stayed with him in the same maisonette where he talked quite a bit about his service with the Royal Ulster Rifles in Cyprus and being in the military police. He was always trying to provide you with a broad view of the world based on his experiences.

I remember Gusty talking about the British tactics of trying to destroy the support for armed groups, particularly in relation to the Mau Mau. He wanted us to be aware of how the British used dirty tricks to demonise groups during conflicts in which they were engaged; don't be surprised at the black propaganda whether it be about your father being an alcoholic or your mother being a prostitute he wanted us to understand that they could and would try anything to break people's standing or morale. This happened to me on a number of occasions when the army would have driven into my home in Jersey Street in armoured cars and purposefully crashed into people's cars. They also would have raided the houses on either side of my mother's. This was all intended to turn people against me and my family in the hope that people would phone the barracks when I appeared at the house to get a bath or some such thing. It didn't work. We countered that by being one step ahead of the army by having safe houses and supporters who wouldn't have been known to the authorities in different streets. Some people volunteered to act as decoys – all you needed was a young fella with no connections who had long hair and was skinny! That was one of the strengths of coming from such a tight-knit community. Equally we had to work hard on a consistent basis to gain the confidence of the loyalist people.

Gusty also drove home to me that I had to be aware that one of three things would happen to myself and the young men who joined the YCV or UVF: one – you'll end up in prison; two – you'll end up maimed; three – you'll end up dead. Those were the sacrifices people had to be prepared to make for God and Ulster, and I had prepared myself for one of those three things, which in my case was 16 years in prison. Of course death was a very tangible possibility and with regard to that I had to develop a coping and protection mechanism. One of the major pitfalls at this time would have been to become psychologically weak. You couldn't develop relationships with people, and if you were to do that they had to be selfish relationships. It was all about you rather than the other person, whether that person be providing you with shelter, information or weapons. I've been with people who within hours have been killed due to being shot or bombs going off, sometimes prematurely, so you actually live it and you see it happening to other people and you wonder when it's going to be your turn. You end up substituting normal human relationships for relationships where people rely on you for protection or to solve their problems. Gusty taught me that a lot of this was psychological, that it was about man management. For example if you had a feeling that somebody under your control had done something wrong you might repeat the accusation to them and then the people you led might feel that you did have a sixth sense or whatever. These people were important to me – we all looked out for each other and trust had to be 100 per cent in those relationships.

During 1972 myself and Gusty obviously talked at length about the contemporary situation and the need for a military strategy. The problem was of course that the IRA didn't wear a uniform or fight out in the open. The UVF modus operandi then was to bring the war to the nationalist community in order to weaken support for the IRA. It didn't work; in fact it reinforced support for the IRA. Gusty reorganised the UVF along British military lines, which wasn't difficult given the history of the 36th Ulster

Division. The adjutant (Gusty) was 'Captain William Johnston' which looking back is interesting because I can remember when Gusty was re-arrested on the Shankill and brought to Springfield Road police station his wife, Louie, and myself were arrested as well. I was questioned because some article had appeared in the *Daily Mirror* or one of the other tabloids that 'Captain Henry Wilson' had overthrown 'Captain William Johnston' and they were accusing me of being Wilson. For some reason the police and military intelligence communicated that this coup had happened within the UVF and that it had involved me and Gusty, which couldn't be further from the truth. It's strange because here were all these historical figures of the 36th Ulster Division being mentioned in Belfast in 1972!

I was in the flat with Gusty and three other volunteers on the day he was rearrested. He got up early while we were still asleep and went out to get Belfast baps and bacon for the breakfast. We would normally take turns to do that, but on this particular day Gusty decided to go ahead and he was captured. I felt frustrated, angry and guilty. There is of course no denying that Gusty was a UVF man but he always maintained his innocence of the murder he had been convicted of.

Revanchist unionists had agitated for the removal of O'Neill in the 1960s and there is a feeling that when Gusty had served his purpose he was dropped like a hot potato. I don't think these anti-O'Neill unionists and others like them who came on further down the line should have been allowed to set the UVF agenda. The UVF should have discredited them with black propaganda or whatever means were necessary. Instead they were able to use the UVF for their own political gain and then set the scene for us in the 1970s by then telling the Protestant people that we were thugs and criminals. It was our fault – we allowed them to do that time and again. These figures then and later on didn't have the guts to stand up and say what they really wanted. If the UVF killed somebody these people would have said that they were going to go on television and condemn the murder but reiterated behind the scenes that they didn't really mean it, that their condemnation was hollow.

Incarceration and life in Long Kesh

In late 1974 one of the three inevitabilities that I had prepared myself and the other YCVs for happened when I was arrested and convicted for my part in a shooting on the lower Falls Road as part of an active service unit of the organisation. I knew there would more than likely be dire consequences for being involved in paramilitarism at some stage so it didn't come as a shock to me when I found myself incarcerated at the age of 19. My mother on the other hand probably found it difficult and although her love for me was unconditional, as any mother's love for their son is, I'm sure she cried herself to sleep on many nights. She coped by maintaining her strong character in public. She was a strong unionist and was the type of person you either really liked or really hated: a bit like myself I suppose! My mother was a very well-read woman who would give advice to people when she thought they needed it.

I once saw a woman who I hadn't seen in years whose husband used to drive the bus to Long Kesh. My mother had become very friendly with this woman and her husband and used to mind their children. My mother was a bit of a comedienne actually, but in hindsight I think that the humour was probably a coping mechanism designed to cover up her feelings of hurt about me being in jail. In reality she was the person who was doing the sentence while I got an education and busied myself with the camaraderie of life in the compounds.

Life in Long Kesh under Gusty was run along strict military lines. Having spent a lot of time with him in 1972 I knew more than most volunteers what to expect and actually relished the discipline he instilled. We had a full uniformed muster parade every Monday morning and every day there was an inspection of each of our 'cubes'[17] to make sure they were clean and that your bed-pack was made. There were hut orderlies who were responsible for cleaning the huts and there was somebody who looked after the ablutions, but on a Sunday everything was taken out of the huts and the place was scrubbed from top to bottom and given a deeper clean. Everybody had a role to play and there was nobody that got off with doing nothing. One of my first roles in the compounds was that of quartermaster for the Headquarter Company. This meant that I was responsible for looking after everything that came in and out of the compounds. That food came in on time and was edible – if it was cold I sent it back out again. We were also given rations by prison staff so it was also my responsibility to ensure that these were used sensibly in the event of a shut-down or a siege in Long Kesh. So at the start when Gusty was there I always had a role to play in meetings with him (C.O. at the time), the officers and whoever the O.C. was with regard to such things as medication and prisoners' welfare. A lot of this was again about man management and delegation and ensuring that everybody felt part of the compound; that there was somebody to arrange and look after physical education and someone else to look after education. It was all about maintaining morale and military discipline.

Representing loyalism and the Protestant working class: politics and community work

A lot of what I learned as a leader both on the outside and in Long Kesh was eventually applicable in a political context when I was voted as leader of the Progressive Unionist Party at their party conference in 2011. Although I had been heavily involved in the PUP and the negotiations that led to the Good Friday Agreement in 1998, and had sat in the Assembly as an MLA for North Belfast until 2003, I had decided to step back from politics and return to community work for a number of years – something that I had been involved in after I was released from prison.

Before my return to politics as leader of the PUP in 2011 I was aware from my work in the community that the Agreement hadn't benefited loyalist working-class communities in Northern Ireland and particularly in areas of north Belfast such as Mount Vernon, where my work is still based. People in these communities have experienced a lot of abuses because of their class, such as abuses of economic rights, human rights and cultural rights. Indeed the loyalist community in particular has been cast by the media and many commentators as a criminal community, as if they are responsible for everything that is bad about the country in which we live. As I have said many times before, Catholics blame the Protestant working class for discrimination, but how can you discriminate if you don't have power in the first place? The Combined Loyalist Military Command stated on declaring the UVF, RHC and UDA ceasefires in October 1994 that they offered 'abject and true remorse' for the innocent people who had lost their lives at the hands of loyalist paramilitaries over the duration of the conflict. With the PUP and the Ulster Democratic Party being involved in that announcement there was a clear message from our loyalist political parties that they agreed with that sentiment.

Sinn Féin on the other hand, 20 years after the ceasefire, refuse to acknowledge that they are linked to an organisation – and that they have many elected members who were involved in that organisation – which was involved in a murderous campaign. Sinn Féin needs to take responsibility for respecting loyalist communities. We are not 'deluded Irishmen' and we are not anti-Irish – we are pro-British and proud of our social, political and cultural heritage and history within the UK.

Working-class people, no matter where they come from, have the same hardships and socio-economic problems. We (the PUP) need to ensure that we have a system of government which safeguards working-class people's access to housing, education, health and employment. We can't just talk about unionists – this has to be about everybody that lives in Northern Ireland. In recent times there have obviously been a lot of arguments over culture. My belief is that if an aspect of culture is only for Catholics or only for Protestants then that is a privilege. What we as the PUP want are rights, not privileges. If we go back to the 1970s and 1980s I suppose we would be highlighting Clause Four and the socialistic aspects of that part of the PUP manifesto, but society has changed. The talk now should plainly not just be about workers' rights, but about the most vulnerable in society. The non-working and underclasses are in dire need of civic and economic investment within their communities. People often ask how we can build a fitting monument or a tribute to all the victims of the Troubles.

I always refer them back to after the Second World War and how the biggest gift that we as British citizens were ever given was the Welfare State. It was a firm foundation for people who felt frightened and disorientated by the recent conflict to rebuild their lives – to rebuild the nation. In theory it allowed soldiers to return home to proper housing, it allowed the bombed cities such as Coventry, London and Belfast to be rebuilt and their people re-empowered, free education and free access to health. Of course the Tories are trying to pull all of this apart and it is likely that they will try to do it more and more while they are in government. As an important component part of the British working class we as loyalists need to be protecting the legacy of the Welfare State. We must shape people's hopes and aspirations around building and maintaining a civic culture so that all have an equal stake in society. If that is successful, future generations in Northern Ireland will hopefully not have to talk about conflict or blood sacrifice.

Notes

1. Tennent Street is a road which runs between the Shankill Road to the west and the Crumlin Road to the north.
2. The protagonist from a series of Western films from the 1940s starring Charles Starrett.
3. Linfield are the most successful Association football club in Ireland. They draw their support from across Northern Ireland and have a strong Protestant and loyalist identity.
4. The shootings referred to here were carried out on 26 June 1966 when a young Catholic barman, Peter Ward, who was enjoying a late-night drink in the Malvern Arms on the Shankill along with some of his co-workers from a city centre hotel was shot dead by UVF men. Although convicted of Ward's

murder, Gusty Spence was always adamant that he did not carry out the killing.

5. The Hammer is the name given to a district in the lower Shankill area due to its unique shape. It is also one of the areas of Belfast which has consistently suffered from high unemployment, poverty and violence.

6. North Street is an arterial road which links the main city centre thoroughfare of Belfast with the lower Shankill.

7. The 'Hula' was a chant Linfield fans used at the time to intimidate other supporters; Brown Square is a small enclave in the lower Shankill close to the interface with Divis Street and the Falls Road.

8. The YCV was the junior wing of the UVF during its original incarnation during the Home Rule crisis and WWI.

9. Billy Hutchinson and fellow YCV member Tom Winstone were both given life sentences for a murder carried out on the Falls Road in October 1974. Tom Winstone is now a key figure in restorative justice practices on the Shankill and is heavily involved with Greater Shankill Alternatives.

10. Eddie Kinner and Martin Snodden were in Long Kesh along with Billy Hutchinson and Gusty Spence. The compound that Spence ruled over is famous for the way in which loyalist prisoners availed of education and became politicised. Kinner, Hutchinson and Spence were later key figures in the Progressive Unionist Party with Kinner and Hutchinson being part of the negotiating teams who were involved in drawing up the Good Friday Agreement of 1998.

11. The Four Step Inn bar on the Shankill Road would have been a meeting place for Linfield supporters. On 29 September 1971 after a European home tie with Belgian side Standard Liège, the bar was blown up by the PIRA.

12. The Balmoral Furniture Company was blown up by the PIRA on 11 December 1971. Four civilians, including two babies, were killed. This event is often cited by many young men at the time as the reason why they joined one of the fledgling loyalist paramilitary groups.

13. The Sea Cadets Corps is an organisation sponsored by the Ministry of Defence and the Royal Navy for young people between the ages of 10 and 18.

14. *Report of the Advisory Committee on Police in Northern Ireland*. Chairman: Baron Hunt, C.B.E., D.S.O. Presented to Parliament by Command of His Excellency the Governor of Northern Ireland October 1969 (Belfast: Her Majesty's Stationery Office, 1969).

15. The site where the Milanda Bakery stood is where the Shankill Road branch of the Department of Health and Social Security Jobs and Benefits office is currently located.

16. The 7th Parachute Regiment Royal Horse Artillery.

17. Cubicles where prisoners slept within each compound.

Index

Lightning Source UK Ltd.
Milton Keynes UK
UKOW06n0117110915

258420UK00004B/81/P